1R

Praise for

The Third Reconstruction

"Peniel E. Joseph is one of the most brilliant and gifted historians in the nation today. With a deft pen and a lucid eye, he limns the outlines of a new struggle for radical equality that has risen from the ashes of two noble but failed efforts in previous eras to make justice sing. *The Third Reconstruction* is a soulful love song to the epic struggles of chastened but hopeful citizens to pursue yet again their long-delayed arrival to the shores of real freedom and true democracy."

—Michael Eric Dyson, author of the *New York Times* bestseller *Tears We Cannot Stop*

"In this searching, often searing, account of our recent past and of our still-unfolding present, Joseph writes in the tradition of Du Bois and of Baldwin as he seeks to delineate how tragedy might give way to true justice. Personal and political, human and historical, Joseph's book is urgent, important, and illuminating."

—Jon Meacham, Pulitzer Prize–winning historian

"In *The Third Reconstruction*, renowned historian Joseph expertly draws on his remarkable breadth of knowledge to tell a powerful and interwoven story about three watershed moments in American history. Brilliantly written and elegantly argued, this book is a gift to all Americans. It offers an honest and compelling account of how change happens, and it forces us all to consider how we might work together to win the fight for racial justice."

—Keisha N. Blain, coeditor of the #1 *New York Times* bestseller *Four Hundred Souls* and award-winning author of *Until I Am Free*

"*The Third Reconstruction* offers a brilliant historical analysis of race relations in twenty-first-century America. Whether he is discussing Barack Obama or Martin Luther King Jr., the Black Power Movement of the Long Sixties or the Black Lives Matter zeitgeist of today, Joseph is superb. He is fierce when it comes to promoting racial equality. *The Third Reconstruction* is an awesome achievement."

—Douglas Brinkley, *New York Times*–bestselling author of *Rosa Parks*

"Anyone genuinely interested in understanding the relationship between America's racial history and our current political and moral turmoil should read every word of *The Third Reconstruction*. For while Joseph writes that 'the clash between reconstruction and redemption is continuing,' he also insists that 'things are afoot that show change is possible,' that 'a new political world is being created,' not least with the work of a new generation of Black grassroots organizers—especially Black women—and, yes, their white supporters. *The Third Reconstruction* is a book that could help us all create that world. As Joseph writes: 'These dark parts of our past underscore how a nightmare can still be a dream.'"

—Charlayne Hunter-Gault, prizewinning journalist

"*The Third Reconstruction* is a powerful and eloquent analysis of the enduring battle between opponents of multiracial democracy and forces of racial change across American history. Drawing parallels to the period of Redemption after the Civil War, Joseph persuasively situates the white backlash to the presidency of Barack Obama—captured in the rise of Donald Trump and MAGA—within the long, but frequently ignored, history of organized white resistance to Black freedom. Part historical investigation and part call to action, *The Third Reconstruction* is a towering achievement that brilliantly meets the moment."

—Tomiko Brown-Nagin, author of *Civil Rights Queen*

"The best books I encounter are always those that make me think, feel, and, most of all, dream. This book didn't just weigh heavy on my mind, it crawled its way into my imagination, shaking up my politics, bringing meaning to my story, and ultimately, igniting my commitment to work for a more loving and just world. *The Third Reconstruction* is not just a must-read, it fills in the gaps in American history and memoir, pulling from the black literary, radical, and religious traditions and thereby becoming what the American jeremiad must be: salvation for the soul of the country and liberation for the heart."

—Danté Stewart, author of *Shoutin' in the Fire*

"Joseph is one of the most important minds alive today, bar none. His latest book, *The Third Reconstruction,* is a masterclass on the painful process America must dare to undertake to become a land of true justice and equity. Like the brilliant *The Sword and The Shield,* *The Third Reconstruction* combines a delightfully readable narrative with elegant academic insights that leave the reader feeling like they got schooled, without having to go back to school. A marvel, and so necessary."   —Van Lathan Jr., author of *Fat, Crazy, and Tired*

THE THIRD
RECONSTRUCTION

ALSO BY PENIEL E. JOSEPH

*The Sword and the Shield: The Revolutionary Lives
of Malcolm X and Martin Luther King Jr.*

Stokely: A Life

*Dark Days, Bright Nights:
From Black Power to Barack Obama*

*Waiting 'til the Midnight Hour:
A Narrative History of Black Power in America*

*The Black Power Movement:
Rethinking the Civil Rights–Black Power Era*

*Neighborhood Rebels:
Black Power at the Local Level*

THE THIRD RECONSTRUCTION

AMERICA'S STRUGGLE FOR RACIAL JUSTICE
IN THE TWENTY-FIRST CENTURY

PENIEL E. JOSEPH

BASIC BOOKS

NEW YORK

Basic Books
Hachette Book Group
1290 Avenue of the Americas, New York, NY 10104
www.basicbooks.com

Printed in the United States of America

First Edition: September 2022

Published by Basic Books, an imprint of Perseus Books, LLC, a subsidiary of
Hachette Book Group, Inc. The Basic Books name and logo is a trademark of the
Hachette Book Group.

The Hachette Speakers Bureau provides a wide range of authors for speaking
events. To find out more, go to www.hachettespeakersbureau.com or call (866)
376-6591.

The publisher is not responsible for websites (or their content) that are not
owned by the publisher.

Library of Congress Cataloging-in-Publication Data

Names: Joseph, Peniel E., author.
Title: The third reconstruction : America's struggle for racial justice in the
    twenty-first century / Peniel Joseph.
Other titles: America's struggle for racial justice in the twenty-first century
Description: First edition. | New York : Basic Books, 2022. | Includes bibliographical
    references and index.
Identifiers: LCCN 2022020255 | ISBN 9781541600744 (hardcover) | ISBN
    9781541600768 (epub)
Subjects: LCSH: African Americans—Social conditions—21st century. | African
    Americans—Civil rights—History—21st century. | United States—Politics and
    government—2009-2017. | United States—Politics and government—2017-2021. |
    United States—Race relations. | Racism—United States. | Racial justice—United
    States—History—21st century. | Joseph, Peniel E.
Classification: LCC E185.615 .J678 2022 | DDC 323.1196/073—dc23/eng/20220428
LC record available at https://lccn.loc.gov/2022020255

ISBNs: 9781541600744 (hardcover), 9781541600768 (ebook)

LSC-C

Printing 1, 2022

CONTENTS

For my mother, Germaine Joseph, and all the Black people, especially Black women, who have led efforts to reconstruct America here and around the world

A NIGHTMARE IS STILL A DREAM

> Here was a land of poignant beauty, streaked
> with hate and blood and shame, where God
> was worshiped wildly, where human beings
> were bought and sold, and where even in the
> twentieth century men are burned alive.
>
> W. E. B. Du Bois, *Black Reconstruction*

GEORGE FLOYD'S TRAGIC MURDER irrevocably shattered myths of racial progress in a country that had elected its first Black president less than a dozen years earlier. Floyd's death was just the latest in a long series of crimes against Black people throughout the nation's history. And yet it was also a pivotal moment. There would, forever it seems, be an America before Floyd's public execution and one after. For me personally, Floyd's murder was a painful reminder of my own vulnerability. At any moment, Black lives could be lost, seemingly without reason. At times I feel like I have spent my entire life watching images of Black people dying at the hands of the police. Floyd's death remains hauntingly present to me still.

I grew up in a pregentrified New York City during the 1980s. My coming-of-age paralleled the emergence of hip-hop. Run-DMC's

THE THIRD RECONSTRUCTION

"Sucker MC's," a propulsive battle rap by a Queens-based trio, became my personal soundtrack during elementary school, and I occasionally saw DMC in my Hollis, Queens, neighborhood. These sightings made me feel like part of a larger Black youth community. Public Enemy's "Fight the Power" became my anthem around the time of my sixteenth birthday, and Salt-N-Pepa's "Push It!" gave Black kids a rare chance to express unfettered sexual liberation, erotic curiosity, and bodily autonomy. But the violence of racial division was inescapable. The effects of racial segregation in housing and education and racial gaps in wealth and income ordered the social, political, and cultural landscape, and they shaped my early life and those of my Gen X peers. In many ways, the music I listened to evolved as I became more aware of the violence, poverty, and racism that scarred my neighborhood. I tried to understand the racially segregated and politically volatile city I called home and make sense of its epic contradictions. Neither Ed Koch, who became mayor around the time I began kindergarten, nor David Dinkins, the city's Great Black Hope, who came into office during my senior year in high school, offered as clear a path forward as hip-hop.

Police brutality respected neither age nor gender. It crushed the elderly, humiliated the young, and destroyed families that looked like mine. And it ran rampant under both a white mayor and a Black one. I remember studying pictures of sixty-six-year-old Eleanor Bumpurs, who died on October 29, 1984, after being shot twice by police officers trying to evict her from public housing. It was a little more than three weeks after my twelfth birthday. She reminded me of my maternal grandmother, whom I had never met in person, unless you count the time she visited from Haiti

2

when I was a baby. My grandmother died around the same time as Bumpurs, from an unexpected illness. But Bumpurs's death at the hands of the police affected me in a different way, because it revealed the stakes of the racial violence of the city.[1] My South Jamaica, Queens, neighborhood regarded police less as guardians dedicated to protecting the community than as powerful sentinels patrolling our streets to ensure that we might never breach our invisible cages.

This reality stood at odds with a rosier portrait of law enforcement and US history taught at the local Catholic school, where my mother had enrolled me after one year at PS 34. My teachers characterized law enforcement as the "good guys," as trusted authorities who were supposed to protect children who looked like me and would look after neighborhoods like mine. My growing understanding of history and my compulsive reading of the New York City tabloids said otherwise. As my social studies teachers regaled us with vivid stories about how the civil rights movement had transformed America, ending racial segregation, securing Black voting rights, and moving the nation closer to Dr. Martin Luther King Jr.'s vision of a "Beloved Community," I began to notice this gap in our perceptions. They supplemented their teachings with posters and television documentaries. Film clips of King's "I Have a Dream" speech at the 1963 March on Washington particularly inspired them, especially when King called for all Americans to look past race toward the deeper character traits that populated individuals' souls. What I failed to notice, until around the eighth grade, was that, year by year, as class photos attested, my school had transitioned from overwhelmingly white to all Black. It had started after the March on Washington and continued during the years after King's assassination. The teachers celebrated what they considered to be the nation's racial progress during those years, without once mentioning that our school reflected the harsh reality of unyielding racial segregation—a segregation fueled by white anxiety over encroaching Black families. Families like mine.

Mom and Me, Jamaica, Queens, New York, 1976. Courtesy of the author.

My Haitian American mother, meanwhile, took deep pride in her understanding of Haiti as a political and cultural key capable of unlocking a pan-African future that included African Americans. She taught me that we were central to Black American freedom struggles, although not many other people recognized it. She frequently told me about Toussaint Louverture and the heroic ingenuity he exhibited in the late 1700s in defeating the French empire and Napoleon Bonaparte. The Haitian Revolution inspired slave rebellions in America and offered a model of citizenship and dignity that helped propel Black activism over the decades and centuries that followed. Without it, the United States would never have been able to secure the Louisiana Purchase. I recognized being Haitian as my birthright and fiercely embraced my Black Americanness. I felt a deep connection with Black America's struggle for full citizenship and dignity, acquiring an empathy for underdogs that drew from my mother's example but was all my own, unencumbered by her temperamental boundaries and generational biases. I was both a proud son of Haiti and a first-generation Black American.[2]

In September 1986, one month before turning fourteen, I started attending an overwhelmingly white high school in Queens. It was there, during that freshman year, that a white person first called me the N-word. The melee that followed landed both of us in the principal's office. Others, I knew, fared far worse than I did. Five days before Christmas that year, Michael Griffith, a twenty-three-year-old Black man, was chased to his death by a white mob in the Howard Beach section of Queens. I have never felt more alone than I did on bus rides to and from school in the immediate aftermath of Griffith's death. I became painfully aware of the geography of racial borders in Queens. Crossing over into the white parts of Flushing felt like entering a combat zone: enemy territory where roving mobs could potentially threaten, attack, or kill me.

Though I had never met Griffith, I felt as if I *knew* him. His death was a concrete example of exactly how much fear and loathing Black men could inspire—that I, having just turned fourteen, might even inspire. Both events, my skirmish and Griffith's death, left me deeply troubled and politically exhilarated. I had long realized how greatly the narrative of civil rights in America in history books differed from my own experience, but now my anger and my grief gave way to an intense study of Black history. What had started as a bonding experience with my mother turned into a lifeline, a support system, and a safe space. Through my study of history, I tried to make sense of it all, and I began to recognize history as a series of stories we tell ourselves in order to understand the world we live in. The characters from these stories could never really die if we continued to study and remember them. Their examples could help me overcome my fear and calm my anxiety. Ultimately they would also enable me to find my own voice as a writer, thinker, and student.

Eyes on the Prize, a transcendent documentary series broadcast on public television during my freshman year of high school, helped me to see my own world with new eyes. Over the course of six hour-long episodes, it showcased both the grandeur and the trials and tribulations of the modern civil rights era. *Eyes* often focused on ordinary Black people who, in the course of their struggles for dignity in pursuit of citizenship rights, revealed the extraordinary resilience of African American culture. The series treated Black people with deep empathy, even reverence. Their stories, it suggested, were worthy of respect; even those on the "lower frequencies" of American society could impart lessons to us all, the lettered and unlettered alike.[3] Episode after episode, the period came alive through intimate, mesmerizing portraits of Black people: sharecroppers who became voting rights activists, single mothers turned welfare rights advocates, prisoners who became political organizers, and many others. *Eyes* afforded as much respect and esteem for ordinary Black people as it did for the legendary exploits of Malcolm X and Martin Luther King Jr. This insight would stay with me and help shape my approach to reading, writing, and studying history in the future. During my senior year of high school, an eight-episode sequel, *Eyes on the Prize II*, premiered. Covering the years from 1965 to 1983, the second series lingered over the Black Power era and showed Stokely Carmichael's rhetorical brilliance, Muhammad Ali's draft resistance and courage in opposing the Vietnam War, King's radicalism, and the movement's political legacy into the 1970s and 1980s. These images would stay with me forever.[4]

And then, in the summer before my seventeenth birthday, I saw Spike Lee's film *Do the Right Thing*, which premiered on July 21, 1989. The film shattered me emotionally and changed my life. It also became a generational touchstone, offering a cinematic portrait of the afterlife of Jim Crow segregation that almost everyone around me seemed afraid to acknowledge. Lee provides the anatomy of a racial rebellion that erupts on a blazingly hot summer day in Brooklyn in the wake of the police murder of a young Black man named Radio Raheem. I loved Radio, but I especially identified with the character Buggin' Out. I enjoyed his fervent, at times comical, efforts to boycott an Italian American–owned pizzeria over the management's failure to include Black people on the restaurant's wall of fame. The character, a stand-in for the lost promise of Black Power–era efforts at community control, reminded me of my own powerlessness, whether in my segregated neighborhood, at my school, or in the country generally. I could relate to the film's tragic final act because as a young Black man I lived with the fear of police violence every day. The heartbreaking depiction of New York police officers choking Radio to death brought me to tears in the theater. Radio, a passionately angry young Black man, is seen throughout the film carrying a boom box blaring Public Enemy's

"Fight the Power" as his personal soundtrack. It reminded me of all that Black people had lost.

The movie's coda drew quotes from Malcolm X preaching Black dignity and from Martin Luther King Jr. promoting Black citizenship. Hearing those words in that context remains stamped in my soul to this day.

The deaths of Eleanor Bumpurs, of Michael Griffith, and yes, of Radio Raheem set me off on a search to heal racism's psychic wounds through history. I weep for that precious Black boy who fashioned personal vulnerability into a suit of intellectual armor. Then and now, I imagined myself wielding African American history as a corrective against historical fallacies that denigrated Black people, as an illuminating shield that new generations could employ to protect their minds, bodies, and souls. Studying Black history provided a balm, one that eased the pain, trauma, and anger brought to the fore by anti-Black violence and premature death. The passion to study broadly, to empathize deeply, and to organize politically still burns within me.

With the distance of time, I now recognize how I processed my anger and grief over Michael Griffith's death in 1986 by turning to history. But until 2020 brought the murder of George Floyd amid a season of sickness and death, I failed to fully consider the possibility that this same practice might serve as a balm to millions of Americans who were seeking, as I did as a fourteen-year-old high school freshman, to process traumatic events.

I mourned Floyd's death with the tears of that young Black boy who remains within me. It was as if he were kin, because in a sense he was. I recognized myself in Floyd's face. I saw my older brother, my cousins, and my deceased father in his bewildered eyes as the life slipped from his body. Floyd's story will forever impact millions of precious Black boys and girls in America, including many who took to the streets in the days, weeks, and months that followed his death, both to demonstrate the value of their own lives and to honor those taken from us too soon. I offer this book to them, and to all Americans, in the belief that these premature deaths are related to a larger story about ourselves that we rarely want to hear, but urgently need to.

W. E. B. Du Bois called America "a land of poignant beauty, streaked with hate and blood and shame, where God was worshiped wildly, where human beings were bought and sold, and where even in the twentieth century men are burned alive," and this unvarnished description continues to resonate deeply.[5] America remains a nation riven by cruel juxtapositions between slavery and freedom, wealth and inequality, beauty and violence. Our history reminds us that the racial juxtapositions of the present are not aberrations; rather, they reflect an unhappy pattern from the past that continues into the present.

Du Bois is perhaps best known for introducing the term "double-consciousness" into the lexicon of the Black experience.[6] By this he meant the duality of being a Black American—neither fully African nor completely American, an enduring "problem" to be fought over in war and wrestled with during peace. But for Du Bois, double-consciousness did not refer simply to Black efforts to forge a coherent identity in a nation scarred by racial slavery. The internal struggle for a clear identity that the outside world recognizes as human is only one aspect of double-consciousness. Within the body politic Black people have been locked in a seemingly infinite struggle against the forces of white supremacy, and the duality at the heart of double-consciousness impacts the entire American project. America itself has a dual identity, reflecting warring ideas about citizenship, freedom, and democracy. There is the America that we might call *reconstructionist*, home to champions of racial democracy, and there is the America that we might call *redemptionist*, a country that papers over racial, class, and gender hierarchies through an allegiance to white supremacy. Since the nation's birth, its racial politics have been shaped by an ongoing battle between reconstructionist America and redemptionist America.[7]

William Edward Burghardt Du Bois remains the most important American scholar and social scientist of the twentieth century. He grew—out of necessity—into the greatest scholar-activist in the history of the nation. The confounding relationship between race and democracy became his métier. More than any other Black thinker of his generation, Du Bois identified Reconstruction, the years of hope and pain following the formal end of slavery, as America's most important origin story. By the time of the Great Depression, he was perhaps Black America's leading intellectual. He had helped found the NAACP in 1909 and had played a key role in its subsequent work, and he had already written a number of important books and essays. But in 1935 he wrote what was arguably his most important book yet, *Black Reconstruction in America, 1860–1880*, about the two Americas that briefly united as one in the aftermath of a bloody Civil War. Du Bois wrote from a sense of tragic responsibility in order to set the record straight about a nation whose pastoral beauty could exist alongside public spectacles of lynching and of white Americans picnicking over the charred remains of burnt Black flesh. The landmark book had been inspired by Du Bois's incisive understanding of the moral failure behind the rise of white supremacy. He viewed Reconstruction as more than just a missed opportunity, interpreting the post–Civil War decades as the nation's second founding. Reconstruction, he said, gave birth to a new America that expansively redefined freedom beyond the parameters of the old. America's Reconstruction era, which lasted a little more than three decades, from the ratification of the Thirteenth Amendment in 1865 to the white riot in Wilmington, North Carolina, in 1898, was a historical watershed.

Black Reconstruction demolished the myths and lies of "Lost Cause" histories that presented the period after slavery's end as a horrible mistake that required the heroic intervention of the Ku Klux Klan to make right. Throughout the early decades of the twentieth century, the Dunning School of Reconstruction history, named for Columbia University historian William Archibald Dunning, who was white, was taught from coast to coast. At Harvard University in the 1930s, a young future president named John F. Kennedy imbibed these lies. Dunning and his supporters viewed themselves, like the white historical characters they wrote about, as "redeeming" America from the mistaken Reconstruction era with its commitment to Black citizenship. By June 11, 1963, President Kennedy had clearly reconsidered the merits of the Lost Cause. That day, he gave his first major nationally televised speech in support of racial justice and equality. A few hours later, Medgar Evers, a Mississippi civil rights activist, was assassinated as he emerged from his car in his own driveway, shot in the back by a white supremacist. "I don't understand the South," Kennedy observed to a close aide. "I'm coming to believe that Thaddeus Stevens was right."

THE THIRD RECONSTRUCTION

Kennedy's invocation of Stevens, a Radical Republican who believed in political and social equality wrought from the punishment and subjugation of Confederates as well as active and passive supporters of the slave power, exemplifies Reconstruction's afterlife during the civil rights era. A son of Vermont turned Pennsylvania Republican, Stevens chaired the House Ways and Means Committee during the Civil War and became a most powerfully effective spokesperson in support of Black citizenship after the war. He battled Andrew Johnson's embrace of white supremacy and looked upon Radical Reconstruction as a method of "perfecting a revolution" intended to irrevocably break the former Confederacy's efforts to restore racial inequality by other means. Aware of the reports that white supremacists, just one year after the end of the Civil War, were "daily putting into secret graves not only hundreds but thousands of the colored people," Stevens became one of the architects of Reconstruction policies aiming to ensure federal protection of Black voting rights, to prevent ex-Confederates from resuming their political domination in the South, and to put an end to widespread anti-Black violence in the former Confederate States. Redemptionists would never forgive his moral clarity in the face of white supremacy during Reconstruction and made sure to sully his legacy to all who would listen, including the young John F. Kennedy.[8]

Du Bois's views about Reconstruction became more widely accepted, but by no means mainstream, during the civil rights era. Like Kennedy, segments of American society tried to square the false history they had been told regarding "Negro domination" in redemptionist histories of the Reconstruction era with the violence, bad faith, and blatant racism gripping the nation.

For Black America, Reconstruction remains a blues-inflected tone poem about the perils and possibilities of Black humanity, democratic renewal, and the pursuit of citizenship and dignity amid the ruins of a world ravaged by racism, war, and violence. Du Bois's work serves as a historical correction, political inspiration, and policy provocation. And the problems that gave rise to these debates, in truth, have never really ended. The racial violence, political divisions, cultural memories, and narrative wars that emerged from the Reconstruction era continue in our own time. The "hate and blood and shame" are still deeply embedded in twenty-first-century America.

But making sense of the events of 2020 requires both short- and long-term historical context. The First Reconstruction era, 1865 to 1898, was followed by decades of Jim Crow, with its mendacious principle of "separate but equal." The Second Reconstruction spanned the heroic period of the civil rights era—from the May 17, 1954, Supreme Court decision in *Brown v. Board of Education of Topeka* to Dr. Martin Luther King Jr.'s April 4, 1968, assassination. And in our time we have come to the Third Reconstruction, the period from the election of Barack Obama as president in 2008 through the recent Black Lives Matter (BLM) protests and all that they have entailed.

The debates, conflicts, and divisions of the Third Reconstruction have been the most volatile yet. The global health pandemic that started in early 2020 revealed beyond doubt how deeply the racial disparities in society have affected Black lives. That disparity is still rooted in the world America built just after the end of slavery. The BLM movement inspired rebellions against police brutality both at home and abroad. It became the largest social protest movement in American history, representing a continuation and expansion of reconstructionist segments within the nation.

Joe Biden became president following the most racially divisive presidential campaign season in US history, and the issues that arose reflected the continuing evolution of redemptionist impulses in our own time. The transformation of President Joe Biden is telling. A generation before taking the Oval Office, Biden had supported a redemptionist notion of Black citizenship; by the time of the 2020 election he had become an advocate of reconstructionist policies. He thus exemplified how politicians from the First Reconstruction era to the present have often moved back and forth between these two poles, at times straddling both of them simultaneously. When two Democrats won Georgia's runoff elections on January 5, 2021, the party took a slim majority in the US Senate. One of those victors, Raphael Warnock, became the first Black person from Georgia in American history to be elected senator. When he spoke, his words evoked the promise born from the height of the Reconstruction era, with its triumphant scenes and its hopes for Black power. In the 2020 and 2021 elections, Black women took a leading and very visible organizing role, especially in expanding voting rights and bringing the issue of criminal justice reform into the foreground. Not to mention that a Black woman, Kamala Harris, was elected vice president of the United States for the first time. All of this took shape along the front lines of a Reconstruction period that has often failed to give Black women the credit they deserve.

The white riot of January 6, 2021, at the US Capitol Building is impossible to understand without reference to earlier, yet strikingly similar, efforts during the First Reconstruction period. In both cases, there were attempts to violently overthrow democratically held elections won with the aid of Black votes. To fully comprehend the challenges and opportunities of this moment, we must take a deep historical dive, one that braids together the most crucial aspects of these three periods and the repeated clashes between the forces of redemption and the forces of reconstruction.

The First Reconstruction established a set of competing political norms and frameworks—reconstructionist and redemptionist—regarding Black citizenship, the virtues of Black dignity, and the future of American democracy.

Reconstructionists fervently believed in a vision of multiracial democracy. Du Bois coined the term "abolition democracy" to describe what seemed to promise a second American founding, one where Black political, economic, and cultural power would give new meaning to citizenship, liberty, freedom, and democracy. The left wing of the First Reconstruction era's political spectrum, sometimes called Radical Republicans, believed in social equality as well as political rights. They sought economic reparations through the redistribution of land in hopes that this, alongside Black men's suffrage, would provide a foundation for Black political power. Black leaders, such as the fugitive slave turned abolitionist journalist Frederick Douglass, sufficiently impressed Abraham Lincoln that the president came to believe that the most intelligent African Americans deserved voting rights. But Lincoln and other moderate Republicans had initially hesitated on the matter of voting rights for Black folk. Lincoln agonized over whether Black people could ever be fully integrated (both racially and otherwise) into the American political family. Slavery, and the anti-Black racism it created, indeed planted seeds of bipartisan doubt about the moral and political worthiness of Black people for full and unfettered citizenship, despite the fact that 200,000 Blacks had fought for the Union in the Civil War.[9]

Black women played a central role in designing a progressive vision of Reconstruction politics, often more far-reaching than what could be imagined by Black and white Radical Republicans, identifying racial, gender, and economic justice as keys to abolition democracy. Ida B. Wells, a journalist and anti-lynching crusader, emerged as one of the nation's most ardent reconstructionists, helping to advance Black power by organizing political clubs and educational networks and creating civic spaces that viewed women as equal partners on the road to freedom.[10] She and others imagined a Black freedom struggle that would transform America's democratic experiment and that would be expansive enough to recognize Black women's personal humanity and political genius. They broke the mold by recognizing that unless and until *all* Black lives mattered, none would. And they combined theory with action, with Black women pursuing their activism in domestic labor, education, and health care as well as other fields. Black women's vision of citizenship enlarged the scope of the nation's democratic imagination, opening up political vistas that would be claimed by subsequent generations as a birthright. But their efforts, forged through the crucible of the First Reconstruction, would not be fully acknowledged until the Third.[11]

Reconstructionists adopted multiple strategies in their efforts to forge a multiracial democracy in the post–Civil War years. They organized along religious, agricultural, political, economic, and civic lines, seeking to make good on federal promises of citizenship

16

following ratification of the Thirteenth Amendment. Over two thousand Black men held public office in the three decades after slavery at the local, state, and federal levels. Reconstructionists filed lawsuits against the imposition of racial segregation, passionately advocated for a new social compact for Black Americans and the rest of the nation, and challenged the onslaught of racial violence under Jim Crow with self-defense and paramilitary units, as well as through migrations westward during the 1870s (and, to a much smaller extent, to Liberia). Reconstructionists embraced America not only as an idea, but as a constantly changing political reality that could evolve into a more perfect union through the collective will of people of conscience.[12]

Redemptionists saw America's political future in a very different way. Out of the blood and ruins of the Confederate rebellion came a vow among white supremacists to "redeem" the South of "Negro domination" or perish. The Confederacy's defeat compelled a change in strategy, but not an abandonment of the brutally immoral tactics to which the redemptionists were accustomed. No longer content to create a self-contained empire of slavery, they now endeavored to transform America into a Southern Nation. Racial terrorism accompanied political, legal, and legislative efforts to reestablish slavery by other means. Reconstructionists exhibited a passionate commitment to achieving the goal of multiracial democracy, but redemptionists matched their level of commitment, and at times violently exceeded them, in their efforts to reestablish white supremacy.

Redemptionists sought to reinscribe slavery's power relations between Blacks and whites through racial terror, through Black Codes that disenfranchised Black voters, and by ending federal protection for Black citizenship. They sought to allow former Confederates to hold political office, while denying Black voting. To claw back their lost power, they resorted to organized violence, fraudulent election claims, and control of Black labor through onerous contracts designed to force African Americans into permanent economic servitude. Like their reconstructionist counterparts, redemptionists used multiple strategies. Their goal was to maintain a racial caste system ensuring that even the least privileged whites would amass more land and wealth; have greater access to jobs, health care, and the justice system; and achieve better outcomes than Blacks. They weaponized political, economic, judicial, and legislative strategies to make this happen. But racial violence proved to be the redemptionists' central political tool, as many of them were ex-Confederates well trained in the art of warfare.

Organized violence against prominent local Black people, including officeholders and other political leaders, ministers, and their families, made reconstructionist efforts to achieve dignity and citizenship both perilous and deadly. Redemptionists stymied Black progress toward economic independence through sharecropping and a debt peonage system that encumbered Black farmers with overwhelming financial burdens. These conditions often made it impossible for them to leave the plantations they had toiled upon under chattel slavery. The convict-lease system criminalized newly freed Black men, women, and children through vagrancy laws that gave the authorities permission to arrest African Americans for petty and quality-of-life crimes. An inability to pay cash bail, fines, and fees set thousands of Blacks down a dark road toward incarceration and personal ruin. Black inmates were then leased to private companies as laborers, and their wages were handed over to local municipalities, which thus extracted financial gains from organized racism.[13] Redemptionists championed public policies that stripped Black voting and citizenship rights. Across the former Confederacy, states passed laws, adopted codes, and enacted policies that made it more difficult for Blacks to serve on juries, hold certain political offices, and exercise the ballot. In some cases, they were barred completely from engaging in these activities.

If some of this sounds familiar, it should. Contemporary voter suppression legislation represents one of redemptionism's most stunning modern legacies. So, too, do mass incarceration, racial profiling, and racially exploitative prison labor. The racial violence directed toward Blacks who tried to vote—or to swim at racially segregated beaches, eat at restaurants, travel on buses and trains, or stay at hotels or motels—during the twentieth century contained a direct throughline to this redemptionist vision of America.[14]

Yet America's historical memory quickly forgot slavery's violence, war's pestilence, and the cowardice of white supremacy in favor of a new story, one rooted in efforts at national reconciliation at the expense of Black dignity and through the denial of Black citizenship. On May 1, 1865, in Charleston, South Carolina, Black Americans organized the first Memorial Day (then called Decoration Day) to honor the 257 Union soldiers buried in unmarked graves inside a former horse-racing track turned Confederate prison. Thousands of Black men, women, and children engaged that day in rituals of memorialization for those who had sacrificed their lives to bring about a new birth of American freedom. By the end of the nineteenth century, Memorial Day parades, celebrations, and commemorations were being held in virtually every part of the nation. Yet the meaning behind these celebrations turned the catastrophe of a war fought over slavery into an altar of national unity, with Union and Confederate veterans alike proclaiming the war as an unfortunate misunderstanding where both sides fought honorably. If racial slavery had produced the chasm of war, it would take the stripping of Black citizenship to broker a new national peace.[15]

Redemptionists portrayed themselves as heroic defenders of a misunderstood South. In their telling, it was the South that was under assault, and it was their duty to keep power out of the hands of impudent Blacks, who they said were unprepared to perform the duties of citizenship in an intelligent manner, let alone serve as competent legislators. But redemptionists also prefigured contemporary racial gaslighting. They were architects of racial oppression, but denied the existence of the edifices they built to stand in the way of Black citizenship. While they sometimes called openly for white supremacist rule as a bulwark against Black voting rights and citizenship, they simultaneously claimed that their righteous indignation had nothing to do with race. A version of white supremacy claiming to be color-blind began to take root during the First Reconstruction. Redemptionists normalized violent intransigence against Black citizenship by advancing the notion that African Americans, having been so recently uplifted from slavery, were simply not ready to assume the burdens of political power. Massacres of Black Americans took place in 1866 in New Orleans and Memphis, less than a year after passage of the Thirteenth Amendment, but the reasons for the massacres were never fully acknowledged, and many denied they even took place.[16]

Redemptionism, over time, became the face of the Democratic Party, a situation that imperiled Black rights and the health of American democracy itself. As redemptionism's star grew, so too did its political influence. Martial conflicts, legislative jockeying, and political debates pitting Democrats against Republicans gave way to bipartisan accord between the major political parties on Black subjugation. Redemptionists successfully knitted together a white supremacist political coalition that rationalized racial oppression on the color-blind model. By simply ignoring the Reconstruction-era constitutional amendments through a bipartisan lack of enforcement, redemptionism became the law of the land. Redemptionists turned white supremacy into a kind of civil religion and civic nationalism. They professed a deep and abiding faith in a Christian God unwilling to force them to submit to Black political domination. They committed wholescale atrocities in defense of an American Dream that they narrated as the exclusive domain of white folk. Redemptionism's greatest magic trick lay in convincing white Americans living outside the South, including, but not limited to, Republicans, to collaborate in the shaping of a new national political order based on racial oppression.

Most importantly, redemption became a core feature of American exceptionalism. American exceptionalism portrays our national history as a kind of bedtime story, with a beginning, a middle, and a triumphantly happy ending. It glosses over deeply embedded themes, including the history of inequality, the history of economic injustice and settler colonialism, and the history of violence against women, Queer people, and Indigenous people, in favor of a narrative highlighting progressive change over time. It ignores the sad reality that a civil war was not sufficient enough a price to purchase Black citizenship and dignity. Instead, it views entrenched patterns of racial violence, Black deaths, and white supremacy as aberrations of an otherwise healthy body politic. Racial slavery, structural violence, systemic racism, and white supremacy are largely absent from this story. The focus is on reconciliation, triumph against evil, and a nation's unbounded ambition for greatness under the beneficence of God himself (the Good Lord is always a He).[17]

American exceptionalism rests on two big lies in particular. The first is that Black people are not human beings. The second is that the first lie never happened.[18]

Even today, a wide range of political actors, organizations, institutions, and citizens support redemptionist politics, even as they might not recognize they are doing so. Redemption's narrative genius, based on the lie of the Lost Cause, was to represent white supremacy as necessary to the fulfillment of the American Dream. This notion, and its corollary, that multiracial democracy only works by diminishing white power—an indignity as unacceptable now in some quarters as it was during Reconstruction—has now been kept alive generationally.

Redemptionists, in short, provide an important context for understanding the Third Reconstruction. White nationalism, the rise of Donald Trump and MAGA, and the events leading to the January 6, 2021, riot at the US Capitol are more than simple political backlash. They represent organized resistance to the presidency of Barack Obama, to the rise of the Black Lives Matter movement, and to the increased visibility of Black, Latinx, Indigenous, Asian American and Pacific Islander, Queer, and immigrant demands on the American body politic for racial and economic justice.[19]

* * *

American history since the end of the Civil War has involved a struggle between reconstructionists and redemptionists for the nation's very soul. The contrasting approaches of these two perspectives have shaped the nation's entire history, not only on matters connected directly to race, but also in how Americans have defined citizenship, the national identity, and democracy since 1865. At the turn of the twentieth century, redemptionist politics were mainstream enough for a resurgence of the Ku Klux Klan to take place (it was refounded in 1915 in Stone Mountain, Georgia, where monuments to white supremacy remain today); to turn *Birth of a Nation*, D. W. Griffith's silent film portraying Reconstruction as a horrible mistake, into a sensation (it was screened for an approving President Woodrow Wilson at the White House); and to justify mass violence in dozens of racist attacks against Blacks around the country, including a massacre in Tulsa, Oklahoma, in 1921 in which white perpetrators murdered over three hundred Black people and razed a prosperous, all-Black neighborhood (Greenwood) to the ground.

Two decades later, during the Franklin Roosevelt administration, the federal government once again championed Black citizenship from above when, in 1941, reconstructionists took advantage of opportunities that had been opened up by the Great Depression to establish the Fair Employment Practices Committee. From below, civil rights activists organized the "Double V" campaign as a way to spread the idea of defeating racial segregation at home and global fascism abroad. In the aftermath of World War II, the racist pseudoscience that had fueled the Klan's rise fell into disfavor, because of its association with the genocidal Nazi regime. The liberation of African third world nations turned racial justice into a global issue, and Black Americans continued to organize, demonstrate, and strategize for citizenship and dignity in a political climate that was proving to be more receptive than that of just a generation before.[20]

During the Second Reconstruction, which, as mentioned earlier, lasted from the *Brown* decision in 1954 until the assassination of Martin Luther King Jr. in 1968, reconstructionists won important legislative victories in bills declaring formal segregation unconstitutional. None were more significant than the 1964 Civil Rights Act and the 1965 Voting Rights Act. The latter represented the biggest threat to redemptionists since the First Reconstruction, because Black political power threatened white supremacy both in the South and in the rest of the nation. As the civil rights struggle unfolded, northern white opposition to racial integration revealed that racism transcended regional differences and geographical boundaries.

America's Second Reconstruction transformed the social compact for Black folk, and the legacies from this period still reverberate nationally. From Presidents John F. Kennedy through Barack Obama, the civil rights era institutionalized a national consensus that supported the struggle for Black citizenship and dignity as a political and moral good. In retrospect, America enjoyed a fifty-year period of national consensus on racial justice between JFK's finest moment as president and the June 25, 2013, *Shelby v. Holder* Supreme Court decision, which gutted the Voting Rights Act. The era was a hinge moment in American history. Those five decades provide the context for the Obama coalition that propelled the first Black president into office and seemed to fulfill the wildest imaginings of nineteenth-century Reconstructionists. For the first time, white Americans were expressing political support for making Black equality a core feature of the nation's democracy. Though *Brown*, in 1954, marks the beginning of the Second Reconstruction, the origin date for the emergence of a national consensus on racial justice could be traced to June 11, 1963, when President Kennedy delivered a televised national address on the issue.[21] No president in American history, not even Lincoln, had advocated in such clear, concise terms for abolition democracy. Although there were setbacks, false starts, outright lies, and performative gestures in the years that followed, and the achievements fell far short of the ambitious goals of reconstructionists, rhetorical support for racial justice proved much better for the nation's democratic health than its opposite.

The Second Reconstruction thus produced an important—and tremendously beneficial—consensus around the value of Black equality to the strength of democracy. The problem, however, was not yet solved. The consensus also helped to mask continuing divisions, especially the fact that although reconstructionists and redemptionists both professed national support for racial justice, they sharply differed on exactly how to achieve this.

The civil rights victories of the 1960s turned long-running battles over the meaning of American democracy into an ongoing (and uncivil) racial cold war, with reconstructionists and redemptionists drawing vastly different lessons from the nation's long history of racial division, violence, and oppression. Reconstructionists touted the federal government as indispensable to completing the still unfinished business of guaranteeing Black dignity and citizenship. At their most radical, they called for not just equal opportunity, but equality in outcomes. In this sense, reconstructionist thought forms the basis for contemporary advocates of anti-racism.[22]

In the wake of the Second Reconstruction, redemptionists pledged support for racial justice, too, but not for federal intervention, which they interpreted as a violation of constitutional principles and the sanctity of states' rights and individual preference. Redemptionists celebrated Black History Month and the MLK holiday, at times doing so alongside reconstructionists. They were convinced that such symbolism offered proof that America was no longer a racist nation, even as, paradoxically, they supported policies that would result in the amplification of Black misery, suffering, and premature death, even if these outcomes were not always the intent. Among the effects were ongoing residential and public school segregation, high rates of unemployment, continuing mass incarceration, and housing discrimination, which largely shut Black families out of the wealth created through home ownership.[23]

As the nation moved into the Third Reconstruction, the racial cold war produced striking juxtapositions between racial progress and setbacks. If one group of reconstructionists considered Barack Obama's election a culmination of over a century of struggle for racial justice, and the beginning of a new multiracial democracy, another interpreted it as illustrating not just the heights but also the limitations of the national consensus on racial equality, which they said focused more on symbolic exemplars of change than on systemic manifestations of transformation.

Donald Trump's ascent to the White House did more than tip the scales in favor of redemptionists. Trump's victory shattered the national consensus forged in the post–World War II era, a process ignited in earnest by the *Shelby v. Holder* ruling, which helped to launch a new era of voter suppression using tactics unseen since the passage of earlier voting rights legislation. Before Trump, figures as disparate as Martin Luther King Jr., Richard Nixon, Hillary Clinton, Ronald Reagan, and Michelle Obama had all expressed public support of and fidelity to a civil rights movement that millions of Americans had opposed in real time. Unmoored from the public embrace of Black equality that had marked the nation's forward-looking stance since the Kennedy administration, America lost its way.

Trump turned the White House into a safe haven for redemptionists for the first time since Woodrow Wilson's era. His rough-hewn brand of racism appeared closer to Andrew Johnson, Lincoln's renegade successor and the first president to face impeachment proceedings (a distinction that Trump would better by becoming the first and only president to face two such efforts in a single term). Trump's naked brand of racial intolerance resembled the pugnacious, racially scapegoating populism of four-term Alabama governor George Wallace, perhaps the most infamous elected official turned racial demagogue of the civil rights era. Some modern-day redemptionists found the Trump-Wallace connection disturbing. These were redemptionists who wished to preserve the rhetorical support for racial justice that had marked the Second Reconstruction. Accordingly, they found naked displays of racism to be an unseemly side of a MAGA movement whose tangible policy results they celebrated. In short, certain redemptionists advocated—and still advocate—for the maintenance of racial privilege while claiming to abhor the most grotesque features of white supremacy. From this vantage point, public school segregation can be rationalized as "parental choice," voter suppression as simply an unfortunate by-product of election security, and mass incarceration as the unintended outcome of good-faith efforts to stop crime. The redemptionist coalition began to undergo fragmentation. Whites motivated by racial discrimination began to split off from those who supported seemingly race-neutral policies that just happened to disproportionately impact Black Americans. There would be further splits as the Trump era progressed.

In spite of these differences, redemptionists maintained unity behind the broad arc of white supremacy that Trump championed. Trump's America unleashed white supremacy's pervasive anti-democratic impulses. Redemptionist ambitions writ large are inherently anti-democratic. Brutal authoritarian goals of keeping Black Americans in chattel slavery fueled Confederate treason, secession, and a Civil War that threatened to destroy the republic from within. Large portions of the Republican Party's political leadership and electoral base remained in the Trump coalition—pleased with his tax policies, his Supreme Court appointees, and the Lost Cause nostalgia for a pre–Great Society America. The devil's bargain had been made.

Reconstructionists have also experienced fractures relating to the racial consensus that was forged during the Second Reconstruction. Radical reconstructionists, best represented by the BLM movement, argued that the nation had long ago lost its moral compass, if it ever had one. For them, Trump's rise, like Richard Nixon's in 1968, for certain Black Power activists, represented a necessary ripping off of the bandage of liberal condescension on the road to finally achieving a different country. Black Reconstructionists identified Trumpism as both a threat to multiracial democracy and a new opportunity to move beyond the suffocating constraints caused by measuring racial progress within the frame of American exceptionalism. They recognized that the racial consensus that was unraveling was unjust to begin with, in that it acknowledged Black equality more symbolically than substantively. They interpreted its apparent demise as the fitting end to an unearned rapprochement. Mainstream reconstructionists were caught off guard by this sudden turn of events. Hadn't Obama's election proven that racial progress, however incremental, remained a steady feature of postwar American history, a shining example of the nation's exceptional past, present, and future? If such characterizations turned out to be incorrect, where would the nation now turn?

History is perhaps the most indispensable tool for understanding these dynamics, their evolution over time, and how we remember or forget their contemporary political impact, ideological influence, and policy legacy. Modern-day reconstructionists are exhilaratingly, if also painfully, aware of their relationship to this longer history. In that sense they have gleaned lessons about citizenship and dignity from the first two Reconstruction periods even as they have consciously expanded the boundaries of the kind of reconstructionism that is possible by drawing on Black feminist thought and the larger tradition of Black political radicalism that have continuously reshaped American democracy (while oftentimes receiving no credit).

Consider the revival of the term "abolition" by contemporary activists and organizations connected to and inspired by the Black Lives Matter movement. Police and prisoner abolitionists seek to end the criminal punishment system in all of its manifestations.

Prison abolitionists advocate the eradication of prisons in the United States in favor of systems of restorative justice, community wellness, and policies promoting mental and physical health, access to healthy foods, and environmentally safe neighborhoods for Black folk.

The term "abolition" now links multiple generations of Black organizers spanning three periods of Reconstruction. Nineteenth-century reconstructionists made the term mean more than just opposition to racial slavery: they used it to signify the creation of a new world, one unbound from a racial caste system and freed from the racial violence that framed America's political order. Abolition democracy fueled the Black Reconstruction period, and Frederick Douglass's political thought and activism embodied the phrase. Douglass demanded Black citizenship and dignity in the aftermath of slavery and denounced anti-Black violence as a violation of the interracial blood that had been spilled to create the second American founding. In *Black Reconstruction*, Du Bois made the phrase an urgent expression of Reconstruction's still unfinished legacy.

The radical Black feminist scholar-activist Angela Davis, one of the leading figures of the Black Power era, set the stage for the second and third generations of reconstructionists to reimagine American society on the terms first set by proponents of abolition democracy.[24] During the 1960s and 1970s, alongside the Black Panther Party and revolutionary activists such as George Jackson and Assata Shakur, Davis helped to cast a national spotlight on America's criminal punishment system. Fired in 1969 from her post as a philosophy professor at the University of California, Los Angeles, by the university's Board of Regents, during the governorship of

INTRODUCTION: A NIGHTMARE IS STILL A DREAM

Ronald Reagan, for her openly Marxist beliefs, Davis became a fugitive, wanted in connection with an attempted prison break in Marin County, California. The search for Davis made international news, as did her apprehension in October 1970. Authorities placed her on trial for allegedly supplying guns in an unsuccessful courthouse take-over by Black revolutionaries that resulted in the death of a white judge. In prison, Davis became a global icon, the face of Black rebellion against a system of racial capitalism, white supremacy, and imperialism that denigrated Black life at every turn. While fighting to defend herself, she authored an extraordinary essay, "Reflections on Black Women's Role in the Community of Slaves," in which she took pains to highlight the political organizing and personal agency of Black women and to draw parallels between the First and Second Reconstructions.

Davis's essay theorized about the role of Black women in confronting sexual assault and rape, about their participation in slave rebellions, and about their engagement in more informal forms of protest, from work slowdowns to the poisoning of their enslavers. Writing from prison in 1971 about antebellum slavery, Davis knitted two generations of Black Reconstructionists together through a genealogy of liberation and resistance, citizenship and dignity, and the historical role of Black women in the pursuit of abolition democracy. She repudiated efforts to pathologize Black families as being victims of Black women's matriarchal control. Davis found herself literally writing for her life, as she was facing the death penalty after being charged with the capital crimes of murder, conspiracy, and kidnapping. Although she was acquitted the next year on all charges, her freedom was far from certain as she was writing, and she channeled the fierce urgency of her personal circumstances and the wider struggle for Black freedom into one bravura essay.[25]

Davis's characterization of Black women's centrality to the project of imagining freedom in a society rooted in racial slavery spoke to contemporary and future generations of Black feminists and radicals. In the twenty-first century, she has continued to speak out, amplifying Du Bois's notion of abolition democracy to advocate for the end of the criminal punishment system, the death penalty, and the militarization of law enforcement. In this work she has become part of the essential spirit of the Third Reconstruction, which includes the aspiration to abolish prisons, reimagine public safety, and end a system of punishment rooted in racial slavery and its afterlife.

It is especially fitting that Davis's political activism and scholarship have now influenced two generations of reconstructionists to rally around the term "abolition" as an urgent declaration of the stakes in the battle against slavery's afterlife. The Black Lives Matter movement has fundamentally transformed the idea of abolition: originally signifying the permanent eradication of slavery itself, it is now used to mean the ending and reimagining of a host of repressive and discriminatory systems and institutions that have continued into our time, including mass incarceration; racial segregation in education and housing; disparities in health care, wellness, and wealth creation; and political disenfranchisement. BLM's abolition democracy builds upon both Davis's essential work and her nineteenth-century forebears, including Du Bois's *Black Reconstruction*, while also amplifying them. In effect, Davis's radical abolitionism, in tying the first Reconstruction with the second one from a prison cell, helped to bequeath the ideals of abolition democracy to the reconstructionists of the twenty-first century, who have now given it perhaps the most far-reaching definition ever.[26]

The Third Reconstruction journeys into the American past to make sense of the present by examining three extraordinary periods of political conflict and transformation. Three watershed historical moments mark the beginning of each of these reconstruction eras. These events have played major roles in shaping how American history, memory, and policy portray the national origin story we teach our children, tell ourselves, and share with the world. In many ways, they represent a living archive of memory, a historical repository that subsequent generations have drawn from, reckoned with, and built upon. The ratification of the Thirteenth Amendment on December 6, 1865, was one of these watershed moments, ending racial slavery and involuntary servitude in America—with the exception of those punished for crimes.[27] The passage of the first Reconstruction amendment formally began an experiment in multiracial democracy lasting more than three decades. It burned brightly for a time before dimming amid the embers of a violent white supremacist coup in Wilmington, North Carolina, in November 1898. The next watershed event in this narrative took place on May 17, 1954, when the United States Supreme Court declared, in *Brown v. Board of Education of Topeka*, that Jim Crow's "separate but equal" principle was unconstitutional, a decision marking the start of America's Second Reconstruction. That period, with deep roots in the political internationalism of the Jazz Age and New Negroes as well as the radical democratic impulses coursing through postwar Black America, lasted a little more than two decades. From the civil-rights-era calls for political reform it evolved into a "Black Power!" cry that attacked structural inequity in bold and belligerent tones. The sun began to set on America's Second Reconstruction with the death of Martin Luther King Jr., a political assassination that placed the nation at a moral fork in the road between the reconstructionist dream of a "Beloved Community" free of racial and economic injustice and a redemptionist vision of law and order. The country, in truth, marched straight down a path that prioritized systems of unnecessary punishment and unequal justice, a direction that has harmed millions of people and still haunts the national soul today.

America's Third Reconstruction began on November 4, 2008, with Barack Obama's historic election as the nation's first Black president.[28] That day upended American democracy in dramatic and subtle ways. Obama's victory, arriving at a time of domestic and international crisis, marked a crossroad in American history. At last, it seemed, reconstructionists had finally won a 143-year struggle for the nation's political soul.

Each of these moments in American history is popularly narrated as furthering the nation's long, inexorable march toward racial progress and the advent of a more perfect union. But this is not true. Although these watershed events—the passage of a constitutional amendment, a Supreme Court decision, and a presidential election—promised to guarantee Black citizenship, they were in fact calls to action and not the end of the story.

America's tortured relationship with the most consequential parts of its history renders us wholly incapable of confronting today's opportunities and crises. Our two earlier periods of national Reconstruction, in the aftermath of racial slavery and the suffocating anti-Black violence of Jim Crow segregation, have in a sense formed two tributaries that have led to our current moment of Reconstruction. Isolating the first two periods from one another would deprive us of the ability to see them as linked struggles to form a new America.[29]

History is a balm capable of healing America's deep-seated racial wounds. To do so we must tell a fuller story about our national past to our present selves. In order to embark on the painful journey of healing our national racial wounds, we must revisit the stories we tell ourselves about America.[30] The struggle for Black citizenship and dignity is the most important part of the story about our national search for truth, justice, and reconciliation. Yet a shared national historical memory of the centrality of Black people to the making of American democracy remains as frustratingly elusive as it is profoundly necessary.

The legacies of racial oppression and injustice that sprang from the First Reconstruction became intertwined in American history, politics, memory, and policy. Reconstruction's afterlife can be witnessed in the racial injustice, economic inequality, and domestic terror that continue today, themes of American history marking the distance between how Americans act and who we proclaim ourselves to be. The deep roots of the present day extend into the nation's past, and this is a process that will continue: we are only at the beginning of the beginning of coming to terms with a new American founding in the aftermath of 2020's racial and political reckoning. Telling the bitter and beautiful parts of this story is the first step. I hope this book allows readers to take a historical journey that enables them to see America and its people through new eyes, and in so doing to understand and to retell a different story about the past, one that speaks to the present with enough grace to transform the nation's future.

CITIZENSHIP

THE FIRST AND ONLY TIME I met Barack Obama, I found him to be truly impressive—and too good to be true. It was December 2007, shortly before a surprise victory in the Iowa caucuses over Hillary Clinton and John Edwards thrust his campaign into the political stratosphere. I managed to attend a Boston rally where an organizer picked me to go onstage to join the carefully or-chestrated multiracial mosaic that would form the backdrop for Obama's campaign speech. Obama greeted each of us with a brief handshake and a smile that I can still recall today. No one snapped a photo—this was well before ubiquitous iPhones and selfies—so I don't have a picture of me with Obama, although I would later be afforded the opportunity to take one with First Lady Michelle Obama. As a Gen Xer, a stubborn part of me is proud of this fact. It serves as a tribute to experiencing life rather than documenting it. As a historian, I regret that I possess no image of the moment, at least to share with my daughter.

That 2007 event formed the completion of a circle of sorts for me. By that point, I had spent more than three years reading about and studying Obama, research inspired by his mesmeriz-ing keynote speech at the 2004 Democratic National Convention in Boston. I had watched that speech live from a hotel room in the Cradle of Liberty, where I happened to be visiting at the time.

He appeared much younger than forty-three, spoke in the familiar cadence of the Black church, and rhetorically traversed racial, economic, and religious fault lines with dexterity and passion. Obama's speaking ability made him a man after my own heart. Transformative Black orators had formed the beating heart of my scholarship on the Black freedom struggle. In his Boston speech, Obama channeled Malcolm X and Martin Luther King Jr. I also heard the mellifluously analytical precision of former US congresswoman and voting rights advocate Barbara Jordan of Texas. And as he spoke, I couldn't help but think about the heroic campaign of Shirley Chisholm, the congresswoman from New York who in 1972—the year I was born—became the first Black woman to run for the Democratic presidential nomination. Obama sprinkled autobiographical snippets throughout his speech, rhetorical jewels that shone brightest when viewed by the sons and daughters of fellow immigrants such as myself.

Although Obama's 2004 address was thrilling, as he launched his own presidential effort in early 2007, and as I listened to him hone a stump speech that grew sharper the longer the campaign season stretched, I considered his election to be just short of impossible. Obama's ability to call America toward realizing its full potential felt exhilaratingly improbable. Ivy League educated, husband to a brilliantly confident Black woman, and the proud father of two Black daughters, Obama presented a portrait of a progressively holistic Black masculinity not often seen in public, let alone in the White House. His name alone, Barack Hussein Obama, seemed more of a literary provocation imagined by Ralph Ellison or Ishmael Reed than that of a real-life future president.

I changed my mind after Iowa. Obama's stunning victory there made him more than just a promising new political figure who might one day be president. Iowa, with its overwhelmingly white population, made millions of Americans, including myself, believe in the politics of hope and change that Obama offered. Black Americans moved from skeptical to passionately hopeful overnight. Over the next ten months, many found themselves deeply engaged in a drama whose stakes grew larger with each passing day. The future of American democracy hinged on whether a Black man could be elected to the highest political office in a land rooted in racial slavery.

I threw myself headfirst into covering the campaign and the candidate, attending house parties for Obama, purchasing T-shirts, and spreading the news to friends, colleagues, and strangers. I wrote op-eds, essays, and eventually a book about the future president, and I covered the presidential election as an on-air historical analyst for *PBS NewsHour*. Obama's ascent meant that representation mattered more than ever. Colleagues of mine at Brandeis University who I didn't think remembered my name congratulated me on my contributions to the history unfolding before our eyes. I became a participant observer, culled by local, national, and global media outlets to place what was happening into historical context. What did it all mean? I had no definitive answer, but certainly found myself enjoying the ride.[1]

I went to Denver in 2008 to attend the Democratic National Convention as part of *PBS NewsHour*'s televised convention coverage. Images of Fannie Lou Hamer and Stokely Carmichael picketing outside of the 1964 DNC in Atlantic City, New Jersey, flashed through my mind as I witnessed Obama's acceptance speech.[2] Back then, Democratic Party powerbrokers had refused to give full recognition to the integrated delegate slate of the Mississippi Freedom Democratic Party at the convention. Now, forty-four years later, a Black man stood poised to accept the Democratic Party's nomination for president. I drank in the moment, but I sighed as I realized that Obama had not mentioned Martin Luther King Jr. by name during his address, which was delivered on the forty-fifth anniversary of the March on Washington. Characterizing King as simply "a preacher from Georgia," I thought, failed to give the martyred symbol of the Second Reconstruction the national recognition and historical acknowledgment that such a sacred moment demanded.[3]

I also traveled to the Republican National Convention in St. Paul, Minnesota, where I listened to delegates who were convinced that John McCain and Sarah Palin would beat the Obama-Biden ticket in a landslide. The convention floor looked eerily monochromatic. There were scarcely any nonwhite delegates in attendance, and everyone seemed happily content with that reality. I imagined the pain that Jackie Robinson must have felt witnessing the horror of the 1964 GOP convention at San Francisco's Cow Palace nominating Barry Goldwater. By 2008, the ultraconservative tenor that at one time had produced shock and awe had become, in Minnesota, normalized. Still, leaving the multiracial bonhomie of Denver behind for the monochromatic whiteness of Minnesota felt jarring.[4]

After voting in Boston on November 4, I flew to Washington, DC, to cover the election night results on air in a northern Virginia studio. I held my emotions in check during the live broadcast.

Though I was outwardly calm, questions swirled through my mind as I tried to make sense of the country's historical travails around race through the prism of my own personal life and Obama's. What happens next? Would a Black president survive physically and politically? How would America treat Michelle Obama? I recalled all the pop culture satires and fantasies about the possibility of a Black president: the 1972 film *The Man*, starring James Earl Jones as the first Black president; the television series *24*, with Dennis Haysbert playing President Palmer; and *Deep Impact* in 1998, featuring Morgan Freeman as commander in chief, with the mellifluous voice to match. But my fantasies about this possibility hardly measured up to the giddiness and joy of its emerging reality.

Obama's victory had not been achieved quite as early as Robert F. Kennedy had presciently suggested in 1961, when, as attorney general, he had said the nation might elect a Black president in thirty or forty years. But now that it had happened, what would it mean? Would there be real change? That night I also thought about Michael Griffith, Eleanor Bumpurs, Sean Bell, Latasha Harlins, and countless other Black people who had been killed by the police or by white mobs. I thought about the structures of violence and punishment that exacted premature death by different means during my lifetime and Obama's. Having read his memoir, *Dreams from My Father*, I knew that Obama and I shared a deep reverence for the civil rights movement, connected to a larger appreciation for Black history and culture. We also both found refuge in reading Black history and literature, as well as in writing, as a way to explain the world to ourselves as much as to others. Obama's public speaking gifts elicited my admiration; he exemplified a long and storied rhetorical tradition that I had experienced firsthand at

New Bethel Baptist Church in Queens, imbibed through extensive study of Black freedom fighters, and sought to emulate in my own seminars, lectures, and speeches.[5]

But there were other aspects of Obama's life that were different from mine. His study of Black history began as a quest to belong, a search for identity as a biracial young man raised in Hawaii and Indonesia; he had barely known his Kenyan father and longed for a community to call home. I had long ago found my home, not just among the Haitian and Black American community that raised me, but in the unapologetically Black world that tethered us together in New York City. In my mother's house on Springfield Boulevard in South Jamaica, Queens, I had learned to embrace Blackness and all of its complexities, and to do so as a responsibility and not a burden. Picket lines and protests shaped my understanding of Black dignity and citizenship. Unlike Obama, I had not attended elite prep schools, a liberal arts college, or an Ivy League university. Instead, I had found my academic footing in state universities, publicly funded institutions that offered working-class Black kids like me undreamed-of possibilities. We had traveled separate roads to a historic election night that forever bound us together.

I found myself captivated by Barack Obama's characterization of America as a land of endless possibilities. A part of me wanted to believe the story he told about the country that I loved but that I felt had never really loved me back. After the evils of racial slavery, the horrors of lynching, the moral sins of Jim Crow, and the continuous denigration of Black humanity, it seemed like a country that couldn't possibly love Black people or become their land of opportunity. It had celebrated only the most convenient aspects of a complex history that had yet to be fully told, a history that perhaps could never be truthfully explained.

Barack Obama effectively told Americans, including me, the best parts of our national story. He narrated American history as an evolutionary journey toward progress. However challenged by the darkest forces of our nature and the most hateful instincts within our humanity, in his telling we were inevitably moving toward justice's illuminating light. He offered the nation a historical genealogy that tied the past and the present together in a manner rhetorically elegant enough to acknowledge our missteps while astutely shepherding us toward a New Jerusalem. That new world would be created out of the sacrifices of earlier generations of men and women courageous enough to believe in a future that was now finally within the nation's collective grasp. All we had to do was reach for it.

Obama's victory speech in Grant Park, Chicago, showcased American democracy at its aspirational best. Forty years after Chicago police officers had brutalized peaceful antiwar and civil rights demonstrators during the 1968 Democratic National Convention, almost a quarter of a million people gathered in celebration of a Black president-elect. In 1968 demonstrators had chanted, "The Whole World Is Watching!" as a public rebuke of the yawning chasm between America's democratic ideals and anti-democratic practices. Now, this same chant represented collective pride instead of shame. In that moment, time froze, and the multiracial democracy envisioned by Frederick Douglass, advocated by Ida B. Wells, extolled in the work of W. E. B. Du Bois, and reflected in the revolutionary lives of Malcolm X and Martin Luther King Jr. seemed to be coming true.

"It's been a long time coming, but tonight because of what we did on this day, in this election, at this defining moment change has come to America," Obama observed to the cheering throng, which in size rivaled the one in attendance at the March on Washington.[6] Obama's historic election night, like the Thirteenth Amendment's passage and the Supreme Court's *Brown* decision, opened up a new political world. All three moments introduced new possibilities for how Americans defined citizenship. The image of Obama standing on stage as president-elect of the United States of America breathed new and animating life into the Thirteenth and *Brown*. The betrayal of the Reconstruction Amendments and the broken promises surrounding *Brown* temporarily faded against the incandescent glow his victory produced. The Black president seemed to embody a new aesthetic of American citizenship. This new reality meant that Black citizenship, for so long violently denied and legally delayed, would flourish against the backdrop of an American presidency that was the first of its kind. In winning the White House, Obama simultaneously, it seemed, successfully redefined citizenship: it now not only included Black folk, but made us the representative exemplar of Americanness.[7]

White people began to treat me differently after Obama's arrival on the world stage. Students, colleagues—even strangers—told me that I reminded them of Obama, that I resembled him, that I sounded like him. This fascination with this historic moment—and its attendant burdens and opportunities—only grew after November 4. I laughed at media coverage that interpreted Obama's victory as ushering in a "postracial" America, painfully aware that racial injustice still festered, and indeed thrived, in all corners of the nation. But between November 4,

2008, and the January 20, 2009, inauguration, the world looked and felt different, even to me.

In Boston over the next two and a half months, white passersby chatted me up every chance they could. Colleagues at Boston universities invited me to their homes for dinner, and strangers complimented me, comparing my speech, my manners, or my smile to the president-elect. In short, my emotions about Obama, like the man himself, contained multitudes. I could not shake my own feelings about America, its relationship to the Black community, and our national inclination to run away from, rather than confront, the histories of racial division, violence, and hatred that choked off so much of our democratic potential. And yet I found myself powerfully drawn to the alternative reading Obama offered the nation. His brand of racial optimism about the future of American democracy and about our ability to shape that future as Black people proved to be invigorating, and for a time, I would share it.

Citizenship—how it is defined, who will have access to it, and whether Black people have the right to possess it—forms the beating heart of all three periods of national Reconstruction. For Barack Obama, the mixed-raced son of a white mother with Kansas roots and a Kenyan father with dreams of earning a PhD from Harvard, citizenship meant incorporating disparate, at times dissonant, strands of his own identity into an elegant personal and political symphony.

Obama learned hard lessons about the complex nature of racial identity in Hawaii, which shaped his personal and professional ambitions in Los Angeles and New York, where he attended college, and in Chicago, where he made his home both before and after law school at Harvard. His time as a community organizer on the West Side of Chicago honed his understanding of the Black experience, while his marriage to Michelle LaVaughn Robinson, who traced her ancestral lineage back to racial slavery, tied him more closely to the grandeur and travails of a Black history that he claimed not so much as a birthright than as a responsibility.

Obama optimistically presented his complex personal biography as a potential source of national unity. "Here's one thing I know for sure," Obama later recalled telling Michelle during a December 2006 meeting to decide whether he would run for president. "I know that the day I raise my right hand and take the oath to be president of the United States, the world will start looking at America differently." "I know," he continued, "that kids all around this country—Black kids, Hispanic kids, kids who don't fit in—they'll see themselves differently, too, their horizons lifted, their possibilities expanded."[8] And for a brief moment, Obama's election did precisely that. Seventy percent of Americans believed that race relations would improve, while slightly more considered the election to be one of the three most significant events for racial progress over the past century. Two-thirds of all voters were hopeful that "a solution to relations between blacks and whites will eventually be worked out," 93 percent of Obama voters were excited about the future, and 95 percent felt pride in the historic victory. With someone like Barack Obama as president, citizenship would at last be open to all Americans, and his presidency would unify us.[9]

Beneath Obama's hopeful vision lay the troubling reality that Blacks had *never* been seen as intelligent, patriotic, or American enough to be citizens in, let alone president of, the United States— in other words, never fully human enough to aspire to the highest political echelons within American democracy. Obama dreamed that his victory might offer the entire Black community the collective recognition of long-denied citizenship. His faith in the redemptive qualities of American democracy updated Reconstruction-era dreams of freedom by means of electoral politics. For Obama, citizenship meant that Black people could be part of a coalition powerful enough to elect the first African American president. In a sense, his election lent proof to the idea that Black citizenship had finally arrived in America. After the Civil War, Frederick Douglass, among others, had extolled the ballot as both a political sword, destined to shape a new reality of Black citizenship, and a civic shield, capable of defending Black lives against the remnants of defeated but vengeful white Confederates-turned-redemptionists. Barack Obama's election seemed to show the fulfillment of Douglass's hopes.[10]

Obama had announced his presidential campaign in February 2007 from the steps of the Old State Capitol in Springfield, Illinois, a place made famous by Abraham Lincoln's "House Divided" address. In that speech, two years before he won the presidency, Lincoln, then a member of the Illinois state legislature in a losing state senate campaign against Stephen Douglass, famously urged national unification in the face of roiling political divisions over slavery. "A house divided against itself cannot stand," he said. "I believe this government cannot endure permanently half slave and half free. I do not expect the Union to be dissolved; I do not expect the house to fall; but I do expect it will cease to be divided. It will become all of one thing, or all the other."[11]

After Lincoln was elected president, after the secession of the Southern states, and after four bloody years of civil war, America's

First Reconstruction period began, and it became a national referendum on Lincoln's prophetic words. The recognition of Black citizenship progressed unevenly during Reconstruction and after, stymied by domestic terrorists, by high-ranking public officials who betrayed democracy, and by statesmen whose leadership proved to be politically indefensible and morally reprehensible. America ceased to be half slave and half free, but it did not cease to be divided against itself. Obama fervently hoped that his election might finally turn America into all of one thing: a multiracial democracy. His very candidacy had posed historically fraught and politically urgent questions. Could America, unable to eradicate the system of the same kind of white supremacy and anti-Black racism that had led to disunion in Lincoln's era, become something different, something new and altogether unrecognizable, if it were led by a Black president?

During his almost two-year-long presidential campaign, Obama answered that question affirmatively. In the process, he embraced not only America's sixteenth president, but also the greatest leader of the greatest social movement in its history, Dr. Martin Luther King Jr. His public admiration for Lincoln's political wisdom and King's moral courage linked Obama to two of the greatest architects of American democracy. King's 1963 "I Have a Dream" speech, delivered against the backdrop of the Lincoln Memorial at the March on Washington, had pushed the nation toward the apex of its Second Reconstruction. King had defined the pursuit of radical Black citizenship as the key to unlocking American democracy's full potential. Turning America's capital into a church pulpit, King had essentially delivered a sermon on the possibilities of democracy, on the pitfalls of white supremacist violence, and on the need for national reconciliation through radical truth-telling. King also subtly called for economic reparations, saying, "We've come to our nation's capital to cash a check."[12] And he stressed the need for the birth of a new American freedom, a new American founding centered on Black citizenship.

Less than four years later, at the Riverside Church in New York City, King had announced himself as a political revolutionary. Breaking with his friend and ally President Lyndon Johnson, King challenged the nation to confront what he characterized as "the fierce urgency of now."[13] By then King was expansively defining Black citizenship not simply as the absence of racial oppression, but as encompassing a universal basic income, decent housing, racially integrated public schools and neighborhoods, and the end of structural violence, racism, and war. This vision of Black citizenship inspired him to criticize the Vietnam War as a tragic failure of American moral and political leadership.[14] The ceaseless killing of Vietnamese innocents was only one part of the collateral damage of a war rooted in America's imperial dreams. The conflict sapped financial and political resources from Johnson's Great Society initiatives; compromised the lives of Black and white soldiers alike, who were fighting and dying overseas for a country that disallowed them from attending the same schools; and curdled the freedom dreams that King had extolled during his March on Washington address.[15]

Obama openly cited King's "fierce urgency of now" phrase to explain why he felt compelled to run for president despite a lack of national political experience; once elected, he would keep a bust of Dr. King in the Oval Office. Obama described politics as more than just a blood sport: it was a calling to public service, one deeply rooted in his emphatic appreciation of Black activists, such as King, who had attempted to redeem America's soul during the Second Reconstruction. But Obama embraced King's early iteration, not his later career. Like many other Americans, Obama loved and admired the parts of King that were easy to love and admire: the young Baptist preacher who transformed, for one brief moment, the capital of the nation into a sacred political space, rather than the revolutionary leader King became.

As the presidential campaign progressed, Obama's references to King grew more elliptical. When he accepted the Democratic nomination for president on the forty-fifth anniversary of the March on Washington, he did not mention King by name. Already apparently recognizing that parts of King's radical legacy might be perceived as a threat to white voters, whose support he needed to become president, Obama characterized the man whom he earlier credited as his inspiration as merely a "young preacher from Georgia."[16] In his victory speech on election night, Obama referred to King as a "young preacher from Atlanta." Like most Americans, Obama felt more comfortable with the hopeful optimism expressed by the young King, whose journey from the Montgomery, Alabama, bus boycott to the March on Washington made him the best-known civil rights leader in American history. This version of King believed that American democracy could be reformed by shared political struggle and sacrifice on the part of both Black and white Americans.

Even as Obama's comments about King grew more ambiguous, however, commentators, politicians, and ordinary people increasingly described Obama as King's heir. It made perfect sense politically for Obama to compare himself to King and to invite such comparisons from others, as imperfect as the analogy was. The Black freedom struggle has a long history of individuals who, out of necessity, were simultaneously movement leaders, preachers, and politicians. Obama capitalized on this appeal, sometimes effortlessly and at other times with great strain. On March 4, 2007, in a speech at Brown Chapel A.M.E. Church in Selma, Alabama, the historic church that had served as a headquarters for voting rights efforts mobilized by King, Obama bathed himself in King's glorious light. He announced himself as the symbol of the "Joshua Generation," the heirs to the unfinished work of the Black community's Moses. "Put on your marching shoes," he exhorted an audience filled with civil rights veterans, including John R. Lewis, the longtime congressman from Georgia, who had personally known and still revered King. In the minds of many former civil rights leaders, including, perhaps especially, Lewis, who was a former chairman of the Student Nonviolent Coordinating Committee, Obama represented the most prominent living example of King's political legacy.[17]

But as would quickly become clear, Obama was not a social movement leader, and his election was not the culmination of the civil rights movement King helped to lead. Obama's election is best viewed as a beginning and not an end, a starting point of a third national project of reconstruction that would unfold in the years that followed. With its extraordinary twists and turns, this Third Reconstruction would more closely resemble its nineteenth-century counterpart than its twentieth-century one.

THE THIRD RECONSTRUCTION

*   *   *

Obama rode into office on a crest of history, bolstered by the combined might of Black voters, whose political power had grown exponentially in the four decades since passage of the Voting Rights Act, and a plurality of white voters who were ready to join the kind of multiracial coalition that had briefly thrived during the First Reconstruction.[18] In this sense, Obama became the symbol of reconstructionists everywhere, his victory the result of nearly a century and a half of struggle to usher the country into an age where it might fully realize the words of the Reconstruction Amendments (the Thirteenth, abolishing racial slavery; the Fourteenth, guaranteeing birthright citizenship; and the Fifteenth, providing Black male voting rights, all ratified between December 6, 1865, and February 3, 1870). Obama received over sixty-nine million votes, at the time the most in American history. Forty-three percent of white Americans cast ballots for a Black president. He won thirty-one states and the District of Columbia in the electoral college, the best showing by a Democratic candidate in a two-way race since Lyndon Johnson's landslide the year before passage of the Voting Rights Act. Obama also managed to return parts of the Old Confederacy into the Democratic fold, scoring victories in North Carolina, Virginia, and Florida, along with a shocking win in Indiana and a near miss in the border state of Missouri. But ironies abounded from the time Obama delivered his election night acceptance speech. After all, America finally elected a Black president only amid two wars raging overseas and the biggest economic collapse since the Great Depression.

America's Third Reconstruction began, similar to the first, in the tumultuous context of a domestic crisis that shook the nation to its very foundation. "Presidential Reconstruction" has traditionally referred to Andrew Johnson's lenient attitude toward the defeated South when he assumed the presidency after Lincoln's assassination. Black folk schooled in America's troubled racial history hoped that Obama's administration might give new meaning to that discredited term. But the limitations of Obama's reconstructionist vision meant those hopes would be disappointed.

Obama's electrifying 2004 keynote speech at the Democratic National Convention in Boston outlined the framework of his reconstructionist political vision. The speech reimagined sectional, regional, and national divides that were rooted in racial slavery and its aftermath, positing that differences between Republican- and Democratic-majority states obscured deep convergences. These convergences, he suggested, could be rediscovered through a civic nationalism rooted in reconstructionist dreams of multiracial democracy. By this time red states made up most of the Old Confederacy and its border states, places that were deeply invested in maintaining slavery's afterlife in systems of anti-Black punishment and poverty. These states were largely ruled by redemptionists who barely concealed the true nature of their politics under the guise of "law and order," small government, and states' rights. Blue states, in contrast, formed archipelagos of reconstruction committed, in varying degrees, to multiracial democracy.

Obama wasn't wrong to point out commonalities between red and blue states. After all, one of the reddest states in America—South Carolina—boasted a Black-majority population during Reconstruction. Others, such as Mississippi, housed powerful examples of Black political power in Black-majority counties. Obama erred, however, in his refusal to confront the deeper history behind present-day political and racial divisions. The civic nationalism he projected largely ignored, rather than confronted, this deeper story. Recognition of this harder version of American history, complete with its innumerable instances of white political fraud, its anti-Black racial violence, and its wholescale betrayal of democracy, is the needed first step toward unification around the American civic identity Obama thoughtfully proposed. One could never work without the other.[19]

When Obama entered onto the national political stage in 2004, he did so delivering (without any sense of irony) a full-throated endorsement of American exceptionalism in a city where, during the antibusing riots of 1976, a white rioter had once stabbed a Black man with a pole flying the American flag. "I stand here knowing that my story is part of the larger American story, that I owe a debt to all of those who came before me, and that, in no other country on earth, is my story even possible," observed Obama. His words offered an eloquent summation of a mythic account of America that electrified millions.[20]

Obama's sincere embrace of American exceptionalism represents an irony of history. American exceptionalism turns on its head the powerful and poetic narrative that W. E. B. Du Bois offered in which anti-Black racial violence was central to the nation's ongoing democratic experiment. It smooths over the rough edges of American history, painting an uplifting portrait of the United States as a freedom-loving, God-fearing, and boldly innovative nation where democracy, citizenship, and dignity have flowered on an unprecedented scale. The nation's ability to self-correct its flaws through liberal democracy, capitalism, and the work of social movements enabled the son of a Kenyan immigrant to win the White House, and the descendant of enslaved African Americans to become First Lady. It's a terrific story, one whose propaganda value as political rhetoric is made all the more powerful by the fact that so many Americans of all backgrounds, including Black folk, believe it. Who wouldn't want to believe that their country of origin is exceptional enough to both recognize and overcome its original sin?

Obama embraced American social movements insofar as they told an essentially optimistic story—a redemptive tale wherein the struggle of abolitionists, feminists, and civil rights activists revealed, over the long course of history, the essentially good nature of the American people alongside democracy's enduring strength. In reality, Reconstruction and its aftermath present a more troubling story, one that didn't result in the ultimate victory of Black Davids over white Goliaths, but the exact opposite. Black dehumanization is the essence of American democracy, a reality that must be faced if we are to ever change it. America's intrinsic national character, far from being the generous and exceptional nation Obama recounted, has exhibited violent disregard for Black people's feelings, well-being, lives, deaths, wants, needs, and future. The only way to change this history is by facing it.

American exceptionalism says that America is unique and superior to other nations in its values and principles. But exceptionalist ideas ignore the profound lie that has been fundamental to the nation's life and institutions from the start: that Black people are not human beings. Defining the Black population as apart from "the human family" enabled antebellum Americans to structure a system of racial capitalism that created wealth, power, and privilege based on the exploitation and punishment of Black bodies. Racial slavery, and the caste system subsequently erected to ensure its perpetuation, enshrined this belief into law, public policy, and economic arrangements that viewed African Americans more as a species of property than actual people. This lie fueled biological racism that promoted Black inferiority; rationalized sexual assault, rape, and forced labor during slavery and the First Reconstruction era; and fostered regional and sectional tensions that escalated into a bloody Civil War.[21] The same lie resonates today in the criminalization of Black bodies that leads to premature death at the hands of law enforcement and the massive warehousing of Black people in America's criminal injustice system; in the wealth, income, and employment gaps between Black and white families; in the continuation of racial segregation in schools and neighborhoods; and in the cultural racism that impacts what the nation values in art, literature, music, higher education, and so much more.[22]

The First Reconstruction marshaled a heroic effort to push back against this lie. The initial results were promising. Black Americans seized the opportunities that became available in politics, labor, education, and religion to fashion an assertive new identity that appeared tantalizingly close to full citizenship. But these new freedoms would be betrayed by some of the very institutions designed to offer protection after slavery. Black efforts to reconstruct American democracy faltered as old enemies and new friends weaponized the lie of racial dehumanization to turn back history's tide at the moment a new nation was being forged. Although Reconstruction planted seeds for future liberation movements, for the time being the lie of Black dehumanization was weaponized in the service of creating a new racial order of white supremacy—one that suspiciously resembled the ancient regime of racial slavery.

Barack Obama offered a reconstructionist vision founded in American exceptionalism. However, reconstruction and American exceptionalism are two incompatible ideas. Exceptionalism remains aloof to dreams of abolition democracy. How could it not? American exceptionalism has been fundamentally shaped by redemptionist visions that refuse to see Black people as human beings and rearrange democratic institutions accordingly.

If American exceptionalism rests on the lie that Black people are not human beings, then, as mentioned in the introduction, it also rests on a second lie: that the first lie never happened. This second lie especially thrived during the Jim Crow era that followed the First Reconstruction. The "Lost Cause" mythology, an interpretation of the Civil War that emerged in the South, depicted the Civil War and Reconstruction as misguided efforts to grant the rights and privileges of citizenship to people unable to handle them. Incredibly, the Freedmen's Bureau, in charge of the first federal effort to assist formerly enslaved people in reuniting with their families, securing fair employment contracts, and getting access to medical assistance, among other duties, was attacked for directing special attention to Blacks—even though Blacks had only just secured a hard-fought but still tentative freedom. Reconstruction-era efforts to pass civil rights, anti-Klan, and criminal justice reform legislation were similarly assailed. Because of the enduring power of the second lie, Black people have experienced a kind of historical and political gaslighting that continues to this day.[23]

Obama did confront the racial ghosts of America's slaveholding past during his final presidential campaign rally, in tiny Manassas, Virginia, on Monday, November 3, election eve. An overwhelmingly white crowd of more than one hundred thousand people had come to hear him discuss the possibilities of American democracy at the site of two bloody Civil War battles (the second one, in 1862, left more than twenty thousand soldiers dead). Before the adoring, festive crowd, Obama noted the significance of ending his campaign in Virginia, home to Richmond, the capital of "the Old Confederacy." He embraced the symbolism of the moment, touting the multiracial makeup of American society as a cornerstone of national unity. Those gathered seemed energized by this optimistic suggestion that national reconciliation could be achieved with Obama's election the next day. As a political exercise, the rally worked perfectly. As an effort to remove the legacies of racial slavery and the stains of white supremacy across the nation, and to finally secure full citizenship for all Americans, the results of Obama's election would be less promising. In the months and years to come, Obama's vision of national unity became entangled with the cords of America's racial past, which hindered its fulfillment in both new and tragically familiar ways. Obama would soon discover, alongside the entire nation, that it was not enough to simply pay symbolic homage to America's past racial horrors. He would need to confront them boldly, unapologetically, and with the same rhetorical brilliance that he used to win the presidency, lest they engulf him and the entire nation in the flames of discord that Kennedy spoke of so eloquently on that late spring evening in 1963.[24]

In its impact, Obama's ascent to the peak of American political power—symbolically, if not substantively—rivaled the ratification of the Thirteenth Amendment. Like the Thirteenth, Obama's election seemed like a historical thunderclap.[25] It heralded the arrival of a new American political order, where the president's very biography announced racism's diminishing grip on the national political soul. Obama himself seemed to exhibit such racial optimism as he basked in the warm afterglow of his history-making victory. On that glorious evening in Grant Park, he proudly proclaimed, "If there is anyone out there who still doubts that America is a place where all things are possible; who still wonders if the dream of our founders is still alive in our time; who still questions the power of our democracy, tonight is your answer."[26] Millions of Americans interpreted Obama's words as oracular, hoping that by shattering the nation's last remaining symbolic barrier, Obama might reconstruct democracy from the inside out, in contrast to the civil rights era's attempts to bring down the walls of segregation from the outside in. Obama had good reason to be confident, boastful even, about the fundamental goodness of the American people and the unparalleled virtues of our democracy. Elected with the largest popular vote total in American history, and with support from 43 percent of white voters, he held up his own candidacy as a national litmus test on the future of racial progress. That evening, at least, America passed with flying colors.[27]

Barack Obama's subsequent eight years in power did profoundly alter the aesthetics of American democracy. They transformed the Founding Fathers' sclerotic vision of politics and citizenship into something at once more hopefully expansive and violently fraught. Millions fervently believed that if the American president looked different from past commanders in chief then large structural and institutional transformations might follow, and that, soon enough, the nation would look different and feel different too. Obama's victory helped to fulfill one of the great ambitions of earlier Reconstruction efforts to showcase the ability of extraordinarily talented Black Americans to assume political leadership. First Lady Michelle Obama, and daughters Sasha and Malia, extended this reimagining of American life by providing a conspicuous vision of a healthy, loving, and thriving Black family that defied still-prevalent racist stereotypes.

But the nation interpreted Obama's triumph as much more as well. America's first Black president became the most iconic commander in chief since George Washington. Obama's Blackness reverberated around the world, bearing witness to America's seemingly endless capacity for reinvention. The victory was heralded as the arrival of a postracial America, one in which the nation's original sin of slavery and its afterlife in the post-Reconstruction Jim Crow era became sanctified through the election of a Black man as commander in chief. The outcome of the election seemed to offer a generation of young people a new vision of US citizenship, and Obama, as a Black man who was the leader of the free world, symbolized and personified that vision. The "Obama coalition" seemed a proof of concept for a powerful alliance of African American, white, Latinx, Asian American, and Native American voters who could embrace the nation's multicultural promise in word and through civic deeds. For a while, the entire nation believed.

But it is important to remember that the Thirteenth Amendment was in some sense one of the most profound bait-and-switch events in American history. It outlawed slavery "except as a punishment for crime"—and this exception would quickly become a gaping loophole. Across the nation, formerly enslaved people and other Black Americans found themselves incarcerated and forced into labor without compensation in ever-growing numbers. The amendment thus did not mark a sharp break from the past but only proved to be the start of a new phase of struggle.[28]

Likewise, the profound racial optimism that marked Obama's rise seems less misplaced than unearned. Obama's presence in the White House accelerated deep-seated racial furies. In the years to come, the Tea Party's racist attacks on the president's character, biography, and origin story (his policies were often an afterthought) emboldened a morally violent agenda that claimed Obama was not even a US citizen.[29] His status as America's first Black president expansively reimagined the contours of citizenship in ways that offered hope that the nation might finally complete the unfinished business of the First and Second Reconstructions. But at the same time, the politics of racial backlash worsened. They loomed larger than many had anticipated even in the heady days and weeks between his election and inauguration, as major media outlets announced a postracial order unmoored from the nation's traumatic racial history.

Tea Party activists attacked Obama as an anti-American subversive and begat a "birther" movement pushing the baseless claim that the president had actually been born in Kenya, and therefore, under Article 2 of the Constitution, could not be president. Donald J. Trump, who up to that point was best known as a TV reality-show star, honed his adversarial techniques as a political scoundrel, relentlessly promoting the mendacious birther-movement lie and eventually riding it all the way to the White House. Neither Obama's Ivy League degrees, nor his best-selling books, nor his election to the United States Senate or the presidency, nor even a copy of his birth certificate would be enough, for millions of white Americans, to prove his citizenship. His public displays of humility, his affectionate relationship with his daughters, and his unabashed love for his wife would be no match for long-standing and violent skepticism about the very idea of Black citizenship. Obama's Blackness became the symbolic site of the enduring struggle between reconstructionists and redemptionists. Negating his citizenship became, by proxy, an effort to deny Black citizenship nationally.

A case of racial profiling in Cambridge, Massachusetts, ended Obama's short-lived first-term honeymoon with white folk. After the mistaken-identity arrest of Henry Louis Gates Jr., a nationally recognized Black scholar, public intellectual, filmmaker, and Harvard University professor, in July 2009 at his own home, Obama departed from his usual caution on race matters by remarking that the police had "acted stupidly."[30] In retrospect, the controversy over the Gates incident illuminated the limits of a Black presidency. Against a backdrop of a global economic recession that disproportionately hurt Black Americans, Obama appeared hesitant to engage, wary of the potential firestorm that occurred anytime white voters perceived America's Black president as unfairly siding with African Americans. In his presidential memoir Obama ruefully recounted how his mild public rebuke of the police during his first year in office had resulted in the biggest drop in white voter approval of his entire administration. For many Americans, his defense of the Black professor violated an unspoken understanding. This version of racial etiquette differed in form, if not in substance, from the Reconstruction-era deference that whites demanded from Blacks under threat of death. So long as Obama comported himself as an "exceptional Negro," one who displayed such an intellectually rigorous and emotionally detached nature that one of his nicknames was "Spock" (after the iconic *Star Trek* character in famous control of his emotions), everything would be all right. Violate this script, and all hell would break loose.[31]

Obama both transcended and upheld aspects of this racial bargain during a March 18, 2008, speech designed to put out the fires of racial controversy stoked by the sermons of the Reverend Jeremiah Wright, a Black Liberation theologian who had served as Obama's pastor for almost two decades in Chicago. Wright's sermons drew from a reading of the Bible inspired by the Black Power era, and conservative media outlets uncovered video snippets of him chastising the United States for its racism, violence, and hypocrisy. In one, he is shown saying, "God damn America!" It was a rhetorical flourish in keeping with the best of the Black church tradition, and purposefully taken out of context to frighten white Americans into abandoning Obama's candidacy. It almost worked.

To recover, Obama attempted to bridge racial divides with references to his own biography. He recounted how even his beloved white grandmother, Madelyn Dunham, nicknamed "Toot," had held fast to stereotypes about the criminality of young Black men.[32] He suggested this was analogous to how Rev. Wright's own journey through the crucible of Jim Crow America had made him prone to see white America as a monolith rather than a mosaic. Too many Black and white people, Obama argued, viewed the world through the static lens of their own racial trauma, rather than acknowledging the progress that made contemporary America different.

Parts of the speech recounted, with remarkable candor, a history of institutional racism that Obama had largely glossed over during the campaign. Pastor Wright lived in an age where "black families could not amass any meaningful wealth to bequeath to future generations," he said. He spoke of the legacy of the dual assaults of state-sanctioned redlining and violence, and how these were the same forces that built racially segregated and economically impoverished Black ghettoes.[33] The heart of the speech, however, was in how it found *moral equivalence* between the festering wound of racial slavery, on the one hand, and, on the other, white resentment over affirmative action and the lie that Blacks received special privileges. But while the speech introduced radical themes (institutional racism, structural violence) that expanded the contours of acceptable race talk, Obama's campaign, even before his presidency began, in a sense reinforced the heavily policed racial boundaries of American exceptionalism.

Obama's presidency would not, as some predicted, represent the culmination of the civil rights movement's efforts to achieve Black dignity and citizenship. President Obama's national and global popularity seemed, during the 2008 campaign season and for a short time after, to signal the death of white supremacy, or at least its national decline. Many white Americans, both liberal and conservative, embraced a racial optimism during this brief interregnum inspired by the idea that America had entered a postracial period. They interpreted Obama's ascension as living proof of this, and of the power of American exceptionalism. For many white voters across the political divide, Obama's appeal rested in not just new beginnings but in how he seemed to mark the end of a specific narrative of racial injustice they had longed to be rid of.

From this perspective, Obama's victory would finally take the narratives that America was an irredeemably racist country and lay them to rest. The day America elected a Black president would provide a national reset on race matters. No more excuses for disparities in Black achievement, no more racial grievances over the past sins committed by long-dead generations of whites. The nation would have a fresh start toward a meritocracy wherein race no longer mattered.

But instead, Obama's presence on the national stage coincided with a resurgence in anti-Black racism. The wild conspiracy theories disputing his citizenship and the racist attacks leveled against both him and First Lady Michelle Obama were just the beginning. The burden of transforming America's tortured racial history in two four-year presidential terms proved impossible, even as its promise helped to catapult Obama to the nation's highest office. And yet Obama's presidency sped up our national reckoning on race and democracy.

Obama's presidency hastened America's rendezvous with a political reckoning that Martin Luther King Jr. had outlined during the final three years of his life. The revolutionary King, anticipating the Defund the Police movement, organized a campaign to defund war as part of his effort to achieve an enduring victory over racial and economic injustice. King famously served as the racial justice conscience for two presidents, John F. Kennedy and Lyndon B. Johnson, and he was not afraid to publicly disagree with, challenge, and criticize them.[34]

In the early 1960s, King urged Kennedy to announce a Second Emancipation Proclamation, convinced that the president's bully pulpit could spur America to make good on a promise of citizenship delayed for a century by racially violent words, laws, and deeds. Kennedy balked at issuing such a proclamation, but he proved himself a man after King's heart on June 11, 1963, with an earnest national address on racial justice that centered Black citizenship as American democracy's beating heart. Blacks were "not yet freed from the bonds of injustice," Kennedy observed. They were "not yet freed from social and economic oppression." Then he added an insight that Black abolitionists, civil rights activists, and organizers had advocated for centuries: "And this Nation, for all its hopes and all its boasts, will not be fully free until all its citizens are free." King prayed for a president who would champion the cause of Black citizenship. History, so it seemed, answered those prayers with the Obama presidency.[35]

But those who hoped that Obama might serve as a combined commander in chief and social movement leader would be bitterly disappointed. Obama seemed unwilling to squarely confront the systematic racism and white supremacy that flourished in spite of his watershed presidency—or, as some said, because of it.

Obama was not a social movement leader, but the conflation helped carry him to the White House. Early on in his campaign, Black voters were skeptical that a Black man could be elected president; later, they feared for Obama's safety. Trepidation about white America's willingness to support such a candidacy gave way over time to the most rapturous embrace of a political figure ever. Inevitably, many did begin to see him as both a presidential candidate and a trailblazing civil rights leader—a combination of the dashing JFK and the righteous MLK in one game-changing historical figure. Obama tapped into an intangible feeling that had fueled Black struggles for citizenship and democracy across a spectrum of ideological, religious, and political stances within the Black community since the Civil War. It was this spirit that had animated the eloquence of Frederick Douglass, the advocacy of Ida B. Wells, the travails of Martin Luther King Jr. and Malcolm X, and the revolutionary spirit of Angela Davis. And that spirit was hope.

The almost superhuman capacity of Black folk to express hope in a brighter future against nearly insurmountable odds led them to support Obama with a kind of love and loyalty that telescoped the dreams of past generations onto one man and his family. On the campaign trail, candidate Obama touted his experiences as a community organizer in Chicago, where he had helped a depressed working-class community gain access to job training, education, and social services. As the campaign became better funded and better organized, Obama took pains to forge relationships with veterans of the civil rights struggle. None proved more pivotal in this regard than John Lewis, the last surviving March on Washington keynote speaker and a man who considered King a mentor, friend, and guide.[36]

On February 27, 2008, Lewis formally endorsed Obama. This was a significant public declaration of support, especially since Lewis had previously endorsed Senator Hillary Clinton. Swept up in the excitement of a campaign that by then had seen Obama win the Georgia primary, Lewis described Obama's candidacy as "the beginning of a new movement in American political history" that began in the minds and hearts of ordinary people. "And I want to be on the side of the people," Lewis explained. Obama heartily accepted Lewis's support; the civil rights activist's close friendship with King, in particular, gave the endorsement historical significance. "John Lewis is an American hero and a giant of the civil rights movement," Obama observed. "I am deeply honored to have his support."[37]

Lewis's support made Jesse Jackson's less necessary. Jackson, whose two campaigns for president in the Democratic primaries of 1984 and 1988 had paved the way for Obama's candidacy, fell out with the senator after a hot mic caught him explaining that he would like to "cut" the young senator's "nuts off" for speaking down to Black people. Jackson was referring (privately, he thought) to Obama's penchant for practicing respectability politics in predominantly Black settings, in order to signal to white audiences that he was unafraid to speak uncomfortable truths to Black America. White politicians had long employed this practice, too. But a Black presidential candidate doing so seemed, to Jackson as well as to others, unseemly.[38]

Obama's embrace of the civil rights movement's lineage offered a bulwark against critics who questioned whether his biracial background gave him sufficient understanding of the struggle for Black freedom in America. Obama clung to the legacy of the movement, to King's image, and to his fast friendship with Lewis in part to repel assaults against his claims of Blackness and citizenship. The effectiveness of the charges against him lay in deftly exploiting doubts about Black people's loyalty and patriotism, two prerequisites of citizenship. In one sense, the attack on Obama's citizenship—and by extension, the Black community's—highlighted an uncomfortable truth. Black people have never truly been able to exercise citizenship. Redemptionists historically reveled in this fact, mobilizing organized political violence—at first locally, and in time nationally—to punish Black people who deigned to advocate for their rights as fully empowered citizens of the republic. All but the most radical nineteenth-century white reconstructionists exhibited concerns, along a wide ideological spectrum, over whether Negroes had been given too much too soon. Could they be trusted to judiciously exercise the right to vote? Did they have the intelligence, capacity, and temperament to hold elected office? Would they squander their new-found freedom, or would they exhibit the tenacity, discipline, and hard work required to succeed?

For too many white people, the question of whether Black Americans would ever truly be fit for citizenship remains open-ended. Within the political and historical framework of American exceptionalism, white redemptionists and reconstructionists at times collude in the belief that Blacks are unfit to exercise citizenship with all its privileges and responsibilities. (Think of the white liberals who took authors Richard J. Herrnstein and Charles Murray seriously when they published *The Bell Curve*, a 1994 book advancing an updated, racist eugenics argument, or the bipartisan support for the war on drugs starting in the 1970s, or for Ronald Reagan's crime policies in the 1980s, or Bill Clinton's crime bill and welfare reform initiatives in the 1990s.)

Obama embraced the civil rights movement as a way of both convincing Black voters that he was one of them and enlisting their support. But his reverence for the civil rights era, as expressed in his memoir and at times in public speeches, also seemed to exhibit an outsider's appreciation for it. He depicted civil rights activists as being endowed with a sense of community rooted in shared sacrifice. Obama's peripatetic childhood made him yearn for belonging to such a community. He found his way through his relationship and marriage to Michelle Obama, his time as a community organizer, and his political engagement.

The man with the unusual name, biracial heritage, and cosmopolitan upbringing became the Blackest president in American history. And his opponents took full advantage of the worst parts of America's past in a way that made this fact a political liability. Conservatives weaponized Obama's Blackness against him, pillorying him as just another ghetto hustler who could never be trusted. The president found this surprising, having spent a lifetime expertly bridging racial divides from Hawaii to Indonesia, Los Angeles to New York, and Chicago to the nation's capital, and having charmed white voters all the way to the White House. It was not just Obama who was under attack: every time Obama experienced the public humiliation levied against him by Republican elected officials, conservative media, and ordinary Tea Party–supporting whites carrying blatantly racist signs at rallies, it represented a wound on the Black American body politic.

Incredibly sensitive to critiques of Obama rooted in anti-Black racism, many Black elected officials and much of the larger Black community gave the president a pass.[39] They closed ranks around Obama in much the same way that W. E. B. Du Bois had advised the Black community to do in 1917, with America poised to enter World War I. Du Bois, in a move he would come to regret, urged Blacks to put aside their pain, their pride, and their passion for justice and join the fight to save democracy around the world, in the hope that their sacrifice would be repaid with full citizenship. That strategy did not work out as planned. The politics of Black solidarity during the Obama era would suffer a similar fate. Large segments of Black Americans viewed the health and political destiny of his administration as being inextricably bound to the future fate and fortune of the entire Black community.[40]

In particular, white supremacist assaults on the president's citizenship and character, not to mention his policies, inspired the active creation of a sanctuary of Black communal love and protection for the First Family that brooked no room for honest criticism of the president's failure to prioritize Black issues even though Blacks were the most loyal part of the coalition that had placed him in office. Obama could thus take parts of the Black community for granted, especially those residing at the lower frequencies, who were more vulnerable to structural violence, racism, and inequality. Obama amplified Black leaders, including Congressman Lewis and the civil rights activist Al Sharpton, with whom he enjoyed a rapport. He marginalized those with whom he did not see eye to eye, including Jesse Jackson and the entire Congressional Black Caucus. This dynamic was as understandable as it was unfortunate. Fealty to Obama diminished the vibrancy and scope of a Black public sphere rooted in vigorous debate, passionate disagreement, and a collective will to speak truth to power on behalf of the enduring goals of citizenship and dignity.

———

As Obama discovered in the wake of the Rev. Jeremiah Wright controversy, Black citizenship seems to remain forever subject to the policing of the white imagination. On this score, Black patriotism is questioned if African Americans express anything less than uncritical support for the entirety of the American project. For Obama, the lesson of Jeremiah Wright proved to be that Americans were ready, indeed eager, to embrace an optimistic vision of racial justice and democracy that smoothed over the rough parts of a history that could seemingly be overcome through eloquent words. Obama's upbeat rhetoric about America and its infinite capacity for change echoed the hopes of earlier generations of activists. Yet his public interrogation of its original sin of racial slavery, and how slavery's afterlife continued to impact Black people, fell far short of what was needed: a recognition of the structural violence, racism, and oppression that still marks the African American experience. Racial optimism in the service of narratives of American exceptionalism fueled Obama's rise to power, but it also limited his capacity to be a president who could heal ancient racial wounds. The former community activist—with rare and powerful exceptions that took place during his final two years in office—proved unwilling to confront the depth and breadth of American racism. On this score he lacked King's political courage, though King was the civil rights leader he most often quoted during his first presidential campaign. That burden would fall on the shoulders of a younger generation of activists who demanded Black dignity with no apologies or equivocations.

Obama explicitly linked his political fortunes to the civil rights movement, but he distanced himself from the Black Power movement. Black Power's embrace of Black nationalism—the politics of self-determination, racial solidarity, and cultural pride in the global expansiveness of Blackness—made its appeal seem too specific for a president who tended toward the universal. What Obama failed to recognize was that Black Power called for universal rights and freedoms for all people through the particular struggle of Black folk. In 1964, when Malcolm X visited the US Senate to watch the white politicians debate the civil rights bill, he observed that Negroes were "beginning to feel black." He meant this in a positive light: the transformation from "Negro" to "Black" was a process Malcolm himself had unequivocally sought to advance.

The civil rights and Black Power eras turned Black identity into a powerful force in the struggle for dignity and citizenship. In 2008 and beyond, that "Black feeling" resonated across America and around the world through the words, images, and actions of Barack Obama. This sentiment impacted liberal integrationists, progressive radicals, feminists, and even some conservatives, who marveled at Obama's history-shattering rise. Paradoxically, the less Black Obama tried to be, the Blacker he became in the global imagination. Every fist bump reinterpreted as a "terrorist fist jab"; every brush-off-the-shoulder homage to rapper Jay-Z; all the speeches that drew, intentionally or not, from the cadences of the Black church; Obama's walk, talk, style, and dress—even when he expressly wished to convey the opposite—had millions feeling Black in a way they never had before. By inviting Black performers to the White House; by singing a verse from soul-singer Al Green's "Let's Stay Together," during a 2012 appearance at Harlem's Apollo Theater; by mentioning his favorite rap artists to journalists, he signaled that his would be a different kind of presidency. Yet in many ways these genuinely appreciative nods to a love of Black expressive culture hid Obama's unwillingness to prioritize the policy concerns of Black voters. What, some began to ask, was the value of a Black president who feared that publicly advocating for Black people could undermine his entire agenda?[41]

As a student of history, Obama understood and admired how ordinary people ignited the greatest change in American society, even as he found himself attracted to iconic figures—from Abraham

Lincoln to John Lewis—who helped to speed history's march through acts of personal courage and stoic grace. During his second term, reconstructionist politics in America entered a new phase as Black Lives Matter came onto the stage. BLM embraced the radical Black citizenship of Martin Luther King Jr. and fused it with Malcolm X's advocacy of radical Black dignity. Its activists drew inspiration from the radical King that Obama rejected.

This new generation of activists followed King's call to build a "Beloved Community," one that guaranteed a living wage, a universal basic income, and decent housing and brought an end to the structures of political and policy violence that scarred Black communities. But it would be Malcolm's thirst for Black dignity in the face of violent oppression that would become their calling card. Obama's election had helped to trigger the historical moment, one that would erupt from the lower frequencies of Black political life and grow into the largest social movement in American history.

On the one hand, BLM's pursuit of radical Black dignity placed it at odds with America's first Black president. And yet without President Obama's stirring example as the aspirational face of American democracy—and as at least a version of Black citizenship—many of the activists who came to be his biggest critics might not have become politically active at all. The inspiration, disappointment, and hope emanating from Barack Obama's 2008 victory and political campaigning helped set the stage—in both positive and negative ways—for the emergence of a movement for radical Black dignity, unleashing a grassroots insurgency and an unanticipated political revolution in the heart of the world's most powerful democracy.[42]

2

DIGNITY

I LEARNED THE TRUE meaning of dignity watching my mother wake up early to take a bus to the train station to work at New York City's Mount Sinai Hospital, and then reverse that process to come home in time to make dinner, five days a week, and sometimes on Saturdays, too. My mother exemplified Black dignity through the spectacular and the mundane. She worked herself to the bone to send me and my older brother to the local Catholic school, while also sending regular remittances back to Haiti to take care of her mother and many other relatives still there: brothers, sisters, cousins, nieces, and nephews. She challenged undermining white supervisors at her workplace. And, unable to visit Haiti for decades because of the radical political associations she had belonged to in her youth, she battled pain and regret. She was unable to visit my grandmother before her unexpected death from an illness that turned into pneumonia.

Watching my mother work and read, and hearing her discussing history, politics, and social movements—often with me—I learned at home to appreciate the intellectual foundations of the struggle for Black dignity. I saw her daily efforts to put food on the table, to pay the mortgage on our modest home, and to navigate a work-life-church balance with grace.

Some moments especially stand out. When I was eight years old, Ronald Reagan won the presidential election over incumbent Jimmy Carter. It was Tuesday, November 4, 1980—twenty-eight years to the day before Barack Obama's election, and Reagan's victory sent up a signal flare—a clear sign that the vast majority of Americans were not just uninterested in recognizing Black humanity, but downright hostile toward us. Mom responded to the news as if we had just lost more than an election. I don't remember her exact words, but the gist of her message, related in her lilting Haitian Kreyol, was this: Ronald Reagan did not like Black people. A quarter century before those same words thrust rapper Kanye West into controversy when he used them to criticize President George W. Bush's handling of Hurricane Katrina, my mom broke it down in private.

She embodied Black dignity at New Bethel Baptist Church, where we attended the Sunday and mid-week services as well as holidays and Vacation Bible School events. Her mellifluous voice helped to overcome her natural shyness when she sang. She prayed intensely, walked uprightly, and conveyed an unmistakable air of dignity that I sought to emulate. Dinner table conversations turned into seminars on Black history, radical politics, and religious faith. Mom defined personal discipline as our sole earthly protection against racist police, random neighborhood violence, and worse. She took pains to remind me that knowledge offered both power and danger. Her exit from Haiti had been hastened by her youthful support for pro-democracy movements in a country scarred by authoritarianism. America represented a kind of political limbo for Mom and other Haitian immigrants: a space of myth and mourning that offered a degree of freedom and safety from regimes of political terror, despite the fact that the US government itself had helped to prop up the Haitian regime they had fled. Always attuned to the reality of the Janus-faced nature of American democracy, she cautioned me to use my voice judiciously and sparingly, lest the same forces that had compelled her to leave Haiti rear their ugly heads in her adopted home. I thought she was being dramatic. Little did I know.

Mom came to the United States from Haiti as a skilled worker, a lab technician who found steady employment and quickly joined Chapter 1199 of the Service Employees International Union (SEIU). The union's campaigns in the 1960s had found support from both Malcolm X and Martin Luther King Jr. During its periodic strikes for better wages, health-care insurance, and other benefits, I accompanied her on picket lines, even while I was still in elementary school. From these experiences I imbibed the profound consequences of political solidarity. This was more than allyship: Black, Puerto Rican, Jewish, Eastern European, West African, and Caribbean union members stood locked arm in arm for a struggle that, even then, felt existential. The more we collectively advocated for ourselves—both those who looked like us and those who didn't—the better our lives became. Such forays into the adult world always seemed to be an adventure to me. I remember people carrying picket signs, drinking coffee from thermoses, and endlessly smoking cigarettes. I could not help but notice how the multiracial character of the assembled protesters contrasted with the crowds I was used to seeing in my all-Black neighborhood in Jamaica, Queens. The radical humanity of workers demanding justice became sewn into the fabric of my being. Black struggles for dignity and citizenship gave direction to—while being deeply embedded within—larger networks of struggle that transcended race, class, gender, and difference.

My childhood reflected a blend of influences. I was a New Yorker—born in Manhattan, I spent my toddler years in Brooklyn and was raised thereafter in Queens. But I was shaped even more by my identity as a Black American and by my mother's Haitian roots. She deserves credit for making certain that I understood the value of our family history and my own role as a first-generation African American. Mom was an expert raconteur, a prodigious reader, an indefatigable book buyer, and an organic intellectual. She could regale me and my older brother with stories about Haiti (maybe about the women who made Toussaint Louverture's revolution successful), with political analysis (breaking down why Reagan's election spelled trouble for Black folk), and with lessons in Black American history (describing her admiration for both Malcolm X and Dr. Martin Luther King Jr.)—often all in one sitting. She railed against anti-Black racism while stubbornly retaining a belief that Haitians were America's hardest-working immigrants. Ever.

Mom became a US citizen in America's bicentennial year, 1976. A deeply nostalgic reverence for America's possibilities for freedom infused her political and intellectual radicalism. She reserved a special place in her heart for John and Bobby Kennedy, who held the rare designation of "good white folk" (*bon moun blan*), a phrase that sounded magical when she said it in Haitian or French. But Mom balanced this reverence with a pragmatic recognition of the United States' historical and continuing exploitation of Haiti, from the 1915 US military occupation of the island, which introduced Jim Crow to the populace, to more recent US support for the dictators who had caused Haitians to flee the island's political instability.

Propelled by US government actions, they had arrived on these shores only to be treated as unworthy of asylum or sanctuary— unlike the *Cubanos blancos*, who were welcomed.

Before I ever read W. E. B. Du Bois, I learned about double consciousness from my mother, who seemed capable of loving and criticizing both the United States and Haiti. She loved history, and she loved that I loved it too. It drew us closer together as silent co-conspirators determined to unravel the secrets of our shared existence as Black people. We loved history's great personalities: its mavericks, political underdogs, and revolutionary leaders, who too often perished before their time. I read C. L. R. James's classic history of the Haitian Revolution, *The Black Jacobins*, for example, courtesy of Mom's personal library.[1] James provided intellectual armor for the road ahead. His transportive storytelling portrayed Haitians as revolutionaries who remade a colony of enslaved Africans into a republic of citizens. Their story had helped to inspire Black abolitionists in America, making them unheralded architects of liberation movements that reshaped the world.

Haiti did more than turn the lofty words of the American and French Revolutions into reality at the foundation of democracy. Haitians rewrote the very concepts of liberty, citizenship, and freedom that reverberated across the Atlantic. Those revisions eventually reached US plantations and slave communities. And they scorched the soul of President Thomas Jefferson, who enacted the first trade embargo against the new republic.

Dignity required a deep sense of community, one that my family managed to forge in sometimes unforgiving terrain. My neighborhood was less African American than it was Black: immigrants from Haiti, Jamaica, Belize, Trinidad and Tobago, and Barbados lived alongside Black Americans whose deep southern roots wound back to antebellum slavery. A smattering of African immigrants also lived on the edges of my reality: Mom's work colleagues, or street vendors we frequented in the city. In my racially segregated, working-class section of Queens, as a young boy I sometimes felt embarrassed watching my mother converse with neighbors, in stores, or at home in Haitian or French or Spanish, depending on the audience. My friends' Black moms just spoke English, and I felt eyes staring at me, and at her, in wonder when these exchanges took place. These feelings quickly subsided the more I learned about Black history in all of its transatlantic, multilingual, and culturally rich complexity, and my embarrassment gave way to pride.

When we first moved to our little section of Queens, it seemed like a slightly decaying Black suburb. As I entered elementary school, things got worse. Petty crime reached the area. Neighborhood kids formed small gangs that might relieve you of a bicycle or a grocery bag; in one instance, kids snatched my mother's purse. Keeping your dignity meant treading carefully in parts of the neighborhood where local teens drank, cursed, and played basketball and handball. If you did not, complex negotiations and subterranean hijinks sometimes ensued. Once, when I was about to run an errand at the local bodega, my mom warned me to stay away from "the bad guys," the corner store "entrepreneurs," who might ask me for a favor that could turn my life into a cautionary tale. As much as my love for Haitian history grounded me, I knew I presented to the world as a regular Black kid from around the way.

The police certainly regarded my being Haitian as a distinction that made no difference.

I came to proudly identify as both a Black American and a Haitian, and, over time, as African, and I was both inspired by the history lessons that I learned at home and on the picket lines and enraged by them. I couldn't help but notice the material differences between my own segregated Black working-class neighborhood in Jamaica and the lily-white part of Queens where I went to high school. Unbeknownst to me, my high school had been founded in the 1950s at the exact moment that racial integration had gotten underway in Queens. It had driven many white students—not just those at my Holy Cross High School, but across America—toward private enclaves. I stepped into this history unaware of the details, but able to sense the emotions that my presence elicited. The first time I ever heard the word "nigger" directed at me by a white person was at Holy Cross. But my experience was only one among many that triggered similar confrontations between Black and white students across the city and the nation.

Black history saved me: It became my North Star, my guide for making sense of my environment. The more I read, the deeper I searched, and the deeper I searched, the vaster the expanse I encountered and the safer I felt. Other generations of Black folk had confronted the same challenges, disappointments, and lies that I was now encountering. I watched *Eyes on the Prize*, and I read *The Autobiography of Malcolm X*, a book that I found myself returning to time and again. Malcolm's journey from childhood trauma, juvenile delinquency, and prison to the heights of radical Black political activism was mesmerizingly instructive to me.[2] He became my role model, a historical figure whom I recognized intimately. As an adult, he had lived in the East Elmhurst section of Queens, which was not so different from my own neighborhood. He had combated racism through courageous truth-telling, the kind that I endeavored to emulate.

History shone a clarifying light on injustices that continued in the present. I felt like John the Baptist, eager and ready to evangelize the gospel of Black dignity anywhere, anyplace, anytime. I helped organize an informal Black history reading group with my school's small coterie of African American students, and I challenged teachers to offer a more inclusive and expansive curriculum. Four years of taking three buses to attend an overwhelmingly white high school shaped my views on racial justice, Black history, and the reality (versus the fantasy) of interracial coalitions in profound ways. I imagined that I would be an organizer like the folks at my mother's hospital union. My admiration for historical mavericks, including Malcolm X, led me to believe that I would apply locally the same insistence on justice that they did nationally.

My future changed by chance. After graduating from high school in 1990 I enrolled at Stony Brook University, a state school that attracted a robust contingent of Black students from the New York City boroughs like myself. Through sheer luck, I met Black professors who mentored and cared for me. Stony Brook's Africana Studies Program, while not yet a department, offered a Black Studies major, an outgrowth of the bruising political struggles of the Black Power era. Struggles for Black dignity during the 1960s reached all the way toward predominantly white suburban enclaves in Long Island, making Stony Brook an unlikely repository of radical Black intellectual and political ferment.

Black Studies professors there continued to fight the good fight against the conservative political backdrop of the Reagan era. Some, such as the poet and Black Arts visionary Amiri Baraka, were famous—political celebrities from the 1960s who had transitioned to college teaching after the revolutionary tides they had helped to create subsided amid the conservative backlash of the 1980s.[3] Others, including the Oxford University–educated Nigerian scholar Olufemi "Femi" Vaughan, served as powerful mentors to me. Femi, who was only a little more than a decade older than I was, helped me to imagine a world where the life of the mind comingled with civic activism from the grassroots all the way to more gilded halls of power. Most worked tirelessly on behalf of Black students in relative anonymity.

At Stony Brook, I found my métier, not as an organizer but as a scholar-activist. When I later moved to Philadelphia, in the early 1990s, to enter a history PhD program at Temple University, however, I still didn't really know what to expect. Just shy of turning twenty-one, I lived in North Philly, a part of the city where segregation, poverty, urban decay, and racism were even more acute than in some parts of Queens. Philadelphia taught me to put aside my New York City ego. I met Sonia Sanchez, the brilliant poet and Black Arts pioneer who, in 1967, at what is now San Francisco State University, had helped found the first Black Studies program in the nation. She became my mentor and quietly began putting things in perspective. A Harlem native, Professor Sanchez had long worked for civil rights. Her humility invariably rubbed off on even the brashest students. Her patience and willingness to share her story, and the story of Black people, cast a spell on me and left an indelible impression on my life. My eventual decision to ask her to be on my PhD exam (and later dissertation) committee grew organically from our conversations and from the classes of hers that I took, including ones on Black feminism and the Black Arts. I found myself privy to a subterranean historical world, the depths of which I realized I had barely yet plumbed.

Philadelphia's jaw-dropping racial history included the May 13, 1985, bombing of MOVE, a grassroots Black naturalist movement that had been targeted by police and local officials since the 1970s. I eventually moved to West Philadelphia about twenty blocks away from where the bombing had taken place. City officials had razed the entire city block that was home to MOVE's headquarters and let it burn to the ground, killing eleven people, including six adults and five children between the ages of seven and thirteen. In the 1990s, remnants of MOVE, the Black Panther Party, and other Black radical organizations in Philadelphia found common cause in supporting Mumia Abu-Jamal, a former Black Panther turned journalist and MOVE supporter.

Abu-Jamal found himself on death row after being accused of killing a police officer in 1981. In Philly, he had joined the ranks of Black revolutionaries who had come to embody the afterlife of the radical movements for Black dignity that flourished during the 1960s and 1970s. These included Assata Shakur, who later went into exile in Cuba after being accused of killing a New Jersey state trooper in 1973 (she remains there as of this writing).[4] I supported Abu-Jamal, convinced of his innocence, and impressed by the compassionate intellect he exhibited in his book *Live from Death Row*, as well as in the tape-recorded dispatches he produced from prison.[5] On the tapes, he discussed how his youthful experiences as a Black Panther had exposed him to the depth and breadth of the criminal punishment system. It was that system that had eradicated the Panthers, bombed MOVE, and placed him on death row for a crime he maintained he did not commit. Ramona Africa, one of two survivors of the 1985 MOVE massacre, helped to organize and lead demonstrations for justice for him. These demonstrations also advocated for reparations for MOVE victims and demanded an end to Philadelphia's systemic racism against—and punishment of—Black people in general and political radicals in particular.[6]

Ramona Africa, Mumia Abu-Jamal, and other Black activists in Philadelphia gave me a new understanding of dignity, spurring me to investigate the deep roots of Black Power politics. They fearlessly criticized not only white supremacy but also narratives of American exceptionalism. Those narratives, they said, had allowed certain parts of the Black community to thrive while others still suffered. By getting access to elite educations, sought-after jobs, and, in some instances, the trappings of celebrity and wealth, these "successes" made the revolutionary politics of the 1960s seem unnecessary to the larger American public. The revolutionary ideals animating the Black Power era had become a distant unrealized dream.

But the Philly activists were not giving up: they demanded that all Black lives matter before that phrase became popular, and their example burrowed itself deeply into my scholarly work. I was a Black Gen Xer in Philly, and we lived our own version of the dreams our parents had carried during the civil rights era. The soulful sounds of Erykah Badu and D'Angelo became our soundtrack, the Neo-Soul background music in cafés populated by a Black bohemian community that became a part of a revival of poetry, protest, and spoken word. Philly's arts and culture scene was just as dynamic as the one I had left back home. And the pursuit of Black dignity through history, rooted in the lessons my mother had taught me as a boy, now became my vocation.

Barack Obama represents one variety of Black dignity. Deeply rooted in an American exceptionalist framework that ties recognition of Black humanity to personal responsibility, this type of dignity proved recognizable to both reconstructionists and redemptionists. But such dignity came at great personal cost. Black folk like Obama were lucky, gifted, and talented enough to reach the Olympian heights, where they received protection against the stubborn fact of white supremacy. Yet the price of this protection curtailed the ability of these new exemplars of Black excellence to practice the courageous truth-telling embodied by the civil rights and Black Power activists whom they lavishly praised and who made their success possible.

Obama's brand of Black dignity did not prevent racial conflict from shadowing his first term, in the form of Birthers, Tea Partyers, and other manifestations of gnawing white resentments. Although Obama was reelected in 2012, this conflict erupted into open warfare during his second term. The US Supreme Court's June 2013 decision in *Shelby v. Holder* gutted the enforcement of the Voting Rights Act, throwing into question the signal policy achievement of the civil rights movement. Unbeknownst to the entire nation, the decision signaled the end of a half-century political epic that made Obama's ascension possible. It also marked one of the pivotal, if misunderstood, moments of the Third Reconstruction.[7] Then, in July, George Zimmerman's acquittal in the 2012 shooting death of Black teenager Trayvon Martin in Florida reopened a racial Pandora's box around police and vigilante violence against Black men, women, boys, and girls. After the verdict, the outraged protests and organized demonstrations of a new generation of civil rights activists turned the social media hashtag #BlackLives-Matter into a clarion call for a new social justice movement.[8]

Connecting individual episodes of violence and painful examples of the miscarriage of justice to the broader context of discrimination in the United States, especially the high rate of Black incarceration, Black Lives Matter activists drew lessons about the prison system from legal scholar Michelle Alexander's best-selling 2010 book *The New Jim Crow*. A searing treatise arguing that the criminal justice system represented an extension of the old Jim Crow racial caste regime in a new guise, the book became a national phenomenon. In the process, it armed policy experts and street activists alike with the weapon of history. The Black Lives Matter movement would make the racism of American law enforcement one of its central concerns.[9]

Black Lives Matter became a national movement with global reverberations, its version of Black dignity a development that altered the course of the Third Reconstruction. BLM defined dignity as connected to, but distinct from, claims of citizenship, and insisted that demands for dignity, both universal and particular, were most forceful when emanating from below. Those who reside at America's lower frequencies, they argued, can best comprehend the nature of the chains that bind them, and are thus better able to identify the keys to their liberation.

In each period of Reconstruction, it has been grassroots, bottom-up, radical Black activism that has brought dignity to the forefront. Radical Black dignity imagines the end of global white supremacy as beginning with society's recognition of the intrinsic worth of Black souls. So while citizenship requires the formal recognition of those who hold power, recognition that is at times granted to respectable proxies (such as Barack Obama) as stand-ins for the entire community, dignity emanates from the pores of the Black quotidian. These are the unnamed lynching victims recorded by Ida B. Wells, the sharecroppers who toiled in anonymity, Malcolm X's "Field Negroes." Citizenship is only as strong, as enduring, and as worthwhile as our acknowledgment of the ordinary human dignity with which, within the Black radical tradition, it is inextricably and adamantly linked. It was in this tradition, and by connecting its claims to national citizenship with a simultaneous insistence on personal dignity, that BLM challenged the very foundations of American democracy.

The policy agenda outlined by the Movement for Black Lives (M4BL)—a coalition of dozens of grassroots racial justice organizations founded in 2014—defined achieving justice for all as a universal human rights project bound up in the particular struggles of Black people.[10] More intimately, the movement linked Martin Luther King Jr.'s critique of militarism, materialism, and racism to the ways in which these crises impact individual and group identities.[11] BLM confronted the reality that racism, sexism, violence, and poverty affect Americans—and the wider global community—differently. Recognizing how all aspects of our identity—including race and class, sexuality and gender, disability and mental health—shape neighborhoods, communities, and public policies is the hallmark of the twenty-first-century reconstructionist politics that BLM helped to establish.

Black Lives Matter offered the Third Reconstruction a new vision of American democracy as deeply rooted in radical Black dignity. In this sense it emerged from the gap between the racial optimism of the Obama era and the melancholy reality of Black life at the lower frequencies during Obama's presidency. BLM stood on the shoulders of previous generations of Black radical activists, but also advanced the concept of radical Black dignity by expanding the range of individuals and groups within the Black community worthy of such recognition. In so doing, BLM activists continued the tradition of reconstructionists whose fervent pursuit of dignity placed them at the leading edge of those advocating for radical abolition democracy.

Obama's presidency opened up previously undreamed of possibilities for Black citizenship. These were met, as they had been during the First Reconstruction era, with political backlash rooted in enduring patterns of racial conflict. This struggle dovetailed into long-standing, unrequited efforts to achieve Black dignity. If Obama's presidency offered new hopes for Black citizenship rooted in old concepts of respectability, BLM's insistence that America recognize all of Black humanity became the latest effort, and perhaps the most powerful one to date, to conjoin the search for citizenship with the need for dignity. Demands for dignity from below would irrevocably reshape conceptions of citizenship and democracy from above.

On Friday, July 19, 2013, President Barack Obama conducted an unusual press conference. The purpose was to discuss the Black community's anger over the recent acquittal of George Zimmerman in the shooting death of seventeen-year-old Trayvon Martin.

Zimmerman, a twenty-eight-year-old self-appointed Neighborhood Watch volunteer, had stalked Trayvon, whom he found suspicious. Trayvon, visiting his father in Florida, was in unfamiliar territory as he walked back to his dad's house after purchasing iced tea and a bag of Skittles at a local store. Zimmerman turned vigilante and pursued Trayvon despite being warned by a 911 dispatcher to let the police handle things. Their encounter led to an altercation, and to Trayvon's death.

Tragedies of race and place that dated back to the First Reconstruction haunted Trayvon's death. Zimmerman, a white-passing Latino, believed he was entitled to assume police powers over Trayvon, a stance that many whites took toward Blacks in the decades following the Civil War. Black bodies were heavily policed and scrutinized then and now, especially when they appeared in unexpected places. Zimmerman's encroachment on Trayvon's space violated the teen's personhood, and this violation led to a struggle and Trayvon's untimely death. But none of that mattered in the eyes of the law. Zimmerman said he had felt threatened by the young Black man—despite the fact that Zimmerman had purposefully stalked him—and received absolution from the system in the form of an acquittal. That acquittal was based on Florida's Stand Your Ground Law, which permits people to use lethal force in self-defense in certain situations in which they fear for their lives. It sparked pain, grief, and outrage in Black America. The White House had released a statement five days earlier, in the verdict's immediate aftermath. In that statement, the president had described America "as a nation of laws." "A jury has spoken," he said, preaching for calm as the best way to honor Trayvon's memory. Trayvon's parents did the same. The statement underwhelmed at best, and it triggered righteous fury among those in the Black community who were now skeptical of Obama's constrained vision of citizenship. The press conference represented another chance for the president to respond to the Black community's pain with empathy and understanding rather than clichés.[12]

At the press conference, Obama went from releasing a statement that could have been issued by many previous occupants of the White House to addressing Trayvon's death in a way that only he could have done. "You know, when Trayvon Martin was first shot, I said that this could have been my son," Obama remarked. "Another way of saying that is Trayvon Martin could have been me, 35 years ago," he continued. Making the most pointed statement on racial injustice thus far in his presidency, Obama further noted the importance of recognizing "that the African-American community is looking at this issue through a set of experiences and a...and a history that...that doesn't go away."[13]

BLM's arrival was fueled by those parts of American history that refuse to go away. Between Obama's Trayvon Martin press conference and the end of his presidency almost four years later, Black Lives Matter confronted these tragic dimensions of history through a moral and political reckoning that recalled the struggles for human dignity that marked the most heroic period of the civil rights and Black Power eras. Flowering unexpectedly within America's unforgiving racial climate, BLM sprang like a concrete rose from the yawning chasm between the bursting optimism of 2008 and the reality that killed Trayvon Martin in 2012. In that reality, a young man who reminded the president of his teenaged self, or who seemed like he could have been his own son, could be shot and killed by a man who stalked him, and justice remained asleep.

Obama may have used King's soaring words to cultivate a sense of kinship with the civil rights generation, but he remained an elected leader, and as such was bound to political rules that placed him at odds with radical anti-racism activism. Paradoxically, becoming America's first Black president limited his ability to advocate for reconstructionist policies capable of transforming Black life at its most vulnerable. Part of the problem was that he was operating within a framework of American exceptionalism. Under exceptionalism, Obama could run for and win the presidency, but the substance of hope and change that could actually be delivered to the communities who supported him the most was subject to sharp lines of demarcation. Obama's personal belief in the idea of American exceptionalism—a nation where all things were possible—made him hew toward the universal, despite the nation's cruel historical treatment of Blacks, and despite the need for particular remedies if the illness of racial injustice was to be cured. Politically, Obama failed to recognize, until well into his second term, that the grounds of racial consensus were shifting. This inability hampered his policy vision, weakened his rhetoric, and placed him on the defensive from attacks on both sides—from both an onslaught of redemptionist vitriol and from the righteous indignation of a new generation of reconstructionists. And the latter would take the fight for racial justice outside the corridors of power in Washington, DC, and into the nation's streets.

BLM activists were wise enough to distinguish between a social justice movement leader and a president, and they emerged as keepers of a sacred flame of Black struggle. BLM's greatest achievement, even more important than policy innovations, public education, and mass demonstrations, was that it both revived and expanded the concepts of Black dignity and citizenship that Martin Luther King Jr. and Malcolm X had articulated during America's Second Reconstruction. BLM led as much as it followed, maturing into the nation's most important movement for intersectional justice, radical democracy, and human rights by shedding the political shortcomings that had plagued the two earlier periods of Reconstruction and embracing the full complexity of Black identity.

The hashtag #BlackLivesMatter, coined by radical Black Queer and feminist activists Ayǫ (formerly Opal) Tometi, Patrisse Cullors, and Alicia Garza in the aftermath of Zimmerman's acquittal, was inspired by the increasingly public spectacle of Black men and women being shot down by law enforcement at the very moment the nation reveled in the election of a Black president. Twenty-first-century technological innovations had made it easier for police to kill Black folk, for bystanders to record and disseminate the killings, and for activists to organize protests, mobilize demonstrations, and leverage moral outrage into effective political action. Grassroots activists working at the intersection of anti-racism, anti-violence, anti-sexism, anti-prison, and anti-poverty activism, Garza, Tometi, and Cullors aimed to spread this slogan around the nation "like wildfire." Working in a long tradition of Black feminist activism with deep roots in the First Reconstruction, they sought to confront the ever-present specter of Black death. Amplifying and echoing the work of Ida B. Wells, they shone a light on the fact that America's racist past was horrifyingly present. The bodies of Black women—such as Rekia Boyd, a twenty-two-year-old killed by Chicago police the same year as Trayvon Martin—laying dead on streets across the nation, they argued, represented only the latest incarnation of what Billie Holiday characterized as the "strange fruit" of the Jim Crow era, made famous in her 1939 protest song.[14]

Like the Black Power movement, Black Lives Matter captured the American imagination, both sparking backlash and inspiring supporters. BLM supporters built on the movement's panoramic critique of American democratic institutions. From its origins in 2013, BLM became an international phenomenon, growing against the backdrop of urban rebellion. New police killings that came to light increased the urgency of the protests. The next to receive national publicity took place in Ferguson, Missouri, in August 2014, where police killed the eighteen-year-old Michael Brown. His death and the ensuing demonstrations brought BLM's signature phrase into the national conversation. Brown's uncovered body had lain on the street for several hours after his death. This horrific event cast a spotlight on the systemic racism within the criminal justice system; on the heels of Trayvon Martin's death and Zimmerman's acquittal, it helped to prime activists to increase their organized grassroots resistance.

In December 2014, when a grand jury in Richmond County, New York, failed to indict a police officer involved in the death of another Black man, Eric Garner, protests erupted again. Officer Daniel Pantaleo had put Garner in a prohibited chokehold in Staten Island, and Garner died within the hour. Although Garner had been killed in July, the month before Brown, the two cases became intertwined in the political imagination of the new generation of Black Reconstructionists. Tens of thousands of young people, predominantly, but not entirely, Black, organized under the BLM banner in the wake of their deaths.

A winter of Black grief over these deaths turned into a spring of political outrage the following April, after another Black man, Freddie Gray, died after suffering spinal injuries while being transported in a police van in Baltimore. The twenty-five-year-old Gray was in a coma by the time the van arrived at the hospital, and he died several days later. His injuries had clearly been caused by police mistreatment, and news of his death spread quickly through the city. Angry demonstrations grew into a political uprising (labeled a "riot" by authorities). Reconstructionists called for justice; redemptionists called for law and order. But the turmoil continued for several weeks. With businesses being damaged and looted and vehicle fires being ignited around the city, a state of emergency was declared and Maryland deployed National Guard troops.

These political uprisings, like the Black rebellions that spread across the United States in almost a decade of consistent urban unrest between 1963 and 1972, resulted from the violent overpolicing of Black folk in America. BLM raised public consciousness about a panoramic array of complex and overlapping issues connected to the nation's system of mass incarceration. With eloquence, conviction, and empirical evidence, activists argued that the criminal justice system served as a catastrophic gateway to many other kinds of racial oppression, including economic exploitation, gender injustice, queerphobia and transphobia, and the marginalization of Black and brown youth, immigrants, the mentally ill, and the indigent.

These systems of oppression were hardly new. White violence against Black folk was ubiquitous during the civil rights era and earlier, with law enforcement consistently being among the greatest perpetrators—an unsurprising fact in light of the history of policing in the United States, and especially its role in ensuring the return of anyone trying to escape racial slavery before the Civil War. Police in America have historically represented the antithesis of Black dignity. The institutionalization of local, state, and federal law enforcement, from the end of the Civil War all the way to the civil rights era, paralleled the rise of the Jim Crow system. The two systems evolved together, each reinforcing, safeguarding, and amplifying the development of the other. Incarceration has likewise been a tool of white supremacy. The system of convict leasing during Jim Crow robbed Black people of their dignity, safety, and citizenship rights, and its continuation can still be seen in the system of mass incarceration today. African American communities have been punished on an unprecedented scale even in our modern era.

The greatest moral breakthrough of the Second Reconstruction took place when activists began to recognize that incarceration in an unjust society represented a badge of honor rather than a mark of shame. King came to this realization gradually, as young people, striding beyond his limited appetite for arrest, began to embrace a "Jail no bail" slogan in the midst of the lunch-counter sit-ins of 1960 and the 1961 Freedom Rides. These activists understood that the police had been brutal guardians of America's color line: engaging in horrific acts of violence, practically deputizing white vigilantes, and often arresting Black victims of racial violence instead of the perpetrators.[15] Yet in the face of racial violence, white narratives of the era were quick to describe Black efforts at self-defense as unwarranted provocations. When the mean season of urban rebellions began in Birmingham, Alabama, in 1963, many whites chastised African American protesters because the protests could spill over into violence and sporadic looting. Critics described them as riots, and official documents characterized them as civil disturbances. But the origins of the urban rebellions were almost always found in police violence against Black communities.[16]

Taking a page from the civil rights movement, BLM demonstrated, marched, and picketed to cast a spotlight on systemic racism within US law enforcement and the larger society. The movement's nonviolent demonstrations weaponized civil disobedience as a disruptive political tactic. Shutting down highways, interrupting brunches in downtown urban centers, staging "die-ins" on college campuses, even taking over microphones at political rallies all became effective tactics for spreading BLM's reconstructionist message. The movement offered a searing critique of structural racism, violence, and economic injustice in America wedded to a larger moral and political reimagining of the nation's future. In this sense, BLM combined Malcolm X's call for radical Black dignity with Martin Luther King Jr.'s advocacy of radical Black citizenship. Ella Baker's Second Reconstruction observation that the best organizations were those that had less hierarchy and more inclusive conceptions of leadership became the BLM movement's North Star. The cause of Black Lives Matter itself, more than any individual figure or leader, would emerge from the maelstrom of Ferguson, Baltimore, and other uprisings.

BLM's inclusive conception of leadership reflected the influence of Black feminist and Queer politics and the tradition of Black women's activism. Before the COVID-19 pandemic ravaged Black communities in 2020, there was the HIV/AIDS crisis, which also disproportionately harmed African Americans, especially Black

Queer and trans folk. Black feminists and Queer activists in the fight against AIDS during the 1980s and 1990s played a critical role in expanding the internal architecture of Black political and policy struggles. They forced racial justice movements to expand conceptions of poverty, violence, health care, family, and community, and the legacy of their work was evident both in BLM's priorities and in its approach to leadership. BLM's efforts to prioritize a Black-feminist and Queer-centered vision of political community and collective organizing purposefully eschewed patriarchal and heteronormative models of leadership prized during the Second Reconstruction.

Black women and Queer activists have historically been some of America's most committed reconstructionists. Audre Lorde, the Black lesbian feminist, theorist, poet, and scholar-activist, is an exemplar on this score. Her commitment to a radically inclusive yet politically expansive vision of abolition democracy set her on a course in the 1960s and 1970s that would, in striking ways, come close to being fulfilled by the BLM movement. Born in Harlem in 1934, a first-generation American and daughter of immigrants from Grenada, as an artist, a divorced mother of two children, and a Black lesbian feminist poet she called on Black women to reclaim all facets of the humanity denied to them within a white supremacist political culture. Lorde's art and activism fit outside of mainstream conceptions of what a Black artist looked like and sounded like. Her essays, poems, and other writings proved generative to the Black radical political and literary traditions that later helped shaped BLM. Lorde thrived within networks of Black feminist radical activism that helped to create Black women's studies as a field of respected scholarly inquiry in the late 1970s and early 1980s. She attended the founding retreat of the Combahee River Collective, a

Black feminist grassroots organization that first gathered over the weekend of July 8–10, 1977, in South Hadley, Massachusetts.

Lorde relentlessly searched for a political vision capacious enough to include all aspects of, and facets within, her evolving Black lesbian feminist self. Her reconstructionist vision identified Black lesbian feminism as global in scope, comprising Queer writers, artists, and activists everywhere. These people, "the most despised, the most oppressed and the most spat upon people within our communities," as she put it, were deserving of recognition as human beings, and this recognition would paradoxically unlock freedom and liberation for all people. Lorde identified Black women's multiple identities as a source of strength, rather than division, within the Black community, as well as within broader communities of struggle against racial, economic, and gender oppression. Her candor about surviving breast cancer opened up new political and intellectual worlds for Black women to reveal the complexity of lives too often experienced in the shadows. Lorde's work reinterpreted difference—the way in which individual Black women's identities, in all of their imperfect glory, profoundly mattered. She dubbed herself "an inheritor of Malcolm X and his tradition," because she was willing to openly discuss the political uses of anger—anger that traveled beyond respectability politics, and that, in so doing, expanded both the recognized and unrecognized boundaries of Blackness. Lorde grew to love and accept the parts of herself that sought radical change, and she demanded a Black politics capacious enough to recognize and celebrate the intersections of difference, identity, citizenship, and dignity.[17]

It is often the most oppressed parts of the Black community that most fully recognize the barriers, slights, and markers of shame and pain rarely visible to others. These were Black folk who, during each period of Reconstruction, out of necessity, sought to remake the world. For instance, Black women led Reconstruction-era efforts to reimagine democracy beyond the suffocating limits of white supremacy. Perhaps none did so more eloquently than Frances Ellen Watkins Harper, the Black feminist speaker, activist, and supporter of abolition democracy. "You white women speak here of rights," she reminded delegates at a political convention in 1866. "I speak of wrongs." Harper's outspoken advocacy of voting rights for Black women, her personal refusal to be Jim Crowed on streetcars and trains, and her vision of an American democracy "bound up together in one great bundle of humanity" helped to blaze the trail that led to the Movement for Black Lives.[18]

Like Barack Obama in 2008, but to different ends, BLM activists in 2014 and 2015 embraced the "fierce urgency of now," words spoken by Martin Luther King Jr. at Riverside Church one year before his assassination. At the same time, their defiant posture, toward white structural violence and the failures of civil rights leaders and elected officials alike, embodied Malcolm X's "by any means necessary" philosophy, which anticipated a coming racial and political reckoning. The new generation of activists rejected the Janus-faced portrait of American racial history that Obama had offered in his campaign-saving address in 2008, with the moral equivalence it drew between Black suffering and white discomfort. BLM transformed mainstream conceptions of Black politics, racial progress, and the civil rights movement. It did so by identifying police brutality as simply one layer of the ongoing structural violence that marginalized Black communities nationwide. The civil rights struggle, activists said, had done too little to overcome the racism embedded in American society and institutions. In short, BLM told America a categorically different story about its history, present, and future than the one that Obama believed. They dared to name the violence, injustice, and evil plaguing the country in a manner that not only challenged redemptionists but also upset certain reconstructionists, who, like Obama, were operating under a playbook whose rules were quickly changing.

Speaking these truths placed the Black Lives Matter movement at odds with Obama and others with similar views. Irony abounded here, especially since Obama owed such a large and public debt to the civil rights activists of an earlier generation, who had risked their lives for citizenship and dignity. Obama's Department of Justice, led by America's first Black attorney general, Eric Holder, did try at the federal level to reduce the scale of mass incarceration. Holder's Justice Department, with Obama's approval, proved receptive to ideas such as providing funding for police-worn body cameras, and releasing nonviolent drug offenders from federal prison, aspects of the criminal justice reform agenda that BLM helped to energize. But BLM's relationship with Obama would prove to be more contentious than cooperative—and for good reason. At its core, the movement vowed to end not only systems of racist violence, poverty, and inequality, but also the political framework of American exceptionalism itself, a framework that had allowed Obama to be elected president. BLM understood, more than even the most politically seasoned actors, that democracy is a discipline—one that requires playing the long game. The movement produced ripples of radical hope that forced Obama to confront an important truth that he had refused to mention during his first term: the malevolent existence of a system of mass incarceration that disproportionately punished Black bodies.

I often wonder how President Obama felt in December 2014 as he met in the White House with seven activists from various local and national organizations representing the radical thrust of the BLM movement. They were community organizers who bore personal scars from being attacked by law enforcement on the streets of Ferguson and other cities for peacefully protesting police brutality. Obama reportedly shared stories of his own time as a community organizer on the West Side of Chicago in the 1980s. Perhaps he recounted how, after graduating from Harvard Law School in 1991 as the first Black person to ever head the *Harvard Law Review*, he had returned to Chi-Town and helped lead a large voter registration drive that helped Bill Clinton become president. Or maybe he withheld that part of the story, because of how Clinton, during his two terms as president, had presided over a massive expansion of the surveillance, arrest, and incarceration of Black Americans through the 1994 Crime Bill. The federal government incentivized states to arrest unprecedented numbers of Americans, who were disproportionately Black, and the states in turn incentivized local cities to do the same. Two years after signing that bill, President Clinton ushered through welfare reform legislation that further criminalized poor Black communities. The system now tied social welfare programs to levels of punishment, making ex-offenders ineligible for public housing, Pell Grants, and other social benefits that had offered hope for the formerly institutionalized.[19]

Black people experienced no mercy from the unprecedented investments America made in its systems of punishment between the Second and Third Reconstructions. The War on Drugs, beginning in the 1970s under President Richard Nixon, took full, soaring flight under President Ronald Reagan in the 1980s, and it continued to secure new resources during the Clinton years. The acceleration of the War on Drugs and the growth of the punishment industry paralleled the War on Poverty's decline and the atrophy of the Great Society's robust policy vision of national reforms.[20] The BLM activists who met Obama at the White House were attempting to confront the ruins of America's past, a history that neither they nor Obama completely understood, but which nonetheless held America in its thrall.

Obama's meeting with the activists put the differences between two versions of citizenship into stark relief: one version, which Obama believed in, framed by American exceptionalism, and another, represented by the members of a new social movement, dedicated to a vision of abolition democracy. "The first time I was teargassed was on the streets of St. Louis," organizer Brittany Packnett explained to Obama. The trauma that she and others had experienced was much like the violence that Obama had often lauded John Lewis for enduring. But when Packnett and other young Black activists described how they had been treated by law enforcement, Obama preached patience. Just three months shy of the fiftieth anniversary of Bloody Sunday in Selma, Alabama, when Lewis and hundreds of others had been viciously assaulted by Alabama state troopers on horseback, Obama listened as activists of a new generation redefined the racial optimism that had fueled his election and insisted that the president and the nation must finally recognize Black humanity.

In their own way, by refusing to defer to the president, the young activists were holding the legacy of the civil rights era in reverence. Sitting in the Oval Office, they challenged Obama to defund police departments, invest in community-based alternatives to punishment and incarceration, and publicly support the kind of radical change the times demanded. Obama, in turn, urged them to recognize that deep systemic change took time. He did not promise to be the Moses of the Black Lives Matter era, as Andrew Johnson had condescendingly vowed to do in a disastrous 1865 meeting with Frederick Douglass.[21] Phil Agnew, one of the cofounders of the Chicago-based organization Dream Defenders, offered an unvarnished assessment of the meeting. "We debated on the power of the vote and the lack of faith in the Democratic Party," Agnew said. "We did not budge."[22] But Obama, eventually, would budge, ever so slightly.

On July 16, 2015, Barack Obama became the first sitting president to visit a federal prison when he toured Federal Correctional Institution El Reno in Oklahoma; two days earlier, taking a page from prison abolitionists, he used the term "mass incarceration" during a speech before the NAACP. These events were part of a weeklong effort to draw attention to the need for reform in the criminal justice system.[23] Still, even as BLM, with clarifying moral courage, publicly challenged the president to acknowledge the terrifying breadth and depth of anti-Black racism in America, Obama characterized great social change as an incremental process that could not be hastened by the passions of the moment. If this made for good politics, it proved to be poor history, for the First Reconstruction had shown how quickly social change could take place when, in the span of just a few years, Black Americans went from chattel slavery to the United States Congress. That was not incrementalism. On the contrary, it was fueled by the abolition democracy of activists such as Frederick Douglass and the Radical Republicans in Congress led by Thaddeus Stevens. The redemptionists, pursuing the continuation of war by other means, and attempting to institute slavery under a new name, ironically inspired the greatest political revolution in American history: Rebel states were compelled to guarantee Black citizenship in exchange for safe passage back to the Union. Organized white violence against Black communities and leaders between 1867 and 1871 grew so preposterously widespread that Congress held public hearings in May 1871 to investigate the hundreds of lynchings and targeted political murders that had taken place in Florida, Kentucky, Alabama, South Carolina, Tennessee, and other states. Perhaps blissfully unaware of this bloodstained history, Obama drew the wrong lessons from the First Reconstruction, placing Abraham Lincoln's efforts to heal a divided nation over and above the radical deeds, actions, and policies that, for a brief time at least, gave Lincoln's words meaning.

In his meeting with the activists, Obama clung to an optimistic reading of American history. But the young organizers who had marched in the streets of Ferguson balanced racial optimism with an Afropessimist understanding that Blackness in America served as a political and institutional marker of the non-human.[24] Black pain offered whites and non-Blacks examples, through ritualized terror, public executions, and systemic degradation, of what it means to be truly vulnerable. The president took major aspects of the American Dream at face value. He found, in his personal experience, America to be a magical place filled with unlimited possibilities. But a nightmare is also a dream.[25]

Obama's racial optimism and political incrementalism had proved to be the key to his personal fortunes and professional successes. In this he modeled the outer reaches of a vision of American exceptionalism that nurtured Black talent and capitalized on Black genius. His ability to operate within the racial justice consensus that began under Kennedy and concluded with his own administration made him reject the political radicalism that had helped birth the First Reconstruction. BLM instead embraced the radical politics of America's First Reconstruction, embarking on a new mission to fulfill the lost promise of abolition democracy, and painfully aware that, despite the enormous symbolism of the Obama presidency, the substance of their future hopes lay in confronting parts of American history that the nation's first Black president never would.

W. E. B. Du Bois famously described Reconstruction as a "brief moment in the sun" prematurely concluded by a brutal turn "again toward slavery." No longer slaves, but not yet citizens, at the Civil War's end, Black Americans regarded democracy as a sacred promise with the nation, a covenant forged by the blood of their ancestors and the sacrifices of the nearly two hundred thousand Black soldiers who had fought for the Union. Reconstruction-era laws and constitutional amendments upended the long-standing assumption that Black humanity could be considered legal property. Black men were granted voting rights, although local whites, especially in the South, tried to prevent them from exercising them. Their gains thus proved only as strong as the local Black political and paramilitary organizing so essential to defending Black lives. Black communities in the Reconstruction-era South formed militias, armed themselves, and turned political organizing into militant spectacles demonstrating their capacity for self-defense, their fierce determination to be free, and their ability to wield political power unfettered by the whims of their former white enslavers.

The extended networks of Black communities politicized every aspect of Reconstruction-era America, from the church and the schoolhouse to state conventions and union leagues. Such local organizing was necessary, because anti-Black sentiment shaped the Reconstruction era as much as Black America's new rights did. Over time, as white supremacist violence begat racist policies—which both strengthened and reflected the logic of the Lost Cause narrative—these networks among Black people became even more crucial. The Lost Cause account of recent history memorialized the morally reprehensible advocates of racial slavery as the unsung heroes of American democracy. The most vicious face of this anti-Black sentiment could be found in white terrorist groups, including the Ku Klux Klan, and the raw terror they incited; a milder form of denying Black citizenship could be found in the machinations of federal, state, and local politicians, who often enacted Black Codes stripping Black people of all meaningful exercise of their newly gained rights. US Supreme Court decisions denied Black people human dignity altogether, banning them from many things in public life, from sitting on juries to taking the same seats as white people on public transportation or using other kinds of public accommodations. The reasoning behind these practices was often stated in demeaning and insulting terms. Ultimately, the post-Reconstruction era of Jim Crow racism weaponized violence, the rule of law, and public policy to create a political reality that punished, imprisoned, segregated, and demonized Black Americans in service of a system of white supremacy that became normalized.[26]

Black Lives Matter forced America to confront this history while simultaneously gazing toward a multiracial future of intersectional justice. BLM, like the civil rights and Black Power movements of the Second Reconstruction era, and like the grassroots Black organizers and politicians of the First Reconstruction era, sought to transform American democracy. And in doing so, its activists drew from both eras: they built on a long tradition of Black political activism that could be traced to the 1860s and 1870s even as they echoed themes from a century later. And they also drew from two strands of radical thought from the Second Reconstruction, providing a structural critique of racism and white supremacy that echoed Malcolm X's advocacy of radical Black dignity while making tactical use of King's nonviolent civil disobedience, finding inspiration in the latter's notion of radical Black citizenship and dreams of a "Beloved Community."

The search for Black dignity during the civil rights era took multiple forms. Churchgoing Black folk dressed in their Sunday best to protest segregated buses in Montgomery, Alabama, sparking a successful boycott in 1955 and 1956. It was that boycott that first propelled the twenty-seven-year-old Martin Luther King Jr. into national prominence. For Rosa Parks, Black dignity meant the dignity of Black women and recognition of their humanity. Long before she fulfilled her important role in the Montgomery Bus Boycott, she had fought against the sexual assault, rape, and brutalization of Black women.[27]

Black college students, soon to be joined by young people around the country, appeared at a "whites only" lunch counter in Greensboro, North Carolina, on February 1, 1960, jump-starting a movement that would lead to the creation of the Student Non-violent Coordinating Committee. SNCC (pronounced "snick") propelled the Black freedom struggle beyond conventional respectability politics.[28] Through direct action at lunch counters and other segregated establishments, these students rejected the idea that respectable Blacks should cause no trouble. Instead they attacked Jim Crow at its roots. By embedding themselves with impoverished rural Black families, from the Mississippi Delta and the Alabama Black Belt to parts of Georgia, Arkansas, and other regions, SNCC engaged in an exaltation of the Black poor that re-imagined the face of Black dignity yet again, and in so doing further transformed the scope of Black citizenship.[29]

Educated elites who practiced Black respectability politics, part of the "Talented Tenth" of America's Black population, to use W. E. B. Du Bois's term, were determined to prove, through their dress, achievements, and comportment, the virtues of Black humanity in a racist world. But these methods ultimately appeased the racists, because they seemed to validate the racist idea that less successful African Americans were to blame for their own predicament. Such politics turned out to be a trap, one that faulted Black behavior—rather than systemic racism and structural violence—for aspects of racial oppression that could never, in reality, be surmounted through education, wealth, and even individual achievement. The battle to overcome Black respectability politics—to understand, for instance, that the young Black men and women who were murdered by the police could not have been saved by wearing pants that were less baggy, or by speaking the King's English—continues to be waged, both within and outside the Black community. SNCC struck an important blow by shifting attention away from the fears and class anxieties of the Black middle class to the secret hearts of the Black poor.[30]

In the 1960s, SNCC activists burrowed into the American democratic imagination by embedding themselves into poor Black communities in the South. Wearing sharecroppers' overalls that signaled their respect for local folkways, they went from sitting at lunch counters in southern cities to discussing how they could help unlettered Black sharecroppers achieve dignity and citizenship on their own terms. Ella Baker, the brilliant organizer, activist, and feminist from North Carolina, served as the group's founder, sounding board, and mentor. Baker knew Martin Luther King Jr. in the 1950s, but she longed to move beyond the church-based, patriarchal, top-down framework that dominated the era's civil rights activism. "Strong people don't need strong leaders," observed Baker, who counseled a new network of seasoned activists who soon joined SNCC, helping them to understand that they were embarking on a conflict about "more than just a hamburger." The stakes were nothing less than the nation's democratic soul.[31]

SNCC activists both revered and challenged their elders. They defied conventional wisdom and pushed the boundaries of acceptable political discourse. The organization redefined democracy by viewing dignity as fundamental to the entire American project both domestically and globally. The activists found their purpose by immersing themselves in the lives of ordinary Black people in the South. They arrived there amid an ongoing struggle for political self-determination and self-love that fortified Black souls suffering under the blistering heat of racial violence, terror, poverty, and misery. They gained new insights about the depth of Black humanity by sharing humble meals with people, sleeping on the dirt floors of shotgun shacks, outrunning racist vigilantes, and mourning the Black dead, both their colleagues and local residents, who sacrificed their very lives in the service of advocating for an expansive notion of human dignity.

Writing in 1961, James Baldwin identified the student movement as the center of a national reconstruction effort that went beyond the "consumption of overcooked hamburgers and tasteless coffee at various sleazy lunch counters." What was at stake, he said, went far deeper than newspaper headlines of the era could fathom. "The goal of the student movement," Baldwin observed, "is nothing less than the liberation of the entire country from its most crippling attitudes and habits." Baldwin fervently hoped that with SNCC leading the way, Black Reconstructionists could achieve a new country, but only if whites possessed the courage to see African Americans as human beings instead of abstractions, stand-ins for those society designated as non-human.[32]

SNCC activists were the ground troops of America's Second Reconstruction. Black women in SNCC, such as Ruby Doris Smith-Robinson, Gwen Patton, Fran Beal, and Judy Richardson, emerged as major organizers. Their radical politics helped bring about a second wave of Black feminism that would go on to decisively shape the Black Power era.[33] SNCC's Stokely Carmichael, John Lewis, Cleveland Sellers, and Diane Nash shaped their generation's vision of abolition democracy. For some of them, including Lewis and Carmichael, defiance of Jim Crow meant jail time (a stint in Mississippi's Parchman Penitentiary allowed Lewis and Carmichael, two future SNCC chairmen, to get better acquainted).[34] Nash helped lead a sit-in movement in Nashville that compelled the city's mayor to publicly acknowledge racial segregation as a moral evil.

SNCC's fervent love of America helped to attract white students to the organization, too, and many of them traveled to Mississippi in the summer of 1964 with the aim of helping to build a new world. The Black students who founded SNCC believed in the Kennedy administration's vision of a "New Frontier," supported the "Freedom Rides" that the Congress of Racial Equality (CORE) had organized to challenge segregation in interstate travel, and pledged themselves to the practice of nonviolent civil disobedience as modeled by Mahatma Gandhi and King.

SNCC activists loved America enough to criticize the nation's wrongs. Their time in the South introduced them to a deeper history of abolition democracy, one that stretched back a generation earlier, to returning World War II veterans who had dared to hope that fighting overseas would make them worthy of citizenship back home, and an even longer past, particularly in Mississippi, where Black men had voted and Black women had helped organize Black communities poised toward political and economic independence.[35]

Like ghosts from the nation's unreconstructed past, SNCC activists haunted the states most violently "redeemed" by white supremacists during the nineteenth century. Mississippi proved key in this regard. In the "Freedom Summer" of 1964, SNCC launched the second experiment in multiracial democracy in Mississippi history, nearly a century after the first had fallen victim to white violence. SNCC's core group of organizers, most of them Black, recruited over a thousand predominantly white volunteers to travel to the state to organize "Freedom Schools," libraries, voter registration drives, civics classes, and more. State officials responded with threats, purchased an armored vehicle to terrorize activists, and circulated the rumor that the students were coming to the state to engage in a bacchanal of interracial sex, drugs, and rock and roll. On June 21, at around 10:00 p.m., just outside of the tiny city of Philadelphia in Neshoba County, three young men—two white and one Black—namely, twenty-year-old Andrew Goodman, twenty-one-year-old James Chaney, and twenty-four-year-old Michael "Mickey" Schwerner, were murdered by a combination of local law enforcement officers and white terrorists. As during the First Reconstruction, it was at times hard to distinguish between the two.

The murders seemed to hurtle the nation back in time. During Reconstruction's first decade, Mississippi had emerged as a center of Black power, especially in the twenty-six counties where African Americans made up more than 60 percent of the population. Black Mississippians flexed their new political muscle as magistrates, supervisors, justices of the peace, and sheriffs, and they sat on racially integrated juries. The pinnacle of Black power in Mississippi arrived in the early evening of February 25, 1870, when Hiram Rhodes Revels, before a packed gallery, became America's first Black US senator. A mixed-raced Black man from North Carolina, after the Civil War Revels had moved to Mississippi and leveraged his experience as a preacher in the African

Methodist Episcopal Church to build a political network in the state. In Mississippi he had worked for the Freedmen's Bureau, risen to be an alderman in Natchez, and been elected to the state legislature before winning his US Senate seat.

But whites in Mississippi regarded local Black power as even more offensive than Black power at the national level. Just five years after Revels's triumph, white supremacy returned to Mississippi with a vengeance. The "Mississippi Plan" of 1875, marked by racial terror against Black political assemblies, by white riots, and by Black Codes, became a blueprint for successful efforts to "redeem" the South from the threat of abolition democracy. Redemptionists used Mississippi as a test case for the region, and over time, for the nation. Facing down the barrel of literal and metaphorical guns, local Black power waned. Majority-Black counties became racially oppressed, feudal spaces where African American lives did not matter. Black deaths in vicious killings offered visual evidence that the era of Black Reconstruction had been a short-lived dream, one that gave way to a living nightmare.[36]

Freedom Summer represented a revival and a continuation of the history of Black Reconstruction in America. The added participation of young white college students and activists from outside the South recalled, while surpassing, the support of northern white allies in the Reconstruction efforts of almost a century earlier. Through Freedom Summer and its other projects, SNCC became an incubator of grassroots political radicalism in the service of Black dignity. Over the coming years, the group's internal debates, conflicts, and eventual ruptures around issues of race, class, gender, imperialism, capitalism, and violence profoundly altered the course of social movements into the 1980s. Its activism proved generative, launching second-wave

Black feminism, fostering a new generation of antiwar protests, and spearheading movements that found kinship in the struggles of Mississippi sharecroppers and African revolutionaries.

In all these ways and more, SNCC anticipated the Black Lives Matter era. SNCC's search for dignity and meaning in the lives of unlettered, but morally exemplary, Black sharecroppers and other rural people found a corollary in the BLM movement a half-century later with its insistence that incarcerated, poor, and Queer people, Black women, and those with mental and physical disabilities were worthy of both dignity and citizenship. BLM's decentralized organizational philosophy also mirrored SNCC's: just as SNCC was home to a wide range of radical outlooks, BLM served as an incubator point for several overlapping, and at times antagonistic, political tendencies. Christian pacifists, Black nationalists, liberal integrationists, Black and white feminists, and Queer and peace activists were all, at various points, part of the group, which straddled civil rights and Black Power identities, sometimes simultaneously.

And Barack Obama's go-it-slow message to BLM activists in 2014 paralleled Attorney General Bobby Kennedy's relationship to SNCC in the early 1960s. Just as Kennedy implored SNCC activists to concentrate on voter registration over confrontational sit-ins, Obama administration officials encouraged BLM activists to focus more on policy than demonstrations that might turn violent. In both instances, and against all odds, the young upstarts partially followed this advice—by committing to both tactics at once—and in the process, in both instances, they started a revolution.

BLM offered an updated version of the tactical civil disobedience and grassroots organizing that SNCC had pioneered during the civil rights era. But from its inception in 2013, it was also inspired by the words of fire that Black Power revolutionaries had brandished. By insisting that Black lives mattered, in the face of racist law enforcement, skeptical politicians, and a disbelieving American public, the movement's participants claimed Malcolm X's project of radical Black dignity as their own. Passionately condemning police violence and embracing prison abolition, they took up some of the major planks of the Black Panther Party's platform, expanding the horizons of radical dignity while altering the parameters of inclusive citizenship.

Malcolm X hovers over America's Third Reconstruction, inspiring the new struggles to end mass incarceration, police brutality, and the War on Drugs and to recognize the universality of Black pain and joy. Malcolm might be described as an advocate for abolition democracy by any means necessary. His bold critique of white supremacy identified America as a southern nation under active redemptionist political rule. What upset Malcolm's critics most was his refusal to lie about Black people's predicament. The slave power, Malcolm argued, won the peace after the Civil War.

The broad outlines of Malcolm X's life have become the stuff of legend. Malcolm Little was born in Omaha, Nebraska, in 1925, and his family moved to Lansing, Michigan, while he was still an infant. He had a trauma-filled childhood during the 1930s, living in poverty after the death of his father under suspicious circumstances when Malcolm was six years old. Malcolm became involved in the criminal underworlds of Harlem and Boston in the 1940s and picked up the nicknames "East Lansing" and "Detroit Red." This activity led to a nearly seven-year jail stint in Massachusetts for robbery. In prison, he joined the Nation of Islam (NOI), a group of unorthodox practitioners of Islam who believed in racial solidarity and economic self-determination; they also believed that their leader, Elijah Muhammad, was the Messenger of God. Malcolm read widely from the prison library and changed his name to "Malcolm X." His new surname of "X" reflected Black people's loss of identity under an American regime of racial slavery that forced human beings to take on the last names of their ostensible "masters." Malcolm's time in the NOI would be an era of personal reconstruction that would animate a national, then global, political reckoning around the very idea of Black dignity, citizenship, and humanity.

By the late 1950s, through a television documentary hosted by Mike Wallace and reported by Black journalist Louis Lomax, Malcolm X and the NOI became household names. Their calls for racial separatism and their indictment of white racism lent a radical edge to a group that publicly eschewed formal political engagement, but nonetheless practiced its own brand of radical Black dignity. To them, this meant Black families living without fear, Black communities economically thriving, and Black souls, even when languishing in prison or experiencing poverty, still being recognized as human and worthy of love. BLM would take Malcolm and the NOI's radical empathy for Black people locked up in systems of punishment, policing, and violence to new heights.[37]

Malcolm X's bold denunciation of white supremacy attracted thousands of new converts to the NOI, many of them drawn to his audacious display of Black intelligence, charismatic speaking style, and ability to outclass a wide range of debate opponents. These opponents included Dr. Martin Luther King Jr., whom Malcolm derided as an Uncle Tom: Malcolm believed that King's nonviolent tactics invited further violence and humiliation to an already beleaguered race. Malcolm's increasing fame and popularity attracted envy and criticism from opponents and allies alike, even as his uncompromising insistence that Black lives mattered made him the personification of the radical Black dignity he championed. His November 1963 speech in Detroit, Michigan, "Message to the Grassroots," offered a blueprint for what he characterized as a Black revolution, one mature and sophisticated enough to recognize white supremacy as a national, rather than a regional, issue, and bold enough to deploy radical strategies—including self-defense and political self-determination, to ultimately defeat it.

By the end of 1963, shortly after describing President John F. Kennedy's assassination as an example of "chickens coming home to roost," Malcolm was suspended by the NOI. By the end of the next year, Malcolm had started two new political organizations, taken the hajj pilgrimage to Mecca, and enjoyed two extensive tours of Africa, where he engaged in high-level diplomacy with heads of state and became Black America's unofficial prime minister. Malcolm underwent a striking political evolution during this time characterized by a new willingness to collaborate with former adversaries, most notably King; a recognition that politically sincere whites could be part of a wider racial justice struggle; and an effort to look beyond America's borders to convince the entire world that the struggle for Black dignity and citizenship represented nothing less than a global human rights movement. These projects were tragically cut short by Malcolm's assassination on February 21, 1965.

Malcolm X is still too often remembered as wielding a political sword, in contrast to Martin Luther King's shield of nonviolence.

Malcolm and Martin did start off as adversaries and then rivals, but over time they became each other's alter egos. King's influence on Malcolm can be seen in the latter's "The Ballot or the Bullet" speech, in which, for the first time, he recognized the need for both dignity and citizenship in order to realize a racially just future. Malcolm interpreted Black political power as part of the solution to the problem of white supremacy, a sentiment that exposed common ground with King. And Malcolm's influence on King can be seen in the final years of King's career, when King made increasingly sharp critiques of white supremacy, offered a warm embrace of Black pride and political self-determination, and engaged in a revolutionary critique of capitalism, war, and violence.

Malcolm X's time in prison, his past criminal acts, and his personal mistakes provide a model of Black Reconstructionism that does not require sainthood or a high-polish gloss. In him we discover a life exemplifying flawed humanity with all its pain and promise, which can be a wonderful gift to us. Malcolm was always more than just the sum of the most brutal aspects of his personal and political experiences. A dedicated father, loyal husband, and man of faith, he also loved ice cream, had a wicked sense of humor, and enjoyed taking photographs and recording movies of his sojourns abroad. By teaching not only that Black lives matter, but also that they can reverberate with a purpose that continues after death, he has left us a profound legacy. He stoked the Promethean fires of Black radical dignity, bequeathing to subsequent generations a spark that would, over time, ignite a new movement for the radical reconstruction of American democracy.

BLM represents a radical call for political dignity, a dignity that must reach beyond simply recognizing Black humanity in formal political structures, institutions, and political participation, however necessary those things may be. BLM activists believe that the recognition of Black humanity begins from within, and that the intrinsic power of the Black radical movement lies in a community-wide celebration and defense of Black life even when the outside world insists on the exact opposite. Black Power challenged the structures of violence, poverty, and racism that stifled Black dreams and suffocated Black lives.

Stokely Carmichael's evolution from civil rights militant to Black Power revolutionary is especially resonant here. Carmichael emerged as one of the boldest critics of white supremacy beginning in 1966.[38] A grassroots organizer voted SNCC chairman over John Lewis in an acrimonious election that virtually ended their friendship, Carmichael became the most visible symbol of Black Power radicalism during the late 1960s. Creeping recognition about the depth and breadth of systemic racism strained relations between Black organizers and their white allies at that time—as well as between different contingents of the Black organizers themselves. Interracial organizing, a hallmark of the early 1960s civil rights movement, had become practically sacrosanct within SNCC, but in a contentious debate, many Black leaders—though not Carmichael—publicly suggested that white activists would better serve the cause of anti-racism by organizing within their own communities. The last of SNCC's white members departed by early 1967, a move that marked the symbolic end of the interracial organizing of the 1960s.

This controversy took place against the backdrop of the rise of the Black Power movement. Black Power came of age alongside the urban political rebellions of the 1960s, triggered by some of the most brutal instances of anti-Black violence in American history. Black Power activists identified the police and law enforcement as part of a sprawling system of racial oppression that enforced brutal punishment and premature death upon African Americans, particularly in impoverished and segregated neighborhoods. Advocates of Black Power demanded community control of schools, police, businesses, and public safety as the first step in liberating the Black community from the bonds, both visible and invisible, of white supremacy that stretched back to racial slavery.

Stokely Carmichael (with coauthor Charles Hamilton) coined the term "institutional racism" to describe the structural nature of racial oppression.[39] Carmichael, born in Trinidad, had moved to Harlem at the age of eleven; his parents had already been in America for nine years (Stokely had been raised by his grandmother and aunts since the age of two). He went to Howard University, where he became a prominent activist, graduating in 1964. Carmichael made his bones as an activist organizing under dangerous conditions in rural Mississippi and Alabama and understood racism's uncanny grip on every facet of America, from its political institutions, to its educational, civic, and economic structures, to its national character. Stokely popularized the slogan "Black Power" when he led a chant using these words at a stop along the March Against Fear, in Greenwood, Mississippi, in June 1966.

The idea of Black Power, which preceded Stokely's use and could be traced back to the era of Marcus Garvey and the New Negro in the twentieth century, and to the radical Black activism of Reconstructionists after slavery, grew from there, and Black Power advocates soon embarked on a mission to reimagine American democracy from the inside out. In one of his most important and powerful speeches, in October 1966, Carmichael addressed the notion of white privilege and American democracy before more than ten thousand students at the University of California at Berkeley. "A new society must be born," Carmichael insisted. "Racism must die," and "economic exploitation of non-whites must end." He then asked a question that BLM would pose again decades later: "How can white society move to see black people as human beings?"[40]

The Black Panther Party (BPP), founded in Oakland, California, on October 15, 1966, answered this question through multiple strategies that combined the martial, paramilitary politics of the First Reconstruction era during the 1860s with the efforts to build radical Black dignity in some of the most impoverished segments of American society that flourished during that same period. Malcolm X's message of radical Black dignity inspired both Carmichael and the Black Panthers. For a short time, Carmichael joined the Panthers as honorary "prime minister." SNCC and the Black Panthers both felt as if their activism represented a living extension of Malcolm's work.

Inspired by Malcolm X, by anti-colonial movements in Africa and Latin America, and by an eclectic reading of Marxism-Leninism and the literature of third world revolution (most notably Frantz Fanon's *The Wretched of the Earth*), the BPP in 1966 issued a twenty-point program calling for the radical transformation of American democracy. The Panthers cut a stylishly combative posture, dressed in black leather jackets, powder blue T-shirts, and berets that recalled the one worn by the Argentinean hero of the Cuban Revolution, Che Guevara. Under the supervision of party founders Huey P. Newton and Bobby Seale, the gun-toting Black militants surveilled the police in Oakland and throughout the East Bay Area in the fall and winter of 1966 on their way to creating a national firestorm. On May 2, 1967, a group of thirty Black Panthers, some of them armed (which was legal under California state law at the time), entered the California State Capitol in Sacramento to protest pending legislation specifically designed to end the BPP's practice of surveilling the police. The BPP's "invasion" of the California Assembly Chamber introduced the nation to the Panthers in bold fashion.[41]

Stokely Carmichael departed America for Conakry, Guinea, in West Africa, by 1969. There, he changed his name to Kwame Ture, in honor of his two mentors, Kwame Nkrumah, the former leader of Ghana and an icon of Pan-Africanism, and Sekou Ture, the president of Guinea. From Africa he continued to advocate for a Black political revolution that he now judged could only be effectively organized from outside of the United States. Periodic tours of colleges and universities brought him back to the States until his untimely death from prostate cancer on November 15, 1998, at the age of fifty-seven. Around 1995, shortly before his cancer diagnosis, I witnessed Kwame Ture deliver a keynote speech in Philadelphia at the University of Pennsylvania. I sat, awestruck, at the power of his words, the passion of his speech, the dignity that emanated from his African robes, and the wisdom reflected in his graying beard. I spoke to him briefly afterward, shaking his hand and nodding when he asked me if I was "working for the liberation of my people."

The BPP's advocacy of armed self-defense drew from a deep wellspring of Black politics. Black political power reached its greatest heights in the South's most remote regions during the First Reconstruction era, a time when paramilitary groups that both supported and protected Black political organizing became the bone and sinew of abolition democracy in the Deep South. Under the watchful eyes of armed Black men and women in a reconstructed South, Black voters were ensured protection. Armed self-defense was essential, given the parallel rise of violent white supremacist organizations aligned with (though independent from) the Democratic Party, the old slave plantocracy, and conservative Republicans who were less interested in Negro rights than political stability.[42]

Within a year of their founding, the Panthers ended their direct patrols of the police (a result of the new law as well as their own efforts to do more than simply surveil) in favor of creating local chapters offering free breakfast programs, health clinics, legal and housing aid, drug rehabilitation, and a prisons busing program that helped people visit loved ones in prison. With a robust presence on both coasts, and chapters in Seattle and Portland; Winston-Salem, North Carolina; New Orleans; and over two dozen other cities, the Panthers at their height during the late 1960s comprised between three thousand and five thousand members in over thirty-five chapters. They endeavored to provide Black folks at the lower frequencies with a kind of political dignity unimagined by the Great Society.

President Lyndon Johnson's Great Society programs, like Franklin Roosevelt's New Deal thirty years earlier, put social welfare at the forefront of US policy. Although Johnson set out to wage an unconditional War on Poverty, America's growing political and financial commitments in Vietnam stymied these efforts. In many ways the Black Panthers became a bridge between the rhetoric of the Great Society and its reality in Black communities nationwide. By 1966, the Black Power movement had given urgent new language to this reality by openly discussing the high rate of Black unemployment, the disproportionate number of Blacks drafted into the military and fighting on the front lines of Vietnam, police brutality, the rising tide of violence in urban cities, and the stubborn persistence of poverty, segregation, violence, and disease after a decade of promises that remained unkept.

The Panthers exposed the soft underbelly of American exceptionalism through decisive action. Their twenty-point program ("What We Want and What We Believe") was inspired by a thirteen-point plank that appeared in the Nation of Islam's newspaper, *Muhammad Speaks*. Black Panther Party cofounders Huey P. Newton and Bobby Seale, who first saw Malcolm speak at a conference in Oakland in 1963, remained devoted to the Black nationalist leader long past his death. The Panthers called for an end to police brutality, the release of Black folks from prison and military service, Black history education in public schools, and an end to racial and economic exploitation within the Black community. They embraced a politics of "revolutionary nationalism"—the anti-racist, anti-imperialist, anti-colonial politics of third world revolutionaries such as Fidel Castro abroad and Malcolm X at home—on their way to becoming socialists who aligned themselves with white "Mother Country" radicals.

The BPP's revolutionary politics evolved into a full-blown anti-imperialist struggle that connected anti-Black racism and economic injustice in America's ghettoes to imperial wars around the world. Its members were organizing chapters of the National

Committee to Combat Fascism by 1969, painfully aware that government surveillance, police brutality, and racial violence threatened to tip American democracy into a full-blown political authoritarianism rooted in anti-Black racism.

The Panthers were also prison abolitionists. Inspired by Malcolm X's example, they turned prisons into fertile grounds for intellectual study in the service of political transformation. The Panthers revered Malcolm as a self-made Black radical organizer, a formerly incarcerated street hustler who loved the Black poor and working-class people. They admired him as a prison intellectual who spread a message of Black liberation to the masses. Malcolm, for the Black Panthers, also modeled a Black masculinity that they strived to emulate: it was confident, intelligent, quick witted, and self-assured, yet humble and vulnerable.

One of the leaders of the Panthers' prisoner rights movement was George Jackson, who, convicted of robbery in California at the age of eighteen, had transformed himself into a radical prison intellectual, theorist, organizer, and activist. He achieved fame through his memoir, *Soledad Brother*, published in 1970. Jackson became a Panther "field marshal" while in prison, writing for the Black Panther newspaper and organizing inmates throughout the California system and beyond. He formed a political partnership and personal relationship with Angela Davis, who had returned to the United States in 1967 after spending time abroad. She had met Stokely Carmichael at an international conference in London that summer. Davis's relationship with Jackson thrust her into a radical prisoner rights movement, which in turn caused her to come under deeper surveillance by law enforcement. FBI director J. Edgar Hoover—the nemesis of Malcolm X and Martin Luther King Jr.—considered the Black Panthers to be the nation's number one internal security threat. They faced illegal harassment, surveillance, incarceration, and at times death at the hands of far-flung local, state, regional, national, and global authorities. Jackson was killed in what authorities alleged was a prison break in 1971, but supporters characterized it as an execution. His death triggered roiling protests at prisons across the nation, the most explosive of which occurred in Attica penitentiary in upstate New York, where a rebellion organized by prisoners to protest inhumane conditions led to the deaths of thirty-nine men (twenty-nine inmates and ten guards) after Governor Nelson Rockefeller ordered the prison to be retaken by force.[43]

At their best, the Panthers advocated for a vision of abolition democracy grounded in the lived experiences of the Black poor, prisoners, and the working class, who were made vulnerable by historical systems of punishment, extractive capitalism, and racism. SNCC, the Panthers, and Black Power touched every facet of American life, from the reimagining of beauty, dance, and aesthetics (as promoted by Black Arts activists); to the creation of Black Studies departments and programs, along with cultural centers, at universities and colleges; to the election of a new generation of Black politicians at the local, state, and federal levels. Perhaps most profoundly, Black Power transformed America's racial consciousness—for all its citizens. The era's political radicalism inspired people of color to more fully embrace the historical and cultural roots of their identities. And Black Power, more so than the mainstream civil rights movement, ended the invisibility of white privilege, rendering it clear for all to see.[44]

BLM's at times angry, passionate, and unremitting criticism of police brutality, violence, and murder of Black bodies recalls aspects of the Black Panther Party's twenty-point program, its search for community control, and its survival programs, which sought to fortify the most vulnerable parts of the Black community against racist violence. The BLM movement, like the Black Power movement, also developed, beginning in 2013, its own iconography. Unlike the Black Power movement, however, BLM eschewed charismatic leaders, blasted patriarchal notions of freedom, and instead put an intersectional analysis of dignity and citizenship, rooted in Black feminism and in abolition democracy as drawn from the Black radical tradition, front and center.

Black Lives Matter activists wisely rejected an either/or model of Black liberation struggle in favor of adapting the nonviolent civil disobedience of the civil rights movement's heroic period, exemplified by SNCC's work in the Deep South, to the radical structural critique of white supremacy and capitalism articulated by Black Power. BLM's inclusive approach to Black politics represented a truly radical redefinition of racial progress. By recognizing the intersectional nature of Black identity, the movement took an important step beyond its predecessors. By placing the lives of trans and Queer Black women, young people, and the poor at the center of the BLM policy agenda, these activists enlarged our collective vision of who belongs in the Black community. In doing so, they expanded the terrain of what it is to be human in a society that, since its inception as a democratic republic founded in racial slavery, has insisted that Black lives did not matter, and that Black people were not human.

The struggle for Black dignity has traveled a path toward universal human rights through the particular experience of racial slavery, Jim Crow segregation, and racial caste in America. By insisting that the most oppressed people within the Black community are worthy of dignity and citizenship, BLM argued that we all remain unfree until liberation comes to those faces at the bottom of the well of Blackness. Until the trans boys and girls traumatized by legislation designed to dehumanize them, Black and Afro-Latinx Queer teenagers with no access to mental health care and HIV/AIDS treatment, and Black women who overwhelmingly head households below the poverty line are recognized as part of our collective American family, we all remain imprisoned.

But even though BLM drew on a range of models, and even though it pushed in important ways beyond the limitations of each of those models, it is clear that it would not have existed without the work that SNCC undertook in the Deep South in the early 1960s. Much as Malcolm X had, the group characterized the struggle for Black dignity as the long-awaited recognition of Black humanity. They dared to salvage the buried remains of Black Reconstruction, grappling with the legacies of that period in some of the same tiny hamlets and small towns where an earlier generation of Black Americans had claimed potential power as a marker of their hard-won freedom. Dressed in sharecropper's overalls, Black folk in SNCC forced America to acknowledge Reconstruction's afterlife: the continued existence of systems of racial oppression, economic exploitation, and personal violence and degradation that were a hallmark of antebellum slavery. These systems continued to thrive, and even expanded, after slavery's formal end. SNCC recognized that the denials of Black dignity and citizenship in Mississippi were not an aberration, but an accurate reflection of the impoverished state of American democracy.

More than fifty years later, BLM embraced SNCC's rich legacy as it leveled a similar critique of the manifold ways that America continued to deny Black humanity. BLM's respect for the work of SNCC activists paralleled Barack Obama's veneration of the civil rights struggles of the same period. But BLM and Obama drew startlingly different lessons from this history. Obama's reading of American history made him a mainstream reconstructionist; in every instance of racial progress, he saw the further perfection of the nation's democratic experiment. As radical reconstructionists deeply influenced by the abolition democracy of SNCC, Malcolm X, and the Black Panthers, and the interpretation of history this entailed, BLM offered a different view.[45]

America's Third Reconstruction, as embodied in the vision of Black citizenship offered by Obama, and the radical Black dignity embraced by BLM, would unfold amid the demise of two interrelated phenomena: the racial consensus that made the first Black president possible and the unraveling of the American exceptionalist political framework that made Black Lives Matter necessary by allowing redemptionist impulses to flourish.

3

BACKLASH

DURING ONE HORRIFIC WEEK in July 2016, with political tensions running high as the presidential election heated up, two Black men in their thirties, Alton Sterling in Louisiana and Philando Castile in Minnesota, were shot and killed by police. Their deaths, captured in viral videos, left me and others in the Black community heartbroken and angry. A year earlier, many of us had hoped that Barack Obama's visit to the federal prison in Oklahoma might be a turning point in the nation's criminal justice policies. Black Lives Matter demonstrations seemed to be exerting the right kind of pressure. Our hopes were dashed by the public executions of Black people by police continuing to come to light on a regular basis.

Matters only escalated when, at a peaceful demonstration in Dallas to protest the killings of Sterling and Castile, a mentally disturbed young Black man murdered five police officers and wounded eight others before being killed by law enforcement in a parking garage standoff. The tragic deaths of the police officers quickly shifted the public conversation once again. Instead of a focus on Sterling and Castile, and the many other young Black men who had been killed by police, it was the sacrifice of the police that took center stage in Dallas over the ensuing days.

Donald Trump had meanwhile been campaigning for Black support by asking the question: "What have you got to lose?" The answer turned out to be everything. Trump weaponized white fears of Black bodies in ways that were both old and new. He tapped into national anxieties over the presence of Black people in so-called white spaces, accusing Democrats of planning to unleash hordes of Black criminals into lily-white suburbs. Trump celebrated police brutality and violence against alleged criminals and even hecklers at campaign events, helping to amplify a climate of racial intolerance that stoked an atmosphere of mutual distrust, fear, and anger between law enforcement and Black Americans.

Donald Trump's election surprised a part of me. Although I had spent the preceding eight years documenting the conservative backlash against Barack Obama's ascent, I never imagined that we could fall into the moral abyss so quickly after the soaring heights of 2008. A part me remained under the spell conjured not only by Obama himself but also by the way large numbers of Americans had embraced him in 2008, and by the smaller portion that kept the faith throughout his presidency. I had hoped that Obama's flawed presidency had managed to pull together a coalition powerful and resilient enough to defend democracy against Trump's redemptionist vision. That group of true believers proved unable to hold back the bursting dam of discontent encapsulated by Trump's slogan, "Make America Great Again," or MAGA.

Another part of me, though, was not surprised by Trump's victory. White backlash contains multitudes. Trump won the day by winning white votes. He secured every economic and gender demographic among whites, including a portion of voters who had previously voted for Obama once or even twice. The US Supreme Court's dismantling of the Voting Rights Act surely helped, as did the fact that the Democratic Party was searching in vain for a post-Obama identity. Portions of the Obama coalition, disillusioned by the previous eight years and uninspired by the prospect of a Hillary Clinton presidency, turned inward. Public figures I admired supported candidates who seemed doomed to lose, such as Bernie Sanders or Jill Stein, sometimes loudly in op-ed pages. These public figures, with reconstructionist impulses, lacked the pragmatic humility of previous generations of Black activists, such as those in the aftermath of the Civil War, who had supported flawed candidates out of a sense of duty to protect American democracy from even worse options. Obama's presence in the White House and the Movement for Black Lives had served to radicalize portions of the electorate dissatisfied with perceived half-measures in the aftermath of the Great Recession. Our main job, I believed, was to protect Black lives and the Black community's future in the short and long terms. Hillary Clinton's flaws did not change that calculus, I would argue in public and private, but to no avail. Trump lost the popular vote but won the presidency by taking three states—Michigan, Wisconsin, and Pennsylvania—where Black voters stayed home in larger numbers than they had during the previous two presidential election cycles.

A deep sadness washed over me the night Donald Trump became the president-elect. I felt despondent over the prospect of raising my young daughter in a country that appeared to be even more racist than I had imagined. Some activists connected to progressive and radical Black politics had seemed to encourage people to sit out the 2016 election, reasoning that both major parties were corrupt—a stance with which I passionately disagreed. The failure by some activists and groups that I admired to distinguish between principled criticism and pragmatic support for the best option for Black people (as opposed to the lesser-of-two-evils argument) proved depressing. I grew impatient with the combination of vanity and apathy in parts of the Black community that I believed should know better. I grew angry over the fact that Trump had won the backing of majorities of every demographic of white voter: men and women, college educated and high school drop-outs, rich and poor, urban, rural, and suburban.[1]

The Trump campaign mastered the public art of remembering and forgetting. MAGA offered a vision of citizenship based on a particular narrative about the nation's history. The Trump campaign's story of the American past characterized white violence and privilege as America's necessary ingredient, the secret sauce that made democracy work. Conversely, Black presence in America, if depicted at all, represented an existential threat to white futures.

This sort of forgetting had its own long history. In 1895, during a South Carolina state convention expressly designed to disenfranchise Black voters, a relatively obscure former US congressman, a Black man named Thomas Miller, described Reconstruction's heyday in the state between 1868 and 1876: "We were eight years in power. We had built schoolhouses, established charitable institutions, built and maintained the penitentiary system, provided for the education of the deaf and dumb, rebuilt the ferries. In short, we had reconstructed the State and placed it upon the road to prosperity."[2]

Miller had spoken amid the democratic ruins that South Carolina had become. He proudly but mournfully recalled the important role Black elected officials had played in reshaping American democracy and setting the state on a road to prosperity. The success of Black politics in Reconstruction-era South Carolina had given proof to the lie of white supremacy. And Blacks, more committed to the promise of multiracial democracy than their white counterparts, had done so much for the collective good. Miller lamented that the architects of this renaissance would be purposefully excluded from participating in the New South. Even as it saluted this legacy of achievement, the speech also succinctly explained how redemptionists benefited from Reconstruction-era policies while ensuring the denial of Black citizenship.[3]

I have often pondered how Miller's haunting words seemed to perfectly describe American democracy by the end of 2016. Miller's eloquent testimony about the paradox of Black Reconstruction doubled as an elegy for the first Black president, so much so that journalist Ta-Nehisi Coates titled his collection of essays on the Obama era *We Were Eight Years in Power*.[4] MAGA imagined an America where Thomas Miller never existed, his absence relegating the most consequential parts of American history null and void. The erasure of Miller, and of Black Reconstruction, from MAGA's vision of American history denies the fuller picture of the national story. Left out is the way in which Black labor, during and after slavery, created undreamed wealth and opportunities for all except the rough hands that picked cotton, washed floors, and tended the hearth of white America.

A growing sense of desperation in the wake of 2016 inspired me to return to the scene of the historical crime, so to speak. Today's acts of national remembering and forgetting are part of a historical cycle that began in the aftermath of a cataclysmic civil war that nearly destroyed America. Yet we seemed more intent than ever on learning the wrong lessons by embracing bad history. I realized that the First Reconstruction had offered the key to understanding the dual aspects of Black consciousness that inspired the racial optimism and pessimism in my own time. Redemption not only stained America's democratic soul, but still festered inside of the American project. "Make America Great Again" reflected a redemptionist vision of America just as surely as "Black Lives Matter" encapsulated reconstructionist dreams of abolition democracy.

The Age of Trump inspired me to move forward by looking back, and I spent the majority of his presidency studying Reconstruction with a new set of eyes. I found solace in the history of the nineteenth century, the first era of Reconstruction. The juxtapositions of that era continued in the present, as did the hypocrisy, the historical amnesia, and, especially, the devaluing of Black life. This other country, I discovered, was actually our own. I came to view redemptionist violence and reconstructionist ambition not as separate and distinct from one another, but as the Janus faces of the nation itself. They existed, across time and space, in tandem with one another. Paradoxically, this revelation gave me hope. The harsh contrasts between stunning progress and violent backlash that contemporary Americans claimed as aberrations were in fact dual and dueling traditions of reconstruction and redemption within the national body politic. Where one appeared, the other was almost certain to follow.[5]

I sometimes wonder if Donald Trump ever heard of Dred Scott. Not enough Americans have. The brutality of Scott's life under chattel slavery and the cruel dismissal of his plea for freedom sped America's path toward violent civil war and remain a source of enduring shame. In 1846, Scott sued for freedom for himself and his second wife, Harriet Scott, claiming residence in free-soil Illinois. The complex case found Scott and his wife returning to Missouri and seeking legal relief, in vain, from slavery's seemingly infinite clutches. Scott's case wound its way to the Supreme Court, which did more than rule against him in 1857. Chief Justice Roger Taney's decision in *Scott v. Sandford* (the misspelled name of Scott's owner, John F. A. Sanford) nationalized racial slavery, negating the long-held legal precedent that slavery's rule ended at the borders of free territories and states.

Taney added insult to injury with words that continue to echo through the present. The court refused to recognize Scott as a "'citizen' within the meaning of the Constitution of the United States." The Supreme Court's assertion that Black people had long been considered "so far inferior, that they had no rights which the white man was bound to respect," outraged freedom-loving people across the nation; heightened the resolve of white Republican Party leaders, most notably Abraham Lincoln, to confront the slave power; and hastened the coming of the Civil War. It also cast bright lines around the questions that would become most visible, and most fiercely contested, during subsequent periods of Reconstruction—questions of democracy, justice, and citizenship.[6]

Trump's rise has often been described as a manifestation of racial backlash—an interpretation that Trump's own behavior did much to encourage. Trump symbolized white mediocrity backed by class privilege, patriarchy, and a long history of racial gaslighting: the practice of denying racist intent while ensuring racially disparate outcomes. In the 1970s, the Department of Justice investigated his real estate mogul father, Fred Trump, for discriminating against prospective Black tenants. As a fame-seeking real estate entrepreneur in the 1980s, Trump himself placed an infamous ad in New York City tabloids calling for the execution of the Central Park Five—five teenagers, four of them Black and one Puerto Rican, who had been accused of brutally raping a white female jogger. The Five were exonerated on December 19, 2002, but Trump never apologized for demanding their deaths. And then, after 2008, as the leading voice of the "birther movement," Trump rose to national political prominence by disputing Barack Obama's citizenship status.

Trump's role as chief cheerleader for the birther lie highlights how white backlash cannot be separated from white America's long-standing refusal to recognize Black citizenship, dignity, and humanity. The *Dred Scott* decision was not the last word on the future of Black citizenship. Neither was the Civil War. After Black Americans won formal citizenship and Black men won the vote during the First Reconstruction, "Mississippi Plans" violently "redeemed" the South from Black power. As Black people migrated to cities North and South, organized white riots in Atlanta, St. Louis, Chicago, Tulsa, Elaine (Arkansas), and Rosewood (Florida) violently targeted their bodies, their hopes, and their dreams.

When Black Americans fought again to secure a full measure of citizenship and dignity during the civil rights era, the "Massive Resistance" campaigns of White Citizens Councils fought to preserve white supremacy. And when Barack Obama's election seemed to promise a new era of multiracial democracy and racial progress, Trump's campaign and its MAGA slogan galvanized a new white nationalism that cohered around the fear of Black citizenship. Trump deftly tapped into the resentment of all strata of white society—its political and economic winners as well as those left behind. MAGA defined Obama's rise as alternatively a threat to their privileged status and as a symptom of their personal and political decline. It promoted nostalgia for a time before there existed a national consensus, however flawed, in support of racial justice.

Many believed that the nostalgia suffusing the desire to "make America great again" reflected a yearning for a return to the pre-civil-rights-era 1950s. But Trump's campaign for a new, twenty-first-century era of racial redemption was rooted in a much longer history of redemptionist politics than that. It expertly trafficked in the same white nationalism, resentment, and racism that helped to destabilize the promise of Black citizenship during the First Reconstruction. And it reflected the enduring political, legal, and narrative power of a Lost Cause ideology that portrayed the Civil War as a reasonable effort by southerners to defend their personal honor. From that perspective, the "Negro Rule" of Reconstruction was a tragic mistake, and Black lives were less valuable than white ones. The red MAGA hat that became for many a symbol of rage against immigration, globalization, and economic inequality was also a stark echo of the red shirts worn by the nineteenth-century white nationalist redeemers who violently fought to eliminate Black political power in the Reconstruction-era South.

A white supremacist politics of redemption has shaped America ever since the Civil War's end. From the very start, the First Reconstruction was met with racial backlash at the local, regional, and national levels. Black agricultural workers more often than not found themselves forced into a new kind of servitude through onerous labor "contracts" enforced through threats of physical violence and sometimes death. Even successful efforts by Black farmers to pool their resources in order to purchase and cultivate land were often stymied or obliterated by organized white violence, legal indifference, and collusion with law enforcement. Southern states passed Black Codes designed to strip African Americans of voting rights, bar them from serving on juries, and humiliate them by segregating public accommodations. The growth of local Black power in southern rural and urban areas sparked racial violence against Black communities in Memphis and New Orleans in 1866, less than a year after the Thirteenth Amendment's ratification. The convict lease system appeared just after slavery ended, aided and abetted by the portion of the Thirteenth Amendment that allowed for servitude as punishment for crimes. The criminalization of Black Americans that had begun during slavery accelerated in the context of freedom as men, women, and children were subjected to forced labor contracts; debt peonage on plantations that echoed the master-slave dynamics of racial slavery; and chain gangs that local towns, hamlets, and cities leased out to private companies to work under conditions that amounted to slavery by another name.[7]

Under Andrew Johnson, a native Tennessean and an unrepentant racist, what became known as "Presidential Reconstruction" promised the restoration of white supremacy throughout the entire South. Titans of the former Confederacy received pardons by the thousands, and the question of Black suffrage hung in the balance until the Radical Republican Congress, led by the abolitionist-democracy impulses of Representative Thaddeus Stevens, impeached Johnson (the Senate failed to convict him by a single vote) and passed legislation that allowed Black folk a brief moment in the political sun. The years between 1868 and 1876 were a golden age of Black political power in a newly remade America. But redemption followed close on the heels of this brief revelry. Redemptionist politics wielded intimidation, fraud, and outright violence to restore white supremacy to the South, and, over time, to the federal government and the entire nation. The Lost Cause, fueled by white grievance, became a political movement, a cultural touchstone, and a policy weapon aimed at the removal of Black Americans from the nation's public sphere.[8]

Gruesome instances of racial violence punctured Reconstruction's hopeful aspirations for Black citizenship and dignity. Racial massacres and organized white riots in Georgia, Alabama, Mississippi, Louisiana, and South Carolina between 1870 and 1876 helped to reverse the tide of local Black political power. Racial terrorists, operating under names such as the Red Shirts and the White Leagues, operated with impunity from the law, and at times in collusion with elected officials. In 1870, a white mob killed nine Blacks in Camilla County in southwestern Georgia, an unpunished outrage that marked the beginning of the end of Black political power in the rural parts of the state. Three years later, more than one hundred Blacks were massacred in Colfax, Louisiana, after white Fusionists (an alliance of conservative Republicans and Democrats) attacked African Americans who had taken over the courthouse to protect the duly elected Republican government. The violence in Georgia and Louisiana served as dress rehearsals for redemptionist campaigns to overthrow Black political power in

Mississippi, Alabama, and other parts of the South. The Mississippi Plan revolved around white men with guns, at times amassing by the thousands, who routed the outnumbered Black paramilitary and Union Leagues attempting to defend their newly won political rights. The heroic efforts ultimately proved to be futile.

The unofficial end of Radical Reconstruction took place in the presidential election year of 1876, in Hamburg, South Carolina. The lone state in the former Confederacy with a majority-Black population, South Carolina struck fear in the hearts of racists everywhere— none more so than Benjamin "Pitchfork" Tillman, a future governor and senator, who got his nickname by saying he would prod his opponent, Grover Cleveland, with a pitchfork. Tillman organized a racist militia group of six thousand Red Shirts that helped return Democrats to power through organized violence and terror against Black folk. The anti-Black violence of this white supremacist militia would become legendary. Tillman's swashbuckling version of white supremacy redefined Reconstruction as an assault on "helpless" white women vulnerable to sexual predation by violent Negroes. Demagogues such as Tillman justified the massacres and lynchings to come as a heroic defense of white female virtue and white manhood. Waves of racial violence plagued national and local elections throughout Reconstruction, with Democrats and Republicans making dual claims to statehouses in Texas, Louisiana, and Arkansas. Fraud, corruption, and gruesome violence became a national crisis with that year's presidential election, when Democrats, already in control of Congress after the 1874 midterms, threatened to reclaim the White House. Florida, Louisiana, and South Carolina each delivered competing slates of Republican and Democratic electors, with the outcome hanging in the balance. Ultimately, the

Grand Old Party agreed to withdraw federal troops from the South
and to stay out of local politics in exchange for the election of its
candidate, Rutherford B. Hayes.[9]

Reconstruction did not end with the election of 1876. However, Black Americans lost the federal government as a partner
in ensuring voting rights, fair treatment before the criminal justice system, honorable labor contracts, and bodily autonomy and
protection of Black children, women, men, and families. Reconstructionist politics continued in archipelagos of fugitive democracy that dotted the national landscape. Blacks managed to find
islands of protection through migration to the West, the North,
and the Midwest; in agricultural cooperatives; and through political organizing. But redemptionist impulses structured the future
framework of American democracy and American citizenship.
The 1896 Supreme Court decision in *Plessy v. Ferguson* ratified the
doctrine of "separate but equal," sanctioning institutional racism
and asserting "social equality" as an ideal unrecognized by the
Constitution. In the court's view, Blacks could be considered equal
under the law even as they were relegated to separate and inferior
schools and public accommodations.

This early form of "color-blind racism" reconciled three decades of redemptionist politics seeking to marginalize and subor-
dinate Black Americans with a Constitution that, as modified by
the Reconstruction Amendments, ostensibly ensured racial equality. Similar claims would be wielded by redemptionists from that
era into our own. The white political coup in Wilmington, North
Carolina, in 1898 represented a brutal summation of decades of
redemptionist violence, outright fraud, racism, and dishonor. Organized white violence spearheaded a massacre that killed dozens

of Black men, including some of Wilmington's leading citizens; drove thousands into the frigid woods in a desperate search for survival; and reimposed racist Democratic Party leadership that disposed of the interracial Fusionist government that brought together Black Republicans and white populists. To add insult to injury, Tillman, the villain of the 1876 massacre in Hamburg, formed part of a rogues' gallery of white supremacists that resurrected the Red Shirts in North Carolina to terrorize unwitting Black citizens.

Echoing Thomas Miller's mournful words, North Carolina's sole Black congressman, George C. White, delivered a farewell address to the US Congress in 1901 that surveyed the ashes of America's democratic landscape. It functioned as an elegy for Black political representation. President William McKinley's refusal to publicly acknowledge the massacre spelled the last gasp of Black power in southern politics for the next seven decades. White, who had proposed federal legislation to aid the survivors of the Wilmington massacre, found his position untenable after redemptionist violence reinstated white rule across the state. In what he termed the "Negroes' temporary farewell to the American congress," White expressed the sentiment of "an outraged, heart-broken, bruised and bleeding" people who nonetheless retained hope to "rise up some day and come again" to the halls of power.[10]

Reconstruction laid out the rough boundaries of a reconfigured democratic republic in which Black citizenship was expansively defined. But redemption violently returned the South back toward a regressive vision of white supremacy. The striking juxtaposition of Reconstruction's multiracial democracy and redemption's white supremacist violence, fraud, and corruption became a core feature of American society ever afterward. The Janus-faced nature of America is reflected in the ongoing conflict between redemptionist and reconstructionist impulses today.

Redemption weaponized white grievance against Black dignity and citizenship. It forged explicit and implicit coalitions of active and passive white supremacists, from hardened ex-Confederates who gleefully participated in racial massacres to politicians, business leaders, clergy, and ordinary citizens who found their own social standing elevated by the wholesale degradation of Black communities, and happily accommodated that degradation as a result. Redemption framed American politics as a zero-sum game in which even the appearance of Black citizenship and racial equality could be interpreted as an assault on white privilege and power. The period set the stage for the regime of racial oppression and white supremacy popularly known as Jim Crow, when the United States violently policed—sometimes literally—a color line that reproduced chattel slavery's power dynamic.

But the term "Jim Crow" obscures as much as it reveals. For redemptionist impulses did far more than create American racial apartheid, although they did certainly achieve this. Racist laws and blatantly oppressive policies that purposefully injured Black Americans were indeed a key legacy of this era. But this was also an era of ritualized violence, violence that viciously curtailed freedmen's and freedwomen's efforts to build lives of dignity, secure economic autonomy, and wield political power both in defense of their lives and in support of multiracial democracy. And it was an era in which historical memory and popular culture intertwined to reinforce racial oppression.

THE THIRD RECONSTRUCTION

The erection of Confederate monuments and statues filled America's built environment with memorials to perpetrators of anti-Black racial violence on a mass scale. Newspapers, cartoonists, writers, and journalists furthered redemptionist lies through caricatures of Blacks as lazy, violent, sexual predators who deserved the waves of anti-Black violence and terror that became commonplace in parts of the South. What is characterized as Jim Crow is in reality a period in American history that witnessed the full flowering of the redemptionist vision of the nation-state. The Confederacy lost the war but resoundingly won the peace. Over time, many northerners came not only to participate in the redemptionist lie, but to embrace the logic behind it. Religious beliefs, scientific racism, phony crime statistics, and fake allegations of rape and sexual assault rationalized racial oppression, which became codified in American law and the nation's political and cultural imagination. Blackness became the main basis for determining who would be included in the American project and who would be destined to forever remain the faces at the bottom of the well.

The mythology of the Lost Cause serves as this tragic era's narrative spine, retold in pulp fiction, in cinema, and in history books, an epic fever dream in which blood-soaked fields of human carnage were required to "redeem" the South's lost honor. It was this mythology—the biggest lie in American history—that Donald Trump threw his support behind when he venerated Confederate heroes and vowed to protect statues commemorating war criminals. Redemption, then and now, seeks the restoration of white supremacy through fraud, cruelty, and state-sanctioned violence. The ultimate point, as Confederate monuments exemplified, remains the perpetual subjugation of Black bodies. As in the case of Dred Scott,

146

redemption interprets the US Constitution, as Justice Taney did, as incapable of recognizing Black humanity, let alone Black citizenship.

A redemptionist drift was baked into even the Second Reconstruction. America's civil rights movement rehearsed many aspects of the First Reconstruction era as Black people at all levels of society engaged in a struggle to make multiracial democracy real. But until the explosive emergence of Black Power in the mid-1960s, claims of Black citizenship remained largely focused on achieving formal equality under the law and enfranchisement through the vote. Larger questions of reparations for racial slavery, economic justice for the Black poor, the eradication of barriers to Black wealth—that is to say, questions related to redistributive justice that were so central during the First Reconstruction era—were mostly in the background. Even during the most remarkably successful phases of the Second Reconstruction, redemption framed the paradigm within which conceptions of Black dignity and freedom could flourish in the public sphere.[11]

Reconstruction-era Ben Tillmans found their successors in the civil rights period's George Wallaces. This new generation of racial demagogues helped to buttress the ideological realignment between the major political parties, and it offered cover for "moderates," such as Richard Nixon, elected president in 1968. Almost immediately after it was achieved through the blood of ordinary people and iconic martyrs, the chipping away of the new racial compact began. Politics in post-civil-rights America centered on relitigating questions thought to have been settled by the first two eras of Reconstruction. The period was characterized by assaults on affirmative action, on racial desegregation in public schools and neighborhoods, and on voting rights.

Meanwhile, the limitations of the Second Reconstruction itself became increasingly clear. At the very moment the Black community and broader American public celebrated the passage of the Civil Rights and Voting Rights Acts, local governments planted seeds that would eventually lead to the crisis of mass incarceration. The social programs of the Great Society contributed to this crisis by federalizing crime control and investing more deeply in forestalling Black rebellion than in promoting the eradication of urban ghettoes, rural poverty, police brutality, and violence. While organized white violence against Black people and Black wealth has historically gone unpunished, the Black urban rebellions against police brutality, structural poverty, and racial oppression of the 1960s inspired perhaps the greatest financial investment in anti-Black public policies in history.[12]

These policies took a range of forms: law enforcement's war against the Black Panthers and other Black Power–era radicals, Richard Nixon's creation of the Drug Enforcement Administration (DEA), the accelerated growth of the prison industrial complex, and the Reagan-era Drug War against crack cocaine, for example. In this new redemptionist backlash, disenfranchisement and disempowerment were accomplished through incarceration rather than through the poll taxes, convict leasing, and Black Codes of the nineteenth century. But much as in the nineteenth century, both Democrats and Republicans sacrificed Black citizenship at the altar of racial caste.

Ronald Reagan's presidency successfully reconfigured the conservative wing of the Republican Party so that it won acceptance even as it championed redemptionist policies. But Democrats such as Bill Clinton continued this policy trajectory while performatively embracing parts of African American history and culture, especially as they related to civil rights. By the late twentieth and early twenty-first centuries, Black punishment was a crucial feature of American social welfare policy as a result of crime and welfare reform bills passed during the 1990s with bipartisan support from Democrats and Republicans.[13]

Rapper Kanye West's claim, during a live fundraiser for the victims of Hurricane Katrina, that "George Bush does not care about Black people," telescoped a 140-year history into a racially combustible soundbite. Bush later characterized the allegation as the most painful single moment of his presidency, a personal insult that he could not reconcile with his cordial feelings toward Blacks and his friendship with two high-profile cabinet members, Condoleezza Rice and Colin Powell, the first two African American secretaries of state in the nation's history. Hurricane Katrina revealed the way in which redemptionist policies had reshaped American democracy for the worse, especially for Black folk. Disinvestment in major cities, social policies designed to punish rather than empower, and the transformation of the War on Poverty to a Drug and Crime War made Black people disproportionately vulnerable to catastrophe. The question was not whether George W. Bush was a racist. It was whether the entire US government (and the media that covered politics) could see Black people as human beings, citizens, and political actors worthy of justice, mercy, and grace.[14]

President Kennedy's extraordinary June 11, 1963, civil rights speech defined racism as a moral issue, an existential threat to democracy, and a blight on the body politic. But toward the end of his speech Kennedy announced that the nation had a right to "expect that the Negro community will be responsible"—as if

Black people, after more than a century of slavery and Jim Crow, still had to pass a test of citizenship. At his best, Lyndon Johnson discussed racial justice with unusual eloquence and power, going so far as to demand "equality of outcomes" and not just equal opportunity. His congressional address after Selma and his Howard University commencement speech exemplify this better side. In other instances, however, especially in the wake of urban rebellions challenging police brutality, racial violence, and structural poverty, Johnson relied on rhetoric rooted in racist tropes—for example, contrasting peaceful protesters and looters in a way that suggested that the latter had no rightful claims of citizenship that whites were bound to respect.

Republican presidents Richard Nixon, Gerald Ford, and Ronald Reagan expanded the rhetoric of "law and order" that defined Black people—rather than anti-Black racism—as an existential threat to white safety and American democracy.[15] But Democrats trafficked in this too. In the aftermath of the urban rebellion in Miami's Overtown neighborhood in 1980, Jimmy Carter admonished residents to fix the problems of urban dislocation, racism, unemployment, and violence themselves. This from a man who ran for president four years earlier as a racial progressive. Bill Clinton's new Democratic politics blamed declining values within Black families—the same disease identified by Daniel Patrick Moynihan's infamous 1965 report—rather than institutional racism. To add insult to injury, Clinton—twice elected in no small part thanks to Black voters—enacted criminal justice and welfare reform policies that helped to accelerate both mass incarceration and the very fracturing of vulnerable families used as a rhetorical bludgeon against Black demands for racial justice and equality.[16]

From this perspective George Bush's sentiment that Kanye West's denunciation proved the most personally hurtful moment of his presidency (which included the disastrous dual wars in Afghanistan and Iraq) makes perfect sense. The son of a former president and vice president with a keen sense of history, Bush did not wish to be viewed as a racist. While he would never be viewed as an anti-racist, he wanted to be regarded as someone who did his part in maintaining the status quo on race matters.

The throughline between Richard Nixon's and Ronald Reagan's America can be found in their ability to knit successful political coalitions united around the politics of white racial grievance. Nostalgia is key to the redemptionist imagination. That imagination produced an intellectual genealogy that purposefully rewrote the history of Reconstruction in a manner that justified the brutal, morally reprehensible, and politically indefensible policies that supported the Jim Crow era. A bipartisan consensus forged in the maelstrom of America's Second Reconstruction substituted racially charged symbols—of crime, drug addiction, welfare, public schools, the King holiday—over dismantling structural racism. Democrats and Republicans engaged in a cold war around race, with the GOP decrying racial justice policy efforts, such as affirmative action, as reverse discrimination, and Democrats touting the expansion of voting rights, racially integrated schools and neighborhoods, and equal employment access as the keys to the kingdom.

But with Republicans winning five of six presidential elections between 1968 and 1988, the Democratic Party under Bill Clinton pivoted on Black equality, with Clinton touting himself as a new Democrat tough on crime and hostile to social welfare.

THE THIRD RECONSTRUCTION

As governor of Arkansas in 1992, in the case of Ricky Ray Rector, Clinton had allowed the execution of a man convicted of murder despite the fact that the prisoner's frontal lobe had been virtually destroyed by a self-inflicted gunshot wound, and that the judge thus should have ruled that he was incompetent to stand trial. In 1992, shortly after Rector's execution, Clinton verbally sparred with Sister Souljah, essentially accusing her of anti-white racism. In many other instances, he reimagined Black equality as a question of personal responsibility rather than systemic racism and structural violence.[17]

A redemptionist vision, one deeply grounded in both white nostalgia over the nation's regime of racial slavery and grievance over that system's demise, skewed American history, policy, and moral and political priorities from Reconstruction to the election of Barack Obama. The first Black president inherited this distorted political reality. Obama would, of course, face both familiar and new forms of white grievance. He also encountered new forms of white nostalgia for a racially segregated past where "Negroes" and "Colored People" knew their place, and where the prospects of a Black president were less of a dream than a nightmare.

The fact that, a little more than three years after Katrina, America elected a Black man as president represents a kind of political miracle, one made possible by the combined might of Black voting power, recovered during the Second Reconstruction, and a once-in-a-lifetime economic calamity that found the nation on the brink of another Great Depression and in search of new hope. Obama shattered redemptionist political and cultural frameworks in which the face of American democracy was permanently, irretrievably, irrevocably white. For redemptionists, he represented a living nightmare. His very existence refuted their claims of racial privilege linked to Black debasement. The symbolism of a Black president, especially one as eloquent, politically astute, and obviously intelligent as Barack Obama, sent a shudder down the collective spines of tens of millions of white Americans. His very presence in the White House served to demolish the entire premise of the Lost Cause, an ideology arguing that Black people were forever unready for citizenship, that Black men were sexual predators, and that Black Americans must remain debased and disenfranchised. Obama's ascent to America's political throne exposed the lie of the redemptionist denigration of Black citizenship for all the world to see. Images of a Black First Family, complete with a brilliant Black First Lady and precociously intelligent First Daughters, exploded long-standing racist myths about Black familial dysfunction. Obama challenged the very foundations of white supremacy not only by winning the presidency, but also by behaving in a matter that definitively proved that Black Americans should have been operating within the halls of power all along.

In short, Obama's cosmopolitan, intellectual bearing, and his belief in a version of American exceptionalism that was inclusive enough to see nonwhites as equal political actors, challenged the ethos, politics, and policies of the Lost Cause in unimaginable ways. But there were inherent flaws in the optimistic reading of American history that Obama offered. Drawing from a deep well of historical knowledge about Black-led social justice movements, BLM activists and organizers recognized those flaws. On the streets of Ferguson, Baltimore, and other cities, they had faced tear-gas attacks and police brutality in real time. This historical knowledge and personal experience allowed them to challenge Obama's notion of citizenship as something granted from above and assert their own vision of Black dignity anchored in grass-roots political demands from below.

Trump, too, saw the limitations inherent in Obama's optimism about America. Trump simply knew his whites. He recognized—perhaps especially because of his own feelings of being humili-ated by President Obama at the White House Correspondents' Association dinner in 2011—that perceived Black advancement threatened white privilege, economic status, and social identity. Obama's imperfect efforts to usher in an age of multiracial democ-racy on a scale unimagined since Reconstruction offered Trump the basis for a counterrevolution. Even as economic indicators revealed that Black Americans suffered disproportionately from the Great Recession, sparked by a housing crisis where they had been overwhelmingly targeted by predatory lenders, Trump cam-paigned on a far different reality. He promised an end to economic inequality for *whites*, who, in his telling, were being victimized by a combination of economic globalization abroad, a flood of illegal immigration at home, and domestic policies that catered to un-deserving and underqualified Blacks and immigrants rather than hardworking white Americans.[18]

The election of Donald Trump in 2016 was a third hinge moment of America's Third Reconstruction, following Obama's 2008 election and the emergence of Black Lives Matter five years later. Trump's election was, in some sense, the logical historical and political out-come of the two earlier moments. Despite ideological and political disagreements over the nature and scale of anti-Black racism and white supremacy in American history, Barack Obama and Black Lives Matter activists shared common ground as fervent reconstructionists. Trump's election and the rise of his MAGA movement represented a racial and political backlash deeply rooted in the history of the First Reconstruction. Trump organized America around redemption politics on an unprecedented scale, achieving a victory that removed the veneer of national consensus around rhetorical support for racial equality that had characterized the post-civil-rights period. White nationalism that transcended religious affiliations, geographic diversity, and generational divisions was Trump's métier. But Trump's brand of populism tapped into the raw racial politics of American history. Much of the anti-Black rhetoric that Trump adopted and popularized during his campaign and presidency had clear antecedents in both the First and Second Reconstructions.

Trump targeted both President Obama and BLM with a redemptionist assault on the meaning of American identity, citizenship, and democracy. The message was simple: A Black president threatened the end of the white nationalist republic that arose from Reconstruction's ashes. Black political power had led once again to white peril. Black activism had produced, once again, disorder on the streets of America's cities. Trump drew from Richard Nixon's 1968 presidential campaign, weaponizing the phrase "law and order" in campaign speeches that portrayed the nation as a dystopian wasteland rife with crime, violence, and pain. But he also offered the insinuations of menace and incompetence much like those once leveled at the multiracial governments of the First Reconstruction. At the 2016 Republican National Convention in Cleveland, Trump highlighted "the president's hometown of

Chicago" as a dangerous wasteland, beset by an epidemic of crime as a result of Obama's "rollback of criminal enforcement."[19]

Racial scapegoating and recriminations were central to the four-day affair in Cleveland, which took place against a national backdrop of Black Lives Matter protests and mourning over the recent deaths of eight law-enforcement officers in Dallas and Baton Rouge. The convention's first day featured Rudy Giuliani, the race-baiting former New York City mayor, excoriating Black Lives Matter protesters and attacking President Obama as racially divisive. The redemptionist messaging continued over the next three days, with a litany of speakers painting a portrait of national decline, rising crime, rampant unemployment, and racial division orchestrated by Obama. Speaker after speaker framed the presidential contest as nothing less than a civilizational clash between God-fearing, law-abiding, Constitution-loving white Americans and radical Black protesters, undocumented criminals from Mexico, and Muslim terrorists. As they promised to "Make America Great Again," the message of perhaps the most chaotic, angry, vulgar presidential nominating convention in modern American history was unmistakably clear: people of color were the enemy.

On the convention's final night, Trump walked on stage to rousing cheers from the overwhelmingly white delegates. "We cannot afford," explained Trump, "to be so politically correct anymore." He proceeded to narrate a parallel universe characterized by rampant violence and lawlessness. Trump cited urban violence in Baltimore, Chicago, and the nation's capital as signs of social decay and pointed to deaths of police officers as an example of escalating national chaos that only his election could end.[20] The crux of Trump's speech might be summed up this way: White Lives

Matter, especially those feeling economic anxiety, racial fear, and the loss of white privilege in a nation transformed by demographic shifts, the loss of manufacturing jobs, and the election of a Black president. To convince whites mesmerized by what W. E. B. Du Bois had called the "public and psychological wages of whiteness" that the road to prosperity might be achieved through racial oppression and scapegoating of people of color at home and abroad, Trump cast everyone from BLM protesters to Syrian refugees and even NATO as existential threats to America.[21]

Having expertly stoked white people's fears, Trump proclaimed himself as their savior. His promise to build a wall to prevent immigrants from entering America served as a perfect metaphor for his campaign and the convention's full-throated embrace of white nationalism. "My greatest compassion will be for our own struggling citizens," Trump said as he joined delegates in cheering "USA! USA!" Using the word "white" before "citizen" was not necessary. Any American faintly aware of the nation's long history of racial violence, division, and recrimination heard Trump's message loud and clear. His campaign's promotion of racial anxiety, fear, and anger was a clarion call for a new era of redemption.

Trump's MAGA campaign moved anti-Blackness from the margins of American politics back to its center, helping to normalize white supremacy in contemporary American politics. Trump made Richard Nixon's appeals to America's worst racial impulses seem elegantly subtle in comparison. Seeking to redeem America from the scourge of Black equality, Trump and his supporters looked less to Nixon than to the Reconstruction-era South Carolina demagogue Ben Tillman and his violent supporters. Trump made little effort to hide his affinity for white supremacy, feigning ignorance, for instance, about receiving enthusiastic support from the notorious white supremacist and former Klan leader David Duke.

White hate groups and racial terrorist organizations had grown exponentially in response to Obama's election, just as hate crimes and assaults on Blacks, Jews, Asian Americans, and other people of color did after Trump took office. Perhaps most notoriously, Trump characterized the white supremacists who marched with tiki torches through Charlottesville, Virginia, in August 2017, in a weekend of protests that left Heather Heyer dead, as "good people." Charlottesville resurrected the redemptionist violence of the First Reconstruction, when white grievance over Republican political rule and Black dignity had led to the formation of the Ku Klux Klan in Pulaski, Tennessee, in 1866. The Klan became the catalyzing force behind a loose network of former Confederates, angry white working-class men, displaced civic and business elites, and grandees of the old slave system who together vowed to end Black power in the former Confederacy. Klan violence during Reconstruction emboldened redemptionist legislative, political, and cultural ambitions. Every massacre, outrage, and "shotgun policy" that went unpunished led to more racist violence, new refusals to defend Black citizenship, and the rapid erection of a society that normalized the punishment, degradation, and murder of Blacks as the cost of peace among whites. Donald Trump's tacit approval of white nationalism in Charlottesville echoed Andrew Johnson's mass pardons of ex-Confederates. In both cases, white supremacists surmised correctly that they had a friend in the White House.[22]

When President Obama and BLM activists met in the White House in 2014, he could not possibly have imagined a Trump presidency.

It is a testament to the young activists who served as this generation's shock troops of democracy that they could. They prepared to fight battles that many thought had been long won. BLM activists, as social movement organizers, were not required to pin an American flag to their clothes to illustrate their patriotism, as Obama and many other elected officials did in the aftermath of the 9/11 terrorist attacks. Instead, they displayed their courageous love for a country that had often failed to love them back through bold acts of public service; through street demonstrations that shut down major highways, and other forms of civil disobedience recalling the civil rights movement's heroic period; and through a phrase, "Black Lives Matter," that became the slogan for a twenty-first-century abolition democracy.

In a very real sense, Trump's presidential campaign and his subsequent victory finally settled the argument between BLM activists and Barack Obama over the meaning of American history. The activists characterized America as an unrepentantly racist nation, one whose system of mass incarceration could be traced directly back to Reconstruction and the redemptionist opposition. Obama pushed back against such views as overly pessimistic, suggesting that they ignored racial progress since the end of slavery, which could be gauged, perhaps best of all, by the presence of a Black man in the Oval Office. But Trump's election repudiated "the bet" upon which Obama had premised his entire political identity—the belief that Americans could transcend racial and political divisions if called to a kind of aspirational citizenship and civic identity.[23] Obama's vision of multiracial democracy papered over the continued existence of the white supremacy behind which MAGA America rallied, content in a belief that racial progress, however incremental, unsteady, and precarious, would lead to a more perfect union.[24]

The events of 2016 upended the fragile national consensus that recognized, sometimes grudgingly and hypocritically, the struggle for Black dignity and citizenship as a political and moral good. It was a stunning end to the widespread rhetorical commitment to the moral and political virtue of civil rights and racial justice that had existed since the presidency of John F. Kennedy. This consensus had proved frustratingly limited. Black folk had often found themselves stuck between a Democratic Party that loved their votes, but remained eager to court white voters through policies that harmed Black interests, on the one hand, and, on the other, a Republican Party that lacked the energy to even pretend to be interested in promoting Black futures. And Barack Obama, for all of his efforts to distance himself from Bill Clinton's politics of triangulation, followed aspects of this same Democratic Party playbook. Obama's dreams of Black citizenship fit squarely within the framework of respectability politics, with Obama going so far as to hector a Morehouse College graduating class about the failure of Black fathers to fulfill their familial responsibilities: "I want to break that cycle where a father is not at home," he said. "Where a father is not helping to raise that son or daughter." The message implied that the college graduates before him might otherwise turn out to be deadbeat dads. It appeared incongruent, insulting even, considering the distance between the target of Obama's criticism and his actual audience. But the moment sent a powerful message to white Americans that Obama was willing to speak harsh truths directly to Black people—even if those "harsh truths" were based on stereotypes.[25]

* * *

Obama premised his entire presidency on the politics of racial optimism. Racial optimists sometimes acknowledge the depth and breadth of America's tragic history of racism, but they see a light at the end of the tunnel, where others see only darkness. For Obama, each instance of racial progress, however incremental, offered further proof of the grandeur of the nation's democratic experiment. Inasmuch as American history, ever since the failures of the First Reconstruction, was filled with false starts, broken promises, and outright lies with respect to racial justice, Obama by necessity smoothed away much of this history's cruel edges. As a candidate, Obama interpreted Black trauma over racial slavery and white resentment against affirmative action as morally equivalent. As president, he was often a deftly eloquent practitioner of respectability politics, quicker to excoriate Black men for abandoning their parental responsibilities than to call out the racism of the criminal punishment system that fractured so many Black families.[26]

A striking duality characterized the Obama era. On the one hand, by virtue of his personal biography, his political ideology, and his embrace of multiracial democracy, Obama represented a clear repudiation of the myth of the Lost Cause. His veneration of Abraham Lincoln, his aspiration to build national consensus beyond racial and historical divides, and his temperamental moderation ensured that white supremacists saw him as a threat. But Obama's racial optimism necessitated a belief in, and a commitment to, another set of myths essential to the postwar national consensus around race. Racial optimism sees racism less as the systemic problem it is than as something more superficial, as peripheral rather than central—it suggests that certain instances of racism might be overcome without the necessity or pain of deep structural reform. And it envisions a two-way street, where Blacks are expected to change their "dysfunctional" behavior in exchange for economic opportunities. Obama's presence in the White House burnished an image of revolutionary change, but in crucial ways, his administration maintained the status quo, at best nibbling around the policy edges of racial inequality for fear of provoking backlash. Trump took full advantage of this duality—of Obama's threat to one set of myths about America and his simultaneous embrace of another—by rallying the forces of white supremacy terrified by the change Obama represented, even as he also exploited the disappointment of those who'd hoped for more fundamental change that never came. The result was a profound historical irony: America's first Black president became the last chief executive to preside over the national consensus on racial matters that had made his own ascension possible.

During the 2008 presidential campaign, Barack Obama narrated a story about the intrinsic goodness of America that millions wanted to hear. He told Americans a story about the country—especially on matters of race—that a majority wanted to believe in even before they knew he existed. Obama became the global exemplar of a paradigm of postwar racial consensus built around a vision of American exceptionalism large enough to include Black folk, but not broad enough to countenance their leadership. He upheld the broad outlines of an already fraying consensus that Black Americans deserved formal equality under law, including by choosing two Black attorneys general (Eric Holder and Loretta Lynch) who were committed to racial justice. But as president, Obama mostly refrained from talking about the struggles for

Black citizenship and dignity, wary of being perceived as providing special favors to his most loyal political constituency. And meanwhile, unbeknownst to him, the consensus he sought to shore up was collapsing under a rising tide of white nationalism. Trump, in contrast, saw it coming, and he saw it long before most journalists, politicians, and ordinary citizens did.

Black Lives Matter told America the story it needed to hear, not the one it wanted to hear. Unlike Obama, BLM advocates refused to straighten the crooked parts of American history or gloss over the deeply entrenched injustice still plaguing American society. Rather, BLM became a bridge between the unearned optimism of the Obama era and the redemptionist dreams of Trump's America, drawing richly from a radical political tradition that historically operated at the lower frequencies of Black life. As the latest adherents of the reconstructionist tradition, BLM represented the leading edge of a radical politics that sought to reconcile past racial traumas with contemporary political challenges through an unvarnished comprehension of American history, absent the racial optimism and American exceptionalism that had characterized the postwar racial consensus. BLM activists instead narrated Black history, from racial slavery to the present, as American history. The movement framed their efforts—in their policy agenda, in speeches, in books written by organizers, and in memoirs authored by founders—as part of a long struggle for Black citizenship and dignity, one that did not necessarily follow a path of linear progress. As they put their bodies on the line, they repudiated both the nostalgia-fueled racial animus that undergirded Trump's growing hold on the national political imagination and Obama's incrementalist vision of racial optimism. And in 2016, the ascension of an overt racist to the White House definitively illustrated BLM's historical and political necessity.

Donald Trump became president by telling Americans the story they had always heard, and one they firmly believed in. Trump did not win the American presidency by serving up some generic narrative of white supremacy. Instead, America sought and received in MAGA something more specific: an updating of a Lost Cause narrative that had been relegated to the fringes of mainstream discourse for nearly six decades, during a long interregnum when America seemed to agree that Black equality was a social, moral, and political good. Racial injustice continued, but signs of a new racial order abounded, perhaps none more seemingly promising than the election of Barack Obama. Tens of millions of white Americans embraced Obama—but just as many, and soon more, balked, angered by the perception, both real and imagined, that white racial privilege had precipitously diminished since the civil rights era. Trump heard their call. "Make America Great Again" succinctly phrased a response that promised white America a new future by turning back the hands of time.

Trump's election underscored the power of narratives in shaping history and reality. Obama tapped into this power to stress national unity under a neoliberal vision of American exceptionalism, one that embraced—at times hypocritically, at times self-righteously—racial justice, and that seemed to represent a definitive break from the Jim Crow era. BLM instead offered an unadorned story of Black struggle against punishment, prison, poverty, and premature death, a narrative stressing that this struggle was not an aberration but a central element of American democracy, making its stain therefore much harder to remove. And Trump promised to restore what had been lost, offering a sepia-toned vision of the 1950s—a time when racial segregation was violently policed—as the model for America's future; and rooting his campaign in lies, such as birtherism, that would prove just as irresistible to white Americans as the Lost Cause lies of brave Confederate soldiers, heroic Klansmen, and ignorant and incapable Negro politicians.

By the end of Obama's presidency, the narrative he offered had faded in favor of Trump's and BLM's. Both Donald Trump and BLM sought, for different reasons, to end America's fragile racial consensus. Trump recognized that Obama's presidency had inspired indignation, anger, and fear in generations of Americans who, like himself, had grown up in a world where even the possibility of a Black president appeared to be a fantasy. He saw that, for millions, Black power represented the end of the American Dream, and that, for these same millions, Obama's presidency signaled the literal fall of the white republic. BLM activists, meanwhile, wished for Obama to see Black life in America through a wider lens than his own improbable autobiography. They resisted characterizing America as a place where all things are possible—because for millions of Black people, it still is not. They understood that millions of Black folks lacked the resources, networks, and opportunities that allowed for Obama's ascent. And much sooner than Obama did, they recognized the deep wells of racial hatred, anti-democratic fervor, and political malfeasance that Trump enthusiastically drew upon.

From Reconstruction to the present, racial backlash has offered an opportunity to shape history in service of political power.

Like many racist demagogues before him, Trump vowed to use that power on behalf of white folk. He inspired millions of voters to gamble that he might succeed where others had failed. Over the course of four of the most tumultuous years in American history, the cost of that bet would be measured in humiliation, human suffering, and lost lives. Blacks would bear these burdens disproportionately—while simultaneously erecting a new vision of leadership that, once again, offered a story about America that many were unprepared to hear.

4

LEADERSHIP

IN 2020, AMERICA MOURNED over the battered image of the national soul. We grieved for the loss of a way of life that, for many of us, had never existed in the first place.

In the first months of the year, the global COVID-19 pandemic unfolded domestically as a national crisis of race and democracy. I anxiously read the reports of the contagion's spread, and I watched in horror as Black folk got sicker faster and died quicker than the members of other demographic groups while living in communities suffering from disproportionate economic misery, from racial segregation, and from too much violence and too few resources. I especially noted the challenges facing Black workers on the pandemic's front lines, who reminded me of my mother and our extended labor union family in Local 1199, and I marveled at their resilience. The health crisis brought to the fore issues of racial equity and racial justice that BLM had been advancing for nearly a decade.[1]

And then, as summer began, new generations of social justice warriors marched arm in arm with grizzled veterans of earlier movements. Together, they dreamed of a future capable of healing a past resurrected that May in the last gasps of a dying man, George Floyd, who called for his mother at the hour of his death. I mourned with Black folk and fellow travelers who organized, empathized, and prayed under the banner of Black Lives Matter. I and millions of others watched, in anger and awe, as monuments of white supremacy that still belligerently dotted the American landscape came tumbling down. And yet, as 2020 turned to 2021, white supremacy came perilously close to ending American democracy itself, with violence of the sort unseen since the First Reconstruction.

All year, as long-simmering racial wounds turned the world's greatest superpower inside out, I found myself contemplating the enduring power of American exceptionalism, now exposed before the entire world as the kind of prideful lie that had allowed Lost Cause narratives to flourish. The United States' Achilles' heel, as the Civil War had illustrated long ago, is the original and ongoing sin of racial slavery. No Black History Month celebrations, no Martin Luther King Jr. and Juneteenth holidays, and not even a Black presidency were enough to expiate the nation's commitment to anti-Black violence, to Black misery, to Black death. But now, a deeper reckoning was under way. It seemed to come all at once, from all sides, touching all institutions from root to stem, inducing a kind of vertigo.

I experienced this disequilibrium alongside the rest of the nation and, in some ways, more acutely than most. As more than two thousand cities erupted in Black Lives Matter demonstrations, much of the world sought refuge in books, histories, narratives, stories that might be able to meet the moment. Suddenly, my historical expertise became a sought-after commodity. My natural vocation became a source of knowledge, of education, and perhaps of absolution to born-again racial justice seekers. Corporate spaces that in the past had ignored me now eagerly sought my counsel. Power brokers made personal calls seeking advice. My words mattered on a new scale. By the end of 2020, interpreting Black history as a path to coming to terms with the heartbreak at the center of the American project became, it seemed, my full-time job.

Whether I was speaking to community activists, to students, to fellow scholars, to elected officials, or to corporate leaders, I was often called on to lend not only my expertise as a public intellectual, but also my personal experience. The responsibility of Blackness is service-oriented leadership within a society bent on killing you. The burden of Blackness is being called upon by white folk to make them feel better about this reality. "Give us some hope, please?" became the unasked question from interlocutors ranging from well-meaning would-be allies to curiosity seekers compelled by circumstances to embark on the high-wire act of performing empathy for all the world to see.

My own complicated truth became, like the dark suits worn by Malcolm X and Martin Luther King Jr., a kind of political armor. In virtual lectures and in numerous television and radio appearances, I told audiences that America had reached a moment of existential inflection. The latest hinge point in our Third Reconstruction offered all of us, collectively, an opportunity to transform American democracy by defeating institutional racism and eradicating white supremacy. It would take the work of generations, and we should see this moment as the start of the beginning, rather than celebrating unearned victories.

Beyond such rhetorical flourishes, I traced the many strands of the Black experience in the present—the genealogies of mass incarceration, anti-Black policing, voter suppression, the racial disparities exacerbated by the pandemic, and the proliferating BLM demonstrations—back to the past, and especially back to the First Reconstruction. History is more than a useful guide, I argued. It shapes the tone and texture of the present. It does not hold all the answers to how we could achieve a better country: one that would refuse to murder, maim, and punish Black people as a matter of course. But it can shine a light on paths already taken, and on the need to travel down new roads that might lead to justice. Black history can bind all of us together, leading us to make different choices in our politics and to pursue policies capable of healing national ailments. My hope is that, in the not-too-distant future, Black history will be recognized as casting a spotlight on universal struggles through the particular. From this vantage point, when recalling the moral tragedy of racial slavery or the shame of the racial massacre in Tulsa, Oklahoma, a new generation will ask not "How could we have done that to them?" but instead, "How could we have done that to us?"[2]

As I sought to illuminate Black history for suddenly curious Americans, I was far from alone. I watched in awe as my generation, and the generation right behind mine, exploded onto the national political scene as torchbearers of Promethean fire, offering to explain the incomprehensible to a public that seemed to require George Floyd's unconscious sacrifice before they were ready to listen. Reconstructionists deployed Black history as both a political sword and a shield amid a national racial reckoning that necessitated, indeed demanded, that Americans plumb the depths of our unspoken historical traumas. On an even greater scale than during the civil rights and Black Power eras, there was an explosion of interest in "elevating"—read acknowledging the existence of—Black entrepreneurs, playwrights and poets, musicians, writers, thinkers, activists, and thought leaders. I contemplated what all the newfound attention to Black voices and Black stories meant in the grander scheme of things and, more importantly, how long the attention would last. Would America's latest contemplation of Black humanity inspire change and transformation, or new systems of violence more pernicious than before? But there was no doubt that a year spent confronting the ruins of our past felt cathartic for millions of Black people. We longed to tell our stories, mourn our dead, and share our grief. To finally be seen. Not as bit players in a narrative written by others, but as central characters in our unfolding national saga. Recognizing Black folk as the beating heart of American democracy shifted tectonic plates within our national political culture. The earth moved after George Floyd exhaled his last breath.[3]

As 2020 unfolded, I found daily inspiration in a new generation of leaders who seized America's attention—often young Black women who practiced a synthesis of educational, journalistic, policy, legal, and artistic social justice activism, and who were as interested in scaling radical knowledge production for masses of Black and multiracial people as they were in mastering conventional electoral politics. The journalist Nikole Hannah-Jones's intellectual leadership in creating the 1619 Project—a multimedia exploration of racial slavery and its legacies, initially published by *The New York Times Magazine* in August 2019 and awarded a Pulitzer Prize in May 2020—inspired a national debate on the uses and abuses of history in crafting American conceptions of race, identity, citizenship, and democracy. It also helped to expansively reimagine what leadership in service to Black dignity and citizenship looked like.

Black history is not immune from historical blinders of patri-archy; nor from an overreliance on documenting the activities of famous, wealthy, and credentialed figures; nor from a reticence to see the world through the eyes of those residing in America's lower frequencies. Stories of prisoners and poor people, of Black LGBTQIA+ communities, and of the disabled and neurodiver-gent rarely figure into our heroic models of civil rights leader-ship. Turning once again to history as a political guide, cultural weathervane, and emotional resource, I dug deeper into the past. I became particularly interested in how parts of the Black commu-nity unable to run for elected office, raised in challenging circum-stances, and faced with the brutality of racial terror had become leaders in earlier periods. Most intriguing during the nineteenth century were the Black women, many of them born during the era of racial slavery to parents living in bondage, who assumed a man-tle of transformational leadership by sharing parts of our national history—including America's long practice of gender-based sexual violence, exploitation, and incarceration—that many others pre-ferred to be left unspoken.

I heard echoes of the pioneering journalist and activist Ida B. Wells, for example, in the dynamic Black women organizers who turned the Movement for Black Lives into a global phenomenon. Like her, they were deeply invested in narrating the full spectrum of Black life, both to one another and for the world. In her heroic fieldwork as an investigative journalist, Wells had documented horrific scenes of lynching, seeking to personalize victims who were doubly massacred: first by the brutality of racial violence, and second in bitterly unfeeling narratives by white journalists that justified their tragic ends by depicting them as violent rapists.

After local whites burned her office and threatened her life, Wells fled north and continued her work. She was primarily based in Chicago, where she married Ferdinand L. Barnett, an attorney, in 1895 (thereafter becoming Ida B. Wells-Barnett). But she also traveled widely and had an international impact. There is poetic symmetry in the fact that it was a young Black woman, Darnella Frazier, who filmed George Floyd's death for the world to see.

Frazier was part of a vast and rising Black Lives Matter generation who captured the world's imagination in 2020. After Floyd's death I watched in awe as brave Black women leaders—such as Tamika Mallory, an organizer of the 2017 Women's March—spoke unvarnished truth to power with a furious eloquence recognizing the fierce urgency of now. Black people had been "in a state of emergency" even before Floyd's death, Mallory declared at a press conference a few days after his May 25, 2020, public lynching in Minneapolis. Language about prison abolition and defunding the police once commonly heard only in grassroots, Black-led social justice organizations suddenly became part of the realest and rawest national conversation about Black dignity and citizenship in American history. I watched in pride as a new generation carried on the Black freedom struggle. They did so not by seeking new answers to old questions, but by asking new questions, in the process transforming the entire framework for discussions of Black history, freedom, and democracy. This new generation—Black women; Queer, feminist, cis, and trans people; activist students and scholars; prisoners and the formerly incarcerated; writers, poets, singers, artists, and mothers—was redefining the parameters of leadership within our community, at the national level, and around the world.

These leaders did not simply resurrect your grandmother's civil rights movement. Instead, they updated the radical journalism of Frederick Douglass and Ida B. Wells and blended it with the prophetic teachings of Martin Luther King Jr. and Malcolm X, with the sacred witness of Fannie Lou Hamer and Ella Baker, and with the abolition democracy of Angela Davis, creating a revolutionary new synthesis that matched the scale of the crisis facing the nation. A year of pandemic, protest, and prophetic witness of Black America's sacrificial dignity in the face of unmitigated suffering produced new models of service-oriented leaders who at once reflected the best within the Black radical tradition and broke generative new ground. BLM activists deployed social media as an organizing tool, effectively publicizing the breadth and depth of the structural violence and systemic racism damaging Black communities. They mobilized large swaths of the nation during the protests of the spring and summer, simultaneously strategizing around policy solutions that profoundly changed the national conversation about criminal punishment reform.

The George Floyd protests created a *justice effect* that reverberated through major American institutions and at the core of the nation's unfolding racial and political reckoning. Demands for the eradication of racism and its supply chains of inequality, poverty, segregation, misery, and death became a focal point of national and even global attention. Racism's uncanny impact on every facet of American life became the subject of national protests, controversy, and soul searching. Prompted by this new generation of leaders, Americans wrestled with the complicity of a wide range of institutions, political actors, and ordinary citizens in reinforcing the denigration of Black humanity in small and large ways:

from National Football League players being punished for taking the knee during the national anthem in protest of police brutality; to the Confederate flags and monuments that still formed a built landscape memorializing white supremacy; to the failure of corporate America to leverage economic power in support of racial justice.

Something magical unfolded during 2020. Making all Black lives matter in theory and in practice seemed possible, even achievable, in our lifetime. And Black women's stories became, if only for a moment, universal, taking on resonance on a scale unimaginable just a year earlier. Narratives centering Black women's experiences, their joys as well as their traumas, became part of the national discourse. Suddenly, Americans proclaimed the names of martyrs killed by unjustified police violence, such as Breonna Taylor. They reckoned with evidence indicating that young Black girls are punished, policed, and marginalized in public schools. In 2020, parts of the American past usually disregarded and abandoned collapsed in on a nation that had long been unaware of the extent of the problem and unprepared to do the hard work required to build and sustain multiracial democracy. Fortunately for America, Black women were prepared to do that work—the work of building the "Beloved Community"—through the same models of grassroots collective leadership that Black women like my mother had embraced for generations, and that now appeared as a guiding light to a country plunged into the shadows of racial discord. Even as one version of the story America had told itself for centuries was shattered, Black women introduced another, more powerful narrative that could possibly suture our wounded souls.[4]

Journalists, pundits, and even historians frequently compared the unfolding racial crisis of 2020 to 1968 and the aftermath of the King assassination. But starting the search for historical analogies a century earlier is more fruitful, because the First Reconstruction is the American origin story that refuses to go away.[5] Even as generations of Black activism in support of citizenship and dignity came together in new ways in the face of new threats in 2020, one could see striking parallels between the present day and both the First and Second Reconstructions.

Just as in the years after the Civil War, for example, 2020 changed the aesthetics of Black leadership from the ground up. As Black women crafted new stories of Black dignity and citizenship, they helped to expansively redefine what leadership means and how it looks. The Black women leaders in the age of Black Lives Matter told America a transformational story about itself. If Malcolm X rightly characterized the nation as a prison for Black people, Black women organizers, strategists, activists, and thought leaders offered tools of both decarceration and liberation. The most exhilarating aspect of Black women's leadership, for me, proved to be its radical racial optimism in the face of withering assaults against our collective humanity. These leaders found hope in sharing stories of resilience in the face of violence, of speaking truth to power while resisting shame, of searching for physical and spiritual wellness and healing in the fertile political gardens of generations past.

The women of Black Lives Matter imagined a world where their stories were considered universal: where they were American stories. They told us about the thousands of school suspensions on the road to juvenile facilities, the hazards of domestic and partner violence, the sexual trafficking of Black girls, the violence against trans women, and the unspoken police brutality that had led to the #SayHerName campaign. Meanwhile, Black women's emergence as the most reliable Democratic Party voters told another story, one too often narrated only from above, about the power, ambition, and strength of grassroots Black women's civic and political vision. The storytellers mattered just as much as the story they told.[6]

———

The COVID-19 pandemic and the racial justice uprisings in 2020 America recalled biblical depictions of God's wrath taking the form of pestilence, famine, and despair. The Book of Exodus—featuring the most famous of these depictions—resonates powerfully within Black religious, political, and cultural traditions. The story of the Israelites fleeing slavery's bondage in Egypt for the land of Canaan, promised to them by God through the prophet Moses, fueled the freedom dreams of enslaved Black people. During the First Reconstruction, in the wake of racial terror, violence, and cruelty, Blacks migrated west to presumably more forgiving territories and states. Black nationalists, pan-Africanists, and a range of other Black political actors debated the ideas about nation-building, migration, and escape to a new land that Exodus evoked.

Later, in the Great Migrations that began after World War I and lasted into the late 1960s, millions of Black folk moved from the South into the North and West, injecting southern Black culture into the political veins of the entire nation. These demographic changes paved the way for a national American cultural milieu forever indebted to the genius of Black folk. The civil rights and Black Power eras sought to turn the idea of Exodus inside out, pursuing a future where America itself was reimagined as a welcoming space for Black communities, a new "promised land" of Black citizenship and dignity.

Black activists also renewed a historical interest in an African continent undergoing rapid decolonization, traveling to African nations and collaborating with their leaders and citizens. In the Black Power era, Du Boisian "double consciousness" became synthesized within a holistic Black identity. The African diaspora provided inspiration and ballast for reimagining the Black past, present, and future. Malcolm X became one of the avatars of this Black Nationalist vision of Exodus when he spent time in Africa during his last year; his quest was to pick up the continent's revolutionary fire and return it, like Prometheus, to the domestic arena of civil rights struggles. And Martin Luther King Jr.'s prophetic role in the civil rights movement made him a modern-day analogue to Moses as well, a spiritual and moral leader who, as he suggested in his final speech, had "seen the promised land," even though he might not reach it.[7]

The idea of Exodus again came to the fore in 2020 against the backdrop of a national racial justice movement that drew perhaps more than twenty-five million people into the streets.[8] Exodus is a story of flight and a reckoning with evil. Both occurred in America during 2020. The flight took place metaphorically, in the form of America's potential departure—its deliverance at last—from its history of comfort with the death of Black people, whether from brutality or hardship, and its arrival to the borders of a new era where it could start the process of becoming a new nation: the one that our ancestors dreamed of, hoped for, and fervently struggled to attain. This reckoning played out in violent struggles over whose narratives would shape the public interpretation of America's past and present, over institutional resources, and over political power, even as the nation seemed to begin that process of transformation before our very eyes.

As protesters gathered the day after George Floyd's murder, first in Minneapolis and then in dozens of other cities, something changed. Demonstrations organized and inspired not by charismatic male leaders but instead by Queer, feminist, and radical Black women inspired a large, multiracial, and multigenerational movement that sought not to escape the nation but instead to remake it from root to stem. More than ever before, large numbers of whites were taking to the streets, too, perhaps inspired by a combination of outrage over Floyd's death, political awareness raised by Black Lives Matter protests since 2013, and exhilaration over the easing of shelter-in-place orders brought on by the pandemic. In their number and their size, the demonstrations soon surpassed the high tide of the civil rights movement's heroic period. And police violence against demonstrators was just as extensive.[9]

A winter of discontent featuring a deadly pandemic, mass unemployment, and Black suffering became a revolutionary moment of biblical reckoning that witnessed the largest multiracial demonstrations promoting Black dignity in history. Many observers compared the protests—and the violence—to 1968, when 125 American cities burned in mourning, grief, and anger in the wake of Martin Luther King Jr.'s assassination.

To be sure, there were certain parallels. King's death marked a tipping point in American racial politics, as did Floyd's. But 1968 also marked the denouement of America's Second Reconstruction. Shortly before King's murder, the Kerner Commission Report, published in March 1968, provided a sober analysis of the roots of that era's racial and political unrest, and particularly the 1967 uprisings in Newark and Detroit. Commissioned by President Johnson, the report diagnosed America's urban crisis as being rooted in structures of white supremacy, institutional racism, violence, and economic injustice, which together formed a feedback loop of unrelenting tragedy. The Kerner Commission became a best-seller and an unheeded warning; it offered the nation a path forward to the multiracial democracy that had been delayed since Reconstruction, but its prescient distillation of the structural violence targeting Black communities was destined to become an artifact of history—though one ready to be taken up by a new generation during the Third Reconstruction.[10]

There were good reasons that the fires this time prompted comparisons to 1968. But at the time of his assassination and the uprisings in its wake, King was a Nobel Prize–winning social justice movement leader, the American Apostle of nonviolence, and the most famous and celebrated Black leader of the era. George Floyd was not, and it is precisely this anonymity that made the uprisings in his memory unique. Compared to King's assassination, Floyd's death moved larger numbers of white Americans to acknowledge systemic racism and the existence of white supremacy. The role of Black women and their allies at the forefront of the Black Lives Matter movement in shaping public consciousness and policy debates over the preceding seven years had been behind this. They had done the work beforehand, helping to influence the way in which Floyd's death was understood and perceived, and especially how it was part of a larger tapestry of structural violence and historical racism against Black bodies.[11]

By June 2020, demonstrations in support of Black dignity had spread to more than two thousand cities, including dozens where the populations were more than 95 percent white. Thousands gathered in predominantly white states such as Utah and Oregon. Hundreds of thousands of protesters swelled into millions who marched across bridges, flooded downtown city centers, and swarmed rural hamlets and small towns calling for an end to structural racism, violence, police brutality, and white supremacy. "Black Lives Matter" signs were accompanied by messages to defund the police, eliminate white privilege, and end racial injustice and economic inequality through radical policy proposals that the Movement for Black Lives had developed and promoted over the previous seven years. Black equality as the beating heart of American democracy proved to be the central message behind the largest social justice mobilization in American history.[12]

The vision that animated this mobilization was a deeply reconstructionist one. That is, it sought to reimagine America as a multiracial democracy through the kind of bold policy advocacy rooted in Reconstruction-era Black politics. In 2020, this reconstructionist vision included calling out the Lost Cause—the redemptionist view of America that has thrived, even during moments of racial progress and the two previous eras of Reconstruction—as a phenomenon that needed to be acknowledged, confronted, and then eradicated. This new era of protest recognized the Trump presidency and the MAGA movement as symptoms of a larger national illness, a disorder deeply embedded in a history of racial injustice that touches every facet of American life and its scarred institutions, policies, and politics in ways that both transcended ideology and amplified partisan political divides. And for several months, support of Black Lives Matter as a group, concept, and movement grew nationally—even as the forces of redemption began to muster a counterassault.[13]

All the while, BLM marked a changing of the guard within Black leadership. America's election of Barack Obama could be seen as the pinnacle of a vision of Black politics that viewed citizenship as something defined by middle-class, upwardly mobile, elite strivers.[14]

The killing of George Floyd telescoped 150 years of American history into just over nine minutes of grueling footage. Thousands of grassroots activists and hundreds of nonprofits, community organizers, and young strategists were prepared for the moment. Many of them had come of age within a dizzying political milieu, one featuring a Black president but where police killings of unarmed Black people were increasing in visibility. Groups like the Movement for Black Lives—a coalition of political, legal, and grassroots organizations seeking to make transformational changes in the criminal justice system, and armed with detailed, transformative policy initiatives—entered the national debate over police brutality and mass incarceration in new and impactful ways. Just as important, they stood ready with a radical new reconstructionist outlook.

The face of Black politics in 2020 moved forward while looking back. It was as if the radical spirit of Ida B. Wells had laid hands on the entire nation, moving the plight of Black bodies from the margins of American political life to its very center. Reconstruction's aspirational legacy of multiracial democracy suddenly gripped large parts of America's democratic imagination, culminating in November in Joe Biden's presidential election in perhaps the most racially charged campaign in American history. And as the year wore on, Black women saved democracy through storytelling that simultaneously critiqued and created. They pointed to long-forgotten wounds as well as newly festering ones, and they exalted fugitive democratic spaces and places, in the process recasting models of Black leadership.

———

Ida B. Wells's legacy cannot be overstated. A native of Holly Springs, Mississippi, she was born into slavery in 1862 and lived through the triumphs and tragedies of Reconstruction-era America. Her parents, Elizabeth and James Wells, a cook and a carpenter, were born into bondage in Virginia and Mississippi, respectively. They died of yellow fever when Ida was just sixteen. Holly Springs became a site of Civil War battles and later had a Freedmen's Bureau headquarters, and Wells's experiences there shaped her future advocacy of abolition democracy.

Wells had grown up surrounded by images of Black dignity. She had watched men and women march in support of the Republican Party–backed Loyal League, declarations of Black political power and citizenship in the face of white paternalism and the Ku Klux Klan's murderous rage. From Holly Springs, she witnessed a world undergoing a profound, even miraculous transformation. White supporters of Black equality rose to the governorship of Mississippi, and forty Black men were elected to the state's Reconstruction legislature. By 1873, Black men had served as the state's superintendent of education, Speaker of the House, and secretary of state. Two Black men from the state, Hiram Revels and later Blanche K. Bruce, became US senators.[15] Wells attended the first "colored" school in Holly Springs, and her father supported Reconstruction policies.

After her parents' death, to take care of her six brothers and sisters, Wells abandoned her studies at Rust University to become a teacher. Two years later, in 1880, she moved with her two younger sisters to Memphis to live with her Aunt Fanny. There she discovered her vocational identity as a crusading journalist for racial justice and abolition democracy in support of Black dignity and citizenship. In 1883, she objected to an effort to remove her from the Ladies' Car to the "Colored Section" of a train in Mississippi. She sued the railroad and won, her $500 award in damages making newspaper headlines, including some that she wrote herself. The 1892 lynching of three Black men in Memphis inspired Wells to launch what would come to be known as her "anti-lynching" campaign. This was in fact America's first organized movement for criminal justice reform in the face of systemic anti-Black racism and violence.[16]

In her anti-lynching campaign, Wells pioneered new forms of policy activism, investigative journalism, and social science research. She visited the sites of lynchings, made these scenes of unspeakable racial violence the focus of fact-finding missions, and shared the results with her increasing numbers of Black readers. Long before the founding of the NAACP and Black Lives Matter, Wells cataloged the brutality of her time for readers in such newspapers as *Free Speech*. "Eight Negroes lynched since last issue of *Free Speech*," began one forensic accounting of racial terror. Her reportage spanned a wide geographical area, from Little Rock, Arkansas, to Anniston, Alabama, and from New Orleans, Louisiana, to Clarksville, Georgia. Wells insisted that the rape allegations commonly used to justify lynchings of Black men hid a far less sinister truth about consensual interracial sex, a fact that would "be very damaging to the moral reputation" of white women if widely understood. Wells fled Memphis in fear of white retaliation in 1892 as a result of the ire such words stirred up. She became one of her generation's most vocal Black leaders, helping to organize opposition to white supremacy over the next thirty years.[17]

In New York City, writing for the *New York Age*, Wells penned an editorial titled "The Truth About Lynching" on June 25, 1892, that distilled the predicament in which Black people found themselves. The "lynch laws," she said, showed that the well-crafted image of the "best men" in the country was a sham; their allegiance was to white supremacy and their lives rested on a foundation of greed, cowardice, and an unwillingness to recognize the shared humanity of Blacks and whites. Wells's editorial exposed the fundamental lie behind redemptionist logic: the reality of this shared humanity could be seen in the mixed-race children—products of rape and sexual assault and of consensual relationships—who populated the entire southern landscape. White men lusted after Black women, Wells asserted, their well-known "preference for Afro-American women" adding a further layer of hypocrisy to grotesque and unjustified assaults against the Black family in American policy and culture.

Myths of Black rape, Wells said, were bound up in efforts to organize racial terror, support white political domination, and prolong the abuse of Black lives. Lynching created a feedback loop in which preconceived notions of Black criminality justified wide-spread racial violence, which was designed not to protect white womanhood, but to maintain white political domination. That domination was threatened by dreams of a new South governed as a multiracial democracy, where even Black women like Wells herself could lead. The editorial laid down a moral gauntlet powerful enough to shake the nation to its foundations. Beyond its initial ten-thousand-copy print run in the *New York Age*, it would be published as a fifteen-cent pamphlet, *Southern Horrors*, using money raised from a New York City benefit organized in Wells's honor. The benefit event attracted hundreds of Black women and led to the establishment of the organizations that would eventually evolve into the National Association of Colored Women.[18]

Wells's advocacy of abolition democracy won the approval of Frederick Douglass, the aging lion of Black citizenship, who lauded her public truth-telling about lynching as an outstanding "service which can never be weighed nor measured." Douglass's compliment anticipated Wells's enormously powerful legacy. Her model of leadership proved to be generative: over the years she has inspired and galvanized networks of both new and seasoned Black women activists. Yet Wells also battled patriarchal assumptions regarding Black leadership. She chafed against the top-down approach to leadership exemplified by W. E. B. Du Bois, whose bravura activism in support of Black equality nonetheless exhibited blind spots when it came to women. Six years Wells's junior, and a newcomer to racial militancy by Wells's standard, the Fisk- and Harvard-educated Du Bois positioned himself as the progressive alternative to Booker T. Washington's politics of racial accommodation. And yet Wells's militancy, determination, relatively humble educational background, and outspoken fearlessness made the urbane Du Bois uncomfortable. He sidelined her in the NAACP when it was established in 1909 even though her work had made the organization's very existence possible.[19]

Wells was a trailblazer: a feminist, wife, mother, citizen, and activist who explained why Black life mattered during an era that violently repudiated this notion every day. She engaged in a political struggle to reimagine democracy by advocating for federal anti-lynching legislation. In the process, she amassed one of the largest databases of anti-Black violence ever collected. Ultimately, she turned journalism into both a sword, cutting through the lies of the Lost Cause, and a shield, defending Black lives from the dual indignity of lynch law and the falsehoods that justified it. Through her investigative surveys of the racial violence of the Reconstruction era and beyond, Wells modeled the political and activist energies that have characterized subsequent generations of Black feminist organizers, writers, and thought leaders as they have sought to transform the scope and scale of Black politics.

———

Ida B. Wells sought not only to defend Black lives jeopardized by white supremacist violence and terror but also to reimagine the American project as a multiracial democracy expansive enough to recognize Black women's practical, theoretical, and political contributions to the nation. As such, her voice has echoed through history.

This echo reached the Second Reconstruction, when Black activism both consciously and unconsciously drew from Wells's radical legacy as it bore witness both to the depth of racial oppression and to the possibilities of multiracial democracy. Ella Baker, the organizer of the Student Nonviolent Coordinating Committee, carried on Wells's tradition of generative political thought and activism in the face of white racial violence and Black patriarchal assumptions concerning the makeup, character, and purpose of leadership. In her admonishment of the sit-in movement, when she said that civil rights was about more than just a hamburger, Baker sought to highlight the sacred work of radical democracy in which the students were engaged. Black activists were placing their bodies on the front lines against systems of white supremacy that were more deeply entrenched in the civil rights era than they had been even in Wells's time.

Meanwhile, Fannie Lou Hamer, from Montgomery County, Mississippi, less than one hundred miles south of Wells's hometown of Holly Springs, also followed Wells's example. Hamer, born into a sharecropping family in Mississippi in 1917, worked as a sharecropper herself until 1962. But by 1962 she was a voting rights activist, and over the next few years she became a grassroots leader and helped to found the Mississippi Freedom Democratic Party. She gave riveting testimony before the Credentials Committee of the Democratic National Convention in 1964. Hamer, like Wells and Baker, offered an example of leadership that, in both style and substance, challenged middle-class, patriarchal, church-based power dynamics within the Black community. She understood Black liberation as embedded in a larger social justice movement. Recognizing that "You are not free, whether you are white or black, until I am free," Hamer expressed reconstructionist sentiments that aspired, ultimately, to the creation of multiracial democracy in America. She went from merely surviving within a violent Jim Crow system, maintained through ritualized lynchings, to becoming one of the best-known faces of the Second Reconstruction.[20] Baker and Hamer, working in the tradition of Wells, and in order to preserve Black lives, made the world think differently about Black bodies.

More than any other activist, Angela Davis's commitment to abolition democracy makes her a living bridge between the Reconstruction-era Black politics that Wells embodied and the Black Lives Matter movement of the twenty-first century.[21] Davis's advocacy of abolition democracy was evident in both her prisoner rights activism, from the late 1960s onward, and her groundbreaking theoretical contributions to concepts of Black dignity, citizenship, freedom, and democracy. The "Free Angela Davis" campaign, which began after her arrest in 1970 and culminated in her acquittal on all charges by the summer of 1972, helped to ignite a radical movement for prison reform, and then prison abolition, that was at once international in scope and local in focus. As they fought for Davis's release and for justice for other incarcerated people, Black women organizers at the grass roots carried Ida B. Wells's torch, spreading the cause of radical struggle for Black humanity, democracy, and citizenship in communities quickly forgotten after the heyday of civil rights victories.[22]

Davis's notion of abolition—of slavery, prison, racism, imperialism, war, sexism, and intersectional injustice—took root within a wider Black radical tradition. Black feminism, as practiced by nineteenth-century reconstructionists such as Wells, would prove key to this tradition. The Second Reconstruction included second-wave Black feminist activists who sought to reimagine Black freedom struggles at the local, national, and global levels. They did this through organizations such as the Third World Women's Alliance, the National Black Feminist Organization, and the Combahee River Collective. Black feminist activists, writers, and theorists such as Audre Lorde, Barbara Smith, and Fran Beal updated and expanded the works of their forebearers through searing discussions of racism and white supremacy; of rape, domestic violence, and sexual assault, both within the Black community and as committed historically by white men; of the racism of white feminist movements; and much more.

Black feminism in the decades after the heyday of the civil rights and Black Power era flourished in fugitive spaces. Universities, churches, community centers, private homes, playgrounds, and prisons became sites for debates and discussions about leadership that rejected definitions of freedom that marginalized the fullness and complexity of Black women's humanity. Lorde, an icon of Black lesbian feminist thought, challenged Black people to define freedom in a way that refused to hide parts of our individual and collective identities deemed unworthy by ancient patriarchal hierarchies, contemporary heterosexual norms, and neoliberal capitalist frameworks. "My fullest concentration of energy is available to me only when I integrate all the parts of who I am, openly," Lorde wrote, "allowing power from particular sources of my living to flow back and forth freely through all my different selves, without the restrictions of externally imposed definition." Black feminism's search for a leadership model capable of honoring all the "different selves" of Black women—and in doing so, honoring the entire spectrum of the Black community—became one of the focal points of the Black radical tradition by the twenty-first century.[23]

Indeed, the rise of twenty-first-century Black women's leadership is rooted in traditions of radical Black activism cultivated during the First Reconstruction, updated and refined during the Second Reconstruction, and fundamentally transformed during the Third Reconstruction. Black feminist politics in the 1980s and 1990s operated on multiple levels, all of which would coalesce in the intersectional impulses that characterize the Black Lives Matter movement. Grassroots activists operating amid the overlapping crises of poverty, structural and domestic violence, the AIDS epidemic, the War on Drugs, and mass incarceration brought together hundreds of organizations that rejected the models of charismatic leadership celebrated in history textbooks and popular culture. During the Age of Ronald Reagan—an era marked by potent stereotypes that cast Black women as "welfare queens," by the criminalization of Black neighborhoods as crack dens, and by the diversion of resources away from the remnants of the Great Society and into the largest prison system in the world—Black women cultivated political, mutual-aid, and collaborative local groups and networks.

Some of these organizers had heard of Ella Baker, and many had not, but they all carried on in her tradition. They were aware of the disconnect between even the most radically outspoken Black male political leaders (for example, Jesse Jackson, during his bravura 1984 and 1988 campaigns for president) and their own quotidian struggles. Activists created organizations that prioritized the struggles of poor Black women, especially those experiencing domestic violence—for example, the National Coalition Against Domestic Violence (NCADV) and the National Coalition Against Sexual Assault (NCASA), which broke new ground in creating spaces for radical Black women organizing against sexual assault, domestic violence, and marginalization during the racially cruel Reagan era.[24] Black Queer activists played an integral role in the post-civil-rights era, organizing groups such as Black AIDS Mobilization (BAM), where scholar-activists such as Cathy Cohen helped to place Black Queer leaders and activists squarely within a radical tradition engaged in a painstaking struggle to recognize all aspects of Black humanity.[25]

Simultaneously, Black feminists engaged in an Ida B. Wells type of narrative war from both above and below. In the quarter century between Angela Davis's 1972 release from prison and her founding—alongside activists Rose Braz and Ruth Gilmore—of Critical Resistance, a radical organization devoted to eradicating systems and structures of anti-Black punishment, incarceration, and violence, Black feminists created transformative intellectual and theoretical frameworks that reimagined the American project. Their words helped popularize radical new narratives of Black liberation and introduced Wells's legacy to new generations. These narrative wars took place in academic, political, nonprofit, legal, corporate, and public policy spaces. They influenced, and were influenced by, radical grassroots community organizers, violence disrupters, neighborhood griots, and local keepers of history—Black feminists, Queer people, and at times progressive cisgender Black men.[26]

The twenty-first-century rise in Black women's leadership—including Black feminist public intellectuals such as Kimberlé Williams Crenshaw and Heather McGhee; the investigative journalist Nikole Hannah-Jones; engaged scholar activists such as Barbara Ransby, Keisha Blain, and Keeanga-Yamahtta Taylor; civil rights leaders such as Sherrilyn Ifill and Stacey Abrams; and social movement leaders such as Alicia Garza, Ayǫ (Opal) Tometi, and Patrisse Cullors—took place against this backdrop. Crenshaw, for instance, became well known nationally through her work as a critical race theory scholar and her popularization of the term "intersectionality." Her work expanded upon the political, intellectual, and theoretical thinking of generations of Black feminists who grappled with how Black women's multiple identities were impacted by systemic racism, violence, and economic inequality.

The Black millennial feminist and Queer activists who launched the #BlackLivesMatter hashtag stood on the shoulders of their forerunners from the Reconstruction, civil rights, and Black Power eras, but they simultaneously innovated new ways of seeing and being. Garza, Tometi, and Cullors turned outrage over Trayvon Martin's 2012 death into the fuel for a new social movement that tapped into networks, political language, organizing sensibilities, and political visions rooted in the same Black radical tradition that had nurtured Ida B. Wells and Angela Davis. At the same time, Black Lives Matter brought new intellectual clarity, moral urgency, and policy specificity to the fore as it amplified reconstructionist sentiments regarding the value of Black life in the face of racial terror and violence.[27]

BLM protests in the aftermath of the deaths of Michael Brown, Eric Garner, and Freddie Gray drew on the language of intersectional justice rooted in second-wave Black feminism; the grassroots activism of Black women, Queer people, and anti-poverty and anti-domestic-violence workers; and the policy advocacy of Black legal scholars, public defenders, and social movement leaders who continued to agitate in the decades before Barack Obama's election and during his time in the White House. Exemplifying a commitment to intersectional justice, the Movement for Black Lives activists argued that Black people can only achieve citizenship and dignity by centering the most vulnerable parts of the community, especially women and children; those who are poor or who are facing housing and food insecurity; those in the LGBTQIA+ communities; and the mentally and physically disabled.

By 2020, the extent of the transformation wrought by this new generation became stunningly clear when, on Sunday, June 14, five days before Juneteenth, thousands of demonstrators converged in Brooklyn for a Black Trans Lives Matter rally, also called the Brooklyn Liberation March. The silent demonstration recalled the ten-thousand-strong NAACP march in 1917—the Silent Parade—held to protest a mean season of racial violence in East St. Louis that had killed hundreds of Black people. The Brooklyn protest highlighted the fact that Black transgender people were disproportionately victims of police violence. In the 2020 event a multiracial crowd of fifteen thousand marched from Grand Army Plaza to Fort Green Park before making their way to the Brooklyn Museum. The protest represented one of the most radically democratic moments in American history.[28]

The Black Trans Lives Matter march reflected the profound reimagining of Black politics, decades in the making, that had taken shape in the neighborhoods, prisons, communities, and streets of America. The idea that all Black lives matter, including the lives of members of the Black LGBTQIA+ communities, had been a cornerstone of BLM's organizing strategy and political philosophy from its 2013 founding. Much of this theorizing had drawn from the practical intellectual and political work that Black women had done between the end of racial slavery and the present. Over many decades, Black women's activism helped to shape Black politics even as the women themselves were often relegated to serving behind the scenes, whether as organizers, agitators, or thought leaders. The term "intersectionality" reflects that work and the long road that Black feminist thinkers, activists, and organizers, from Ida B. Wells to the present, traveled to formulate their ideas. If the civil rights movement sought, through the 1963 March on Washington, to turn America into a mass movement meeting, in 2020 BLM succeeded, for the first time in American history, in transforming the entire nation into a classroom.[29]

———

Black feminism's search for liberation paralleled wider currents in American life in 2020, especially those sparked by the *New York Times* 1619 Project. The initiative was the brainchild of journalist Nikole Hannah-Jones, who consciously channeled the legacy of anti-lynching crusader Ida B. Wells into the twenty-first century. Challenging America's origin story, the 1619 Project opened up new worlds of social, political, and intellectual inquiry. Like many breakthroughs, it also elicited both hearty praise and vicious condemnation. Racial slavery, the wealth it produced, the moral compromises it engendered, and the lies that concealed painful and ugly aspects of the nation's history all suddenly took center stage. The project's debut on the four-hundredth anniversary of the arrival of the first enslaved Africans on the shores of Virginia at Jamestown served as a prelude to everything that happened in 2020.

The 1619 Project started as long-form journalism in the August 14, 2019, issue of *The New York Times Magazine*; eventually it would include a podcast, live events, and a best-selling book. Reactions to this potent entrée into the narrative wars over the meaning of American citizenship, identity, freedom, and democracy continued to unfold as partisan bickering divided the nation during campaign season and thereafter. Reconstructionists embraced the 1619 Project as a long overdue corrective to Lost Cause mythology and narratives of American exceptionalism. Public school educators around the nation used its multimedia resources in their efforts to tell their students a deeper history of America. But the more the accolades grew, the greater the backlash became. Redemptionists challenged the 1619 Project's historical validity and scholarly rigor. Eventually, they successfully passed legislation, including in my own adopted home state of Texas, to bar the teaching of American history in ways that touched upon racism, slavery, and white supremacy.[30]

Hannah-Jones's work updated Wells's heroic political and intellectual crusade against lynching into a state-of-the-art vivisection of racial slavery's afterlife in the twenty-first century. Her journalism, like Wells's, turned one of W. E. B. Du Bois's observations on its head. Du Bois had described a question that had constantly confronted him but that went unasked: How does it feel to be a problem? In Hannah-Jones's historical excavation of our national origin story, echoing Wells, Black people not only were not the problem, but they also might be, against all odds, our only hope for salvaging the American democratic project. By arguing that the year 1619 represented the nation's birth just as well as 1776 did, since racial slavery proved to be the greatest economic engine for all that came after, the 1619 Project became perhaps the most powerful popular distillation of reconstructionist sentiment ever conceived.

As the project told it, in the series of essays in *The New York Times Magazine* by an all-star team of journalists and scholars, drawing on cutting-edge research on the history and afterlife of slavery, the economics of slavery implicated more than southern plantation owners. Racial slavery was also central to debates over the Constitution and to the language of the Declaration of Independence; it shaped the creation of supply chains of power and privilege that allowed for economic innovation in domestic banking and international finance; and it provided the foundation for the expansion of the continental United States and the growth of its hemispheric and global political and economic ambitions. It also institutionalized the supply chains of misery and inequality in the form of racial segregation, economic theft, violence, and unequal treatment that still touch virtually every aspect of contemporary American life. As the essays implicitly and explicitly argued, these forces continue to shape our national destiny. The 1619 Project held up an unblinking mirror to a nation that had steadily refused to undertake self-examination on the subject of race.

The pushback came immediately, and it only grew over the course of 2020 as teachers began to draw upon or adopt the 1619 Project's resources. Senator Tom Cotton of Arkansas, a Republican, characterized the Founding Fathers as viewing slavery as a "necessary evil," and seemed to suggest that he agreed with that assessment (a charge he later denied). In the Senate, he proceeded to introduce the Saving American History Act, legislation to ban federal funding for the teaching of the 1619 Project in public schools. These efforts were similar to many others in the history of political backlash against reconstructionist attempts to confront America's long and brutal history of anti-Black racism. The attacks on the 1619 Project paralleled the GOP voter suppression efforts that were taking place at the same time, and both would reach frightening new levels of legislative effectiveness the next year.[31]

The pushback was so fierce in part because the 1619 Project was only the leading edge of the efforts to reckon honestly with America's history that were playing out in full view of the public in the spring and summer of 2020. Confederate monuments came tumbling down (while monuments celebrating those who profited from slavery were toppled in England and beyond). And it was not just Confederate generals, politicians, and other sympathizers who came under scrutiny. President Theodore Roosevelt's support for biological racism against Blacks and other nonwhite people inspired new rounds of criticism. So did Thomas Jefferson's notoriously racist views on Black intelligence. History museums, art galleries, and other sites of commemoration of American history that had been shaped more by redemptionists than reconstructionists came under new and unprecedented pressure.[32]

———

Nearly a century ago, W. E. B. Du Bois's *Black Reconstruction* offered a powerful salvo against Lost Cause narratives depicting Reconstruction's failures as the self-inflicted wounds of Blacks unable to handle the responsibilities of citizenship and unwilling to carry themselves with human dignity. Du Bois instead described efforts by free Black people, alongside anti-racist whites, to forge a new birth of American freedom—to secure the abolition democracy that was the cutting edge of the nation's democratic experiment. And in 2020, the Movement for Black Lives pushed the struggle for abolition democracy to the very center of American life, expanding its meaning to include movements to abolish mass incarceration, the death penalty, and other structures of anti-Black racial violence. BLM's vision of an American democracy that prioritizes the most historically marginalized members of the Black community represented a bold and radical effort to make this newest period of Reconstruction the nation's last.[33]

Black communities experienced institutional racism and economic impoverishment long before George Floyd's death. Racial segregation is rooted in a long history of racial terror and violence in America and a corresponding history of this reality being silenced by the forces of white supremacy. In the early months of 2020, COVID-19 amplified widespread preexisting racial inequities that threatened both the legacy of the civil rights movement and the strength and resilience of American democracy. Structural racism and white supremacy, as embodied in the presidency of Donald J. Trump, played out in the federal response to the pandemic. Black workers were more likely to be in jobs that made them particularly vulnerable both to getting sick and dying and to being subject to layoffs and closures that led to economic ruin. Black prisoners—including many in local jails, such as New York City's notorious Rikers Island, who were awaiting trial and unable to afford bail—faced a high risk of exposure by virtue of their cramped living quarters. Black small business owners found themselves overwhelmingly excluded from government bailouts that instead directed financial payouts to some of the nation's largest corporations.

It was against this backdrop that George Floyd's death reinvigorated the Black Lives Matter protests that had first erupted in 2013. Within twenty-four hours of George Floyd's death, protesters gathered in Minneapolis, turning the site of his murder into a living memorial filled with expressions of love, grief, and rage. Three days later, a protest targeting the Third Precinct, where the four police officers complicit in Floyd's death worked, turned violent and left the building in ashes. Within a week, hundreds of demonstrations in cities as diverse as Atlanta, Anchorage, Los Angeles, and Salt Lake City erupted.

The multiracial nature of the protests astonished the nation, exhilarating supporters and appalling critics. The overwhelming majority of protests—93 percent, by one estimate—were peaceful. Some drifted into sporadic looting and theft, and in a few cases, the determination to express rage, anger, and grief—not simply over Floyd's death, but over the larger structures of racial and economic inequality that made such killings routine—devolved into chaos. But the most disturbing displays of violence came from the police, who were deployed not just against Black demonstrators but white ones as well. The image of police in Buffalo, New York, knocking an elderly white protester onto the sidewalk, causing serious injury, went viral. The scene offered the nation a small hint of the kind of state-sanctioned, profoundly unjust punishment and brutality that Black people have routinely experienced since their arrival on the nation's shores.[34]

BLM inspired reconstructionist politics from below. The movement's demands were both particular and general. Its particular goals centered on a massive set of radical policy reforms seeking the transformation of America's criminal punishment system and the far-flung ecosystem that nourished it. This agenda called for a radical redistribution of local, state, and national resources away from punishment and incarceration to investment, restorative justice, and anti-racism. Practically speaking, this meant shifting funding from law enforcement into mental health, drug rehabilitation, housing, education, and other investments designed to promote Black health and wellness rather than incarceration and death.[35]

BLM's general impulses were in certain ways even more revolutionary than its specific proposals. Organizers identified police violence as the central spoke in the wheel of American exceptionalism. Eradicating the nation's sprawling punishment system, they argued, could end the structures of violence, poverty, and death that have historically denigrated Black bodies. This framework was the necessary response to the nation's long and catastrophic history of using the police to enforce a color line that prevents Black Americans not only from achieving citizenship and dignity, but from even aspiring to do so through political organizing and movement building. The struggle for Black equality as defined by BLM meant defeating the ancient regime of white supremacy and replacing it with a new political reality wherein *all* Black lives mattered. This aim could only be achieved through a focus on the particular struggle of Black people and by defeating the political and narrative frameworks that supported America's racial status quo.

Their deceptively simple argument since 2013 had been that the criminal justice system extended its tentacles of racial and economic oppression into social welfare, education, housing, and employment. And after Floyd's death, that argument went mainstream. Calls to reimagine public safety by "defunding" the police injected urgent new language into the wider public debate about the value of Black lives in America. Grassroots Black Reconstructionists turned "Defund the Police" into a radical political axiom, making it the focus of posters and signs and even painting it in gigantic yellow letters on a street near the White House. The phrase's narrative power could be seen both by the passionate nationwide support it received and by the ferocity of the opposition it evoked. "Defund the Police" derived its political impact, its policy influence, and its controversy from its narrative power. Like the phrase "Black Lives Matter," it told the nation an important story—not the one it wanted to hear but the one it needed to.[36]

As "Defund the Police" went mainstream, so, too, did calls for intersectional justice, attentive to the myriad ways that different identities—racial, class, sexual orientation and gender identification, mental health, and citizenship status—interacted in the policies and politics that shaped the lives of Americans. As a new era of Black Reconstruction transformed American democracy amid a global pandemic, a plague of police brutality, and the scourge of poverty, racism, and violence, the search for Black humanity became a metaphor for multiracial groups of Americans burdened by the weight of structural violence and oppression. With its call for intersectional justice, BLM extended and amplified both Martin Luther King Jr.'s vision of radical Black citizenship and Malcolm X's vision of radical Black dignity.

The pandemic, police brutality, racial segregation, and mass unemployment affected the entire country, but their impacts differed based on wealth, geography, family and kinship networks, housing access, social media and Internet availability, and the environment. Access to twenty-first-century citizenship revolved around deeply entrenched racial divides that in turn affected economic status and varied depending on gender, disability, sexual orientation, and gender identification. What critics dismissed as "identity politics" in fact reflected the most widespread public acknowledgment in the nation's history of the true complexity of white supremacy in all its myriad forms. In a year filled with historical moments, the national reckoning on race and democracy that identified white supremacy as a disease eating away at the body politic proved to be the most significant.

George Floyd's death opened up new political worlds. The political fires that flared in American cities during the spring and summer of 2020 represented the power of a Black Lives Matter movement that had been preparing for the arrival of a hinge moment in American history since 2013. Once, police violence, brutality, and even murder had been seen as disconnected from the political structures that allowed some people and not others access to excellent schools, clean air and water, safe neighborhoods, good jobs, and thriving futures. Within the crucible of 2020's national and political reckoning on racial injustice, economic inequality, and the ever-present threat of violence from local, state, and federal authorities against peaceful demonstrators, and illuminated by history, these connections now came into sharp relief. The result was a national conversation not only about criminal justice and policing, but also about democratic institutions in American society writ large. (Nor were these issues of anti-Black racism, white supremacy, and systemic economic oppression only being discussed in America. International sympathy protests in cities such as Berlin, Munich, London, and Oxford paralleled the reckoning in America, helping to make the Movement for Black Lives perhaps the largest international human rights project ever conceived.) As in the two earlier periods of Reconstruction, in 2020 we arrived, bloodied and battered, but still hopeful, as a new generation, at the moment of a new opportunity to reach toward the creation of a new country, one both unencumbered by its tragic racial past and strengthened by a public commitment to repairing and healing racial wounds through the practice of justice.

In the wake of George Floyd's murder, Black Lives Matter demonstrations, after originating as rearguard, reconstructionist efforts to advocate for Black dignity and citizenship during the Age of Obama, evolved into a frontal assault on the American democratic imagination. The protests redrew the lines of acceptable discourse within Black politics and asserted a new kind of leadership. Black women emerged as some of the protests' leading architects. The dynamic role of Black feminist and Queer organizers, activists, artists, and elected officials was reflected in the growing iconography surrounding Breonna Taylor, a twenty-six-year-old emergency room technician killed after midnight on March 13, 2020 (over two months before Floyd's murder), in a raid by Louisville, Kentucky, police who misidentified her and her boyfriend as drug dealers. Taylor became, alongside Floyd, the face of the demands for an end to anti-Black police violence and a national symbol of the BLM protests. Her countenance graced the cover of *Vanity Fair* and helped to expand the literal and metaphorical boundaries of Black politics. In 2020, Black women's long-standing efforts to reimagine Black politics moved from the margins of political and intellectual discourse in America to its center.[37]

In 2008, brown hands that once picked cotton helped to elect America's first Black president. In 2020, Black folk, led by unapologetically Queer and radically feminist women, articulated the most expansive vision of Black politics in history, and in so doing reimagined American democracy. This is not to suggest that intraracial ideological struggles, conflicts, disagreements, and confrontations ceased to exist. But the frameworks for these disputes, as well as the basis for multiracial and interracial coalitions, fundamentally changed. Nowhere could this be seen more clearly than in the way that local governments scrambled to respond to the groundswell created by Black-led grassroots political movements advocating for the redistribution of wealth and the end of punishment in poor communities.

———

While Nikole Hannah-Jones and the 1619 Project carried on the spirit of Ida B. Wells's journalistic crusades, and while Black Lives Matter took her radical critiques of anti-Black violence into the streets, it was Stacey Abrams who served as a crucial bridge linking Wells's abolition democracy to progressive electoral politics. Abrams, a former Georgia state legislator, emerged in 2020 as a legitimate contender for the Democratic Party's vice-presidential nomination. And she reflected Black women activists' historical resilience in the face of political setbacks and racist backlash.

A graduate of Spelman College, Yale Law School, and the LBJ School of Public Affairs at the University of Texas, as minority leader of the Georgia House of Representatives from 2011 to 2017 Abrams was the first woman to lead either party in the state's General Assembly. Her dreams of becoming the nation's first Black female governor were dashed by voter suppression tactics successfully deployed by her opponent, Brian Kemp, in 2018 (as Georgia's secretary of state, he was responsible for administering state elections). Kemp wielded vintage redemptionist tactics to become Georgia's governor, including reducing the number of polling locations, voting machines, and early voting hours in Black neighborhoods.

Following this bitter loss, Abrams rolled up her sleeves and went back to work. Her gubernatorial campaign inspired a generation of new voters, and it honed her efforts to make voting rights activism a cornerstone of twenty-first-century Black politics and American democracy. By 2020, Abrams was leading the most dynamic grassroots voter awareness campaign in Georgia's history. She personally recruited Raphael Warnock, the pastor of Ebenezer Baptist Church—Dr. Martin Luther King Jr.'s former pulpit—to run for the US Senate that year. In the midst of the pandemic, she advocated fervently on behalf of a new racial and social economic compact between local, state, and federal governments and the most vulnerable workers, disproportionately Black, oftentimes women, and almost always overlooked. A brilliant political strategist, a published novelist, and an inspirational speaker, Abrams blew the lid off of racist, patriarchal, and white supremacist notions of leadership.[38]

Abrams's political leadership reflected a national landscape being reordered by the disturbances in the streets. Some of these energies recalled the urban political rebellions of the 1960s, but the cast of actors—including millions of white demonstrators—looked different, and so did their political demands. The race for the presidency became a proving ground that underscored this point. For perhaps the first time in American history, the existence of structural racism and the need to defeat it became the central theme of a presidential campaign. Black elected officials, including former president Barack Obama, scrambled to catch up with the political radicalism emanating from parts of their constituencies they had long taken for granted.

Kamala Harris, then a senator from California, received the memo. A graduate of Howard University, a member of Alpha Kappa Alpha sorority, and a former San Francisco district attorney and California attorney general, Harris had made her political bones during the tough on crime, War on Drugs era that led to the mass incarceration crisis. Only the second Black woman ever elected to the US Senate, she was one of just three African Americans in the entire one-hundred-member body. As she campaigned for the presidential nomination, Harris pivoted, taking pains to present herself during primary season, with mixed results, as a "progressive prosecutor" more interested in justice than punishment.

Harris was not the only candidate to attract the interest of Black voters, however. They listened to a range of candidates in the months leading up to the primaries. One of these was the radically progressive senator Bernie Sanders of Vermont, whose movement attracted a number of high-profile Black people, such as hip-hop artist and activist Killer Mike and former Ohio state senator Nina Turner. Another was the more centrist Joe Biden, whose political partnership with Barack Obama as vice president and support from Jim Clyburn, a congressman from South Carolina, helped him forge important relationships with Black primary voters. It was widely recognized that Black voters could decide the Democratic Party's presidential nomination.

Ultimately, Black voters gave Joe Biden decisive support, particularly in the South Carolina primary. They judged the former vice president as standing the best chance of securing enough white votes to return the Obama coalition back to the White House. This thinking proved not only wise, but prescient, when Biden's victory in November proved he was likely the only Democratic candidate capable of amassing a broad enough coalition to defeat Trump. Some Black voters, especially those coming of age during the BLM demonstrations, criticized Biden as a relic of a not-too-distant racist past, focusing not on his time as Obama's second-in-command, but instead on his support for punishing policies—most notably Clinton's 1994 Crime Bill—that he once spoke proudly of authoring. But during the 2020 campaign, Biden, like Harris, pivoted, expressing support for police and criminal justice reforms. These promises left grassroots activists dissatisfied, at best, and skeptical, at worst, but reassured Black voters in a number of states that he could win the general election and remove Donald Trump from office.[39]

Black women have been the most reliable voters in the Democratic Party's base, yet they have consistently been shortchanged within the transactional nature of party politics. Despite voting overwhelmingly for Democrats in local, state, and national elections, they remain underrepresented as elected and appointed officials and in the all-too-important, but often forgotten, ecosystem of consultants and advisers in the public and private sector.

The George Floyd rebellions placed new pressure on Biden to pick a Black woman as vice president. For many of the activists engaging in both public street protests and private negotiations for resources, power, and policies aimed at dismantling structural racism, Stacey Abrams would have been the ideal choice.[40]

The behind-the-scenes push for Abrams to become Biden's running mate helped to refashion traditional ideas about Black leadership. Abrams's intellectual abilities, strategic brilliance, and outspoken candor were now publicly defined as assets to embrace rather than liabilities to be downplayed. She confidently answered questions about her qualifications, noting that she would make an "excellent running mate" and pointing out her proven track record in expanding the Democratic electorate in Georgia. Abrams bridged the gap between familiar kinds of Black politics and a new approach with deep roots in the First Reconstruction era. She resembled Reconstruction-era Black women who, under both the withering external oppression of white supremacy and the stultifying patriarchy within Black communities, had broken new ground, defiantly tilling unplowed democratic soil. Seeds planted during the First Reconstruction era, cultivated in the heat of the civil rights conflicts of the Second Reconstruction, now bore fruit as Abrams and other members of a new generation of Black leaders took on the task of furthering the cause of Black equality.[41]

Kamala Harris was not as powerful an exemplar as Abrams of this new approach to Black politics. Harris's political ascendance on the national stage, her presidential campaign, and her eventual role as Joe Biden's running mate took shape initially within the political framework that Barack Obama personified. Obama and Harris were both Black politicians comfortable with their uniquely hybrid racial ancestry—Harris's economist father, Dr. Donald Harris, hailed from Jamaica, and she and her younger sister had been raised primarily by their late Indian mother, Shyamala Gopalan Harris. And both Obama and Harris sought to transcend these origins by becoming multiracial exemplars of American exceptionalism. When the matter of Black lives became central to American politics, it upended this familiar framework and inspired Harris to support criminal justice reform, at least at the edges of the system.

Biden's ultimate choice of Harris over Abrams as his running mate reflected the large gap between grassroots visions of radical democracy and a Democratic Party establishment more comfortable with the status quo. A US senator, from that perspective, seemed safer than a political insurgent who was as interested in building a movement as she was in winning an election. Nevertheless, the grassroots energies that made the selection of Harris possible had emanated from the bottom up—the organizing by Black women activists as personified, in mainstream politics, by Abrams's example. Harris's ascension to the role of Biden's running mate, in other words, hinged on the transformation of Black politics occurring at the grass roots, where Black feminist activists and organizers had marshaled the votes, the political and personal resources, and the democratic vision to compel the Democratic Party to place a Black woman on the ticket. Twelve years after Black voters helped make history by electing Barack Obama, they once again took a leap of political faith by betting on Joe Biden in the hope that he could defeat Donald Trump. Along the way, Black folk exerted enough political pressure to ensure that, for the first time in American history, a Black woman would help to lead a major party's campaign for the White House.

———

Reconstructionists fundamentally transformed American politics in 2020 and proved crucial to the success of the Biden-Harris ticket. Black Lives Matter became the vanguard of a national social justice movement that attracted the largest number of white supporters in American history. The year's demonstrations and confrontations with law enforcement, the removal of Confederate statues, the recognition of the value of Black lives on social and corporate media, and the new connections forged to social justice movements around the world combined to create a powerful new story of American democracy, one centering Black women as change agents, visionaries, and thought leaders. Joe Biden and Kamala Harris became the political beneficiaries of a movement and a moment whose expansive, radically democratic, experientially intersectional vision far outstripped their own.

America's Third Reconstruction lent new dimensions to an old story. In the summer of 2020, reconstructionists and redemptionists battled for the nation's soul through demonstrations, policy debates, cultural wars, and political campaigns that laid bare the manner in which America's troubled racial past had directly led to the political reckoning of the present. Black bodies under assault by police officers revealed bitter truths about Reconstruction's unfinished business. Many Black leaders who had long attempted to till seemingly unfertile political soil, in anticipation—or, more likely, in hope—of such a moment, now helped to refashion the politics of reconstruction, respectfully acknowledging a long tradition of racial justice activism while engaging in innovative new modes of organizing.[42] Because of the work done over months, years, decades, and lifetimes, hundreds of grassroots, Black-led racial justice organizations stood at the ready to offer a bold new vision of American democracy in the face of the global pandemic, the enduring pestilence of racial injustice, and historic protests that called the nation forward to build a "Beloved Community." The trial by political fire of the first BLM moment in 2013–2014 had prepared thousands of Black activists, many of them trained in Black feminist and intersectional organizations, groups, and coalitions, to offer a radical political vision of American democracy. Black politics now attained the kind of moral high ground last occupied during the civil rights era.[43]

But this time there would be no Martin Luther King Jr. to lead the way. Instead, Black women would be the most prominent voices in Black politics. Many of them had cut their teeth advocating for prison abolition, an end to mass incarceration, and policies to aid poor, incarcerated, and low-income members of the Black community. Black women organizers embodied a patchwork quilt of the possible. Their political organizing found deep roots in a Black radical organizing tradition that drew heavily on lessons from Black feminist political victories and defeats since the civil rights era. These Black women manifested the radical energies birthed in the political ferment of the nation's First Reconstruction, when activists such as Ida B. Wells crafted an expansive vision of American democracy. Indeed, Black women indelibly shaped America's three Reconstruction periods, each time battling racism, patriarchal violence, sexism, and dehumanization.

But more than that, they emerged as key architects of an expansive democratic vision. Unable to legally vote during the First Reconstruction, Black women marched alongside, and sometimes led, a Black political community taking shape against the backdrop of a violent period. Through organizing based on political, intellectual, and religious foundations, Black women became, alongside Black men, co-architects of a new American freedom. Fashioning hopeful democratic vistas became their métier generation after generation as they persisted despite the catastrophic racial violence around them—violence that delayed Black citizenship and denied Black dignity. Their legacy survived long past America's collective betrayal of its First Reconstruction.[44] And in 2020, their heirs in a new generation of activists redefined Black politics in theory and practice, reimagining ideas of citizenship, freedom, and democracy in ways that both reaffirmed long-standing Black political struggles and challenged the framework of American exceptionalism within which much of Black politics had long operated.

———

As 2020 unfolded, history seemed to collapse upon itself. Like an episode of the Black *Lovecraft Country*—a sci-fi, fantasy, horror mash-up that premiered that August, and expertly blended 1950s B-movie tropes with that era's Jim Crow reality—the second half of 2020 featured dazzling juxtapositions. Images of multiracial solidarity stood alongside those of the police brutalizing peaceful multiracial demonstrators, recalling iconic—and iconically bloody—civil rights scenes from Birmingham and Selma during the 1960s. Protesters tearing down Confederate flags and statues gave the nation an overdue lesson on how the built environment can contribute to systemic racism and help foster structures of violence, poverty, and alienation. Against the backdrop of Supreme Court–assisted voter suppression, Black voting power was on full display, most powerfully in the Peach State. In the shadow of Stone Mountain's monument to the Klan, Georgia turned from red to blue, and then, in January 2021 in a runoff election, chose its first Black US senator. And then there was Donald Trump, whose virulent brand of whiteness grew more desperate as his grip on power slipped.

More than eighty-one million Americans, part of the largest voter turnout in the nation's history, cast their ballots for Joe Biden and Kamala Harris in November 2020, sending Barack Obama's vice president and the first Black woman to the White House. But seventy-four million voted for the continuation of Trump's redemptionist presidency—the second largest popular vote total in American history. America's most hyperbolically racist president received, in his second campaign, over eleven million more votes than he did in his first. It was the kind of ugly reality that would give the blues the blues. Biden's victory sparked outrage among Trump's MAGA supporters, and Trump refused to admit defeat. Instead he unleashed his Big Lie, alleging—just as nineteenth-century white supremacists frequently did of Reconstruction-era governments—that the election had been marred by fraud. Black voters were the culprits in Trump's racist fantasy, and his supporters feasted on these lies as millions became convinced that the election had been stolen.

Three months before Election Day, the tone of Barack Obama's August 19, 2020, speech at the Democratic National Convention had shown that perhaps the most optimistic Black leader of his generation had undergone a remarkable transformation. Sixteen years after his DNC keynote electrified the nation and set him on the path to the presidency, a somber Obama bluntly confessed that democracy itself hung in the balance. John Lewis's recent death from cancer lent Obama's words urgency. He reminisced about Lewis confiding "that he had looked it up, and it turned out that on the very day that I was born, he was marching into a jail cell, trying to end Jim Crow segregation in the South." Obama's warning tacitly acknowledged parts of the nation's history that he had refused to confront as president, especially during his December 2014 meeting with the Black Lives Matter organizers.

To his credit, Obama—the man whose election to the nation's highest office had helped to jumpstart the Third Reconstruction—had evolved with the times. His 2020 DNC speech was a clear-eyed recognition of the dark political forces at work that were attempting to exacerbate racial divisions, punish Black-led social movements, and hasten the demise of American democracy through voter suppression, misinformation, bad-faith political negotiations, and naked violence. Yet Obama's caution—both in terms of his personal temperament and in terms of his political calculations—remained. His objection, after the election, that the slogan "Defund the police" risked alienating potential allies missed the entire point of a phrase that sums up American history since the First Reconstruction in three elegant words. Sometimes the best strategy to achieve freedom is simply an unapologetic demand for it. An enduring truth about racial progress in America is that individual acts of heroism, no matter how spectacular, are never enough. BLM activists recognized this reality in ways that Obama never quite managed to.[45]

George Floyd's public execution, refracted through the high politics of the Obama and Trump administrations, the grassroots activism of Black Lives Matter, and the bottom-feeding racial violence of white supremacists, represented the tipping point of the Third Reconstruction. In its wake, the Third Reconstruction toppled ancient totems of white supremacy, inspired massive demonstrations, spurred long-awaited policy changes, and ignited perhaps the biggest round of racial soul searching in our nation's history.

In 2020, the reckoning that Ida B. Wells had called for unfolded before the eyes of the world. Despite its historical roots in the First and Second Reconstructions, its immediate origins could be found in the frustrated hopes of 2008, and the notion that America could be absolved of its original sin of racial slavery through the election of a Black president. Instead, this postracial fantasy—a fantasy of unearned healing between the descendants of enslaved Blacks, legally defined as a species of property, and the descendants of those who presumed to be their owners—faltered against harsh American realities. As in the first two periods of Reconstruction, in the third period racial progress met with violent retrenchment. We still live in a nation where, during and long after the First Reconstruction, God-fearing whites routinely burned Black folk alive. James Baldwin's challenge to Americans to "end the racial nightmare, and achieve our country, and change the history of the world," reminds each of us of the sacred work that remains.[46]

FREEDOM

> It is of the utmost importance for white
> people to see the Negroes as people like
> themselves. Otherwise, the whites will not be
> able to see themselves as they are.
>
> JAMES BALDWIN, 1961

THE STRUGGLE OVER REDEMPTIONIST and reconstructionist visions of America's future unfolded in cinematic fashion over the course of three Wednesdays in January 2021.

Wednesday, January 6, dawned with the news of the victories of Raphael Warnock and Jon Ossoff in Georgia's runoff elections—making the two men the first Black and the first Jewish senators from the state, respectively, and giving the Democratic Party control of both houses of Congress, though by slim margins. Later that day, thousands of overwhelmingly white demonstrators stormed the US Capitol in a riot triggered by white rage against Black citizenship. President Donald J. Trump's mendacious allegations of election fraud had spurred the mob to violence—and those allegations were founded on a disbelief that Black voters could truly have formed the backbone of Joe Biden's victory. Capitol rioters stormed the citadel of American democracy after being wound up by the president himself in an early morning rally, where, in a futile effort to halt the official ratification of the electoral college results, he implored his followers to show "strength."

The violence at the Capitol elicited shock, anger, and sadness over the state of American democracy. There was surprise that the red-MAGA-hat-wearing rioters so easily breached the perimeters of the Capitol. The mob, which included armed military veterans and off-duty law enforcement officers, roamed inside the Capitol Rotunda, defiling a sacred democratic space by waving Confederate flags and anti-Semitic symbols. Black activists noted the difference between law enforcement's kid-glove treatment of the white rioters and their treatment of Black Lives Matter protesters the previous summer. With BLM, facing down largely peaceful protesters, heavily armed National Guard units had formed an impenetrable defense around the Capitol Building. But on January 6, some cops posed for selfies with the MAGA activists. The insurrectionists denounced the incoming president as a usurper, condemned BLM as subversive, and repeated Trump's lies that predominantly Black voters in Atlanta, Detroit, and Milwaukee, in particular, had committed widespread election fraud. The violence at the Capitol left five people dead, including a Capitol Police officer. A second officer at the scene would die by suicide a short time later. Images of rioters traipsing through the building in search of the offices of Democratic representatives, with plans to intimidate them, kidnap them, or worse, became seared into the national consciousness.

I watched the day unfold as if witnessing the climax of a lurid but familiar brand of cinema verité. I recognized the familiar rhythms of the anti-Black racist violence engulfing the Capitol, seeing its resemblance to patterns that remained both deeply embedded in our history and stubbornly unrecognized. America's First and Second Reconstructions had both featured striking moments of racial and democratic progress alongside unspeakable acts of violence and political regression. Our time mirrored—indeed grew out of—those times. Assaults on democracy in the wake of successful struggles for Black citizenship and dignity have been a hallmark of all three periods of Reconstruction. The tragic march of white supremacists in Charlottesville, Virginia, in August 2017 was similar. That event and the Capitol insurrection reflected the politics of racial backlash in the Third Reconstruction. The white rage unleashed at the Capitol, seemingly far removed from the jubilation the previous night in Georgia, was in fact part of a historical nexus that tied both moments intimately together. They were both part of the same struggle to define what freedom would look like in the twenty-first century.

On the second Wednesday of the new year, January 13, 2021, Donald Trump was impeached for the second time. This was unprecedented: with just a week left in his term, he became the first sitting US president to be impeached twice. Democrats in the House of Representatives, joined by a handful of Republican allies, charged him with a single article of impeachment: incitement of insurrection. Emboldened by Biden's victory and the Georgia senate runoffs, which together would give them full control of the legislative and executive branches of the federal government beginning on January 20, they began impeachment procedures in an effort to reclaim some of the honor lost at the Capitol the week before as they had fled the rioters in fear. The formal impeachment process commenced with clarifying recognition that it would fail, with Trump's acquittal in the Senate all but assured, as a conviction would have required a two-thirds vote. But America's national honor demanded nothing less.

Joe Biden and Kamala Harris were sworn in on the third Wednesday in January. Against a brisk wind, Biden took the oath of office just before noon. Harris became the forty-ninth vice president and the first woman, the first African American, and the first person of South Asian descent to hold the office. She made history by standing on the towering shoulders of generations of Black women whose struggles against racism, patriarchy, and violence had helped to expand the nation's political imagination and democratic vision. Black women's legendary efforts to shape a new world paid off in bold ways that month. They could rightly claim to have reshaped America's democratic future through their efforts in Georgia and nationwide. That Black feminist genius would be on full display during the presidential inauguration.

A beaming Harris took the vice-presidential oath from US Supreme Court Justice Sonia Sotomayor, another daughter of immigrants, who had beat long odds to sit on the nation's highest court. Although Harris assumed the office of the vice presidency at a less hopeful time than when Barack Obama was inaugurated twelve years before, the moment was no less historically important. Harris and Obama enjoyed a fist bump after her swearing in, basking in the shared recognition of being the only two Black people in American history to occupy their offices. Obama's eight years in power had illustrated, for all the world to see, the clashing visions of freedom and democracy between reconstructionists and redemptionists. If the Trump presidency threatened to permanently foreclose the promise of the nation's great democratic experiment, 2020's political and racial reckoning spread ripples of defiant hope in the wake of plague, pandemic, and protest. Harris's inauguration brought with it at least a glimmer of that hope, signs of the racial progress that had led Obama, on the night of his victory speech in Grant Park, Chicago, in 2008, to boast that "America is a place where all things are possible."

Amanda Gorman, the twenty-two-year-old Black youth poet laureate of the United States, encapsulated the moment's striking racial and political juxtapositions. Her poem "The Hill We Climb" became an international sensation, a glorious literary hymn that called on the nation to move forward by taking a searing trip into its past. History doesn't repeat itself so much as rhyme, and in America, that has meant patterns of recurring generational racial trauma and conflict tempered by soaring movements for justice with brief moments in the sun. Gorman powerfully reminded us that "being American is about more than a pride we inherit." The great responsibility of citizenship lies in our collective ability to acknowledge and recognize "the past we step into and how we repair it."[1]

And on April 7, 2022, a little over a year into President Biden's term, Judge Ketanji Brown Jackson became the first African American woman to be confirmed as a US Supreme Court justice. Jackson's triumph came fifty-five years to the week after one of Dr. Martin Luther King Jr.'s most important speeches, "A Time to Break Silence," in which he came out against the Vietnam War. Viewed through the lens of what has changed—and what hasn't—since King's words at Riverside Church, Jackson's confirmation represents one aspect of what Dr. King that day called a "bitter...but beautiful struggle" for America's soul—a struggle that he helped to lead during the civil rights era, and a battle that continues to this day.

Jackson exemplifies Black women's centrality to the hard work of democracy and promises to be a pathbreaking associate justice. Her past colleagues, her friends, and the members of her family hold her in reverence, illustrating a side of her personal and professional journey obscured by the messiness of the Senate confirmation hearings. Jackson's dedication to family, her candor in discussing the difficulties of attaining work-life balance while sustaining a demanding career and raising two daughters, and her grace in the face of withering attacks deeply rooted in the country's still unresolved assault on Black women's personhood and humanity all show an incredible amount of fortitude that places her in a longer tradition of Black women trailblazers, including Constance Baker Motley, the first Black woman appointed to a federal bench.

Ketanji Brown Jackson's confirmation attests to the political heights reached during this Third Reconstruction, a period that finds large portions of America willing to courageously embark on a dangerous mission to recover its purpose, redeem the national political soul, and restore the lost honor of American citizenship. Judge Jackson's confirmation—like a rose that grows amid the concrete—is one of those beautiful moments that Black women's activism helped bring forth from Reconstruction to the present and that should be celebrated even as we remain diligently aware of the journey that lies ahead.

———

CONCLUSION: FREEDOM

The First Reconstruction, from the December 1865 ratification of the Thirteenth Amendment abolishing slavery to the November 1898 white supremacist racial massacre and political coup in Wilmington, North Carolina, marked America's first experiment in multiracial democracy. This experiment witnessed the triumphant passage of constitutional amendments ending racial slavery, establishing birthright citizenship, and providing voting rights for Black men while offering the basis for the future expansion of the franchise to women. But Black citizenship threatened America's racial and economic order, and racial violence, anti-Black public policies, and white fear of Black power led to the restoration of white supremacy.

The South's political "redemption" meant the introduction of convict-lease systems as a new form of racial profiling and incarceration; the establishment of peonage and sharecropping, which normalized the exploitation of Black labor; and the denial of voting rights, which brought even the nominal appearance of Black citizenship to an end for all practical purposes. White supremacy reached its apex at the end of the nineteenth century just when the country should have been celebrating the elevation of Black Americans from slavery to citizenship and equality within just over one generation. Slavery's central role in sparking the Civil War was forgotten, replaced by racist mythology, a Lost Cause narrative that W. E. B. Du Bois would spend his life challenging. The Lost Cause misremembered the Civil War as an honorable disagreement over "states' rights." It erected monuments to war criminals, traitors, and domestic terrorists who had betrayed the United States. The Confederacy lost the war but won the peace, and in so doing, indefinitely delayed Black citizenship and true freedom for all Americans.

To admit that much of the racial progress experienced since the Civil War took place within a framework of American exceptionalism that has limited prospects for Black citizenship and dignity, and thus constrained the freedom dreams of an entire nation, is not to suggest that *all* is lost. It merely forces us to confront moral and political truths we have been collectively reluctant to acknowledge about how a living history has actively shaped our present and might impact our future. The pastoral beauty that Du Bois described in *Black Reconstruction* framed scenes of lynching. Black suffering and death have taken place alongside white celebrations of family, faith, and friendship—sometimes becoming the occasion for them. These juxtapositions may be characterized as horrific, tragic, and even unforgivable, but they are no mere aberrations. They are not passive historical wrongs awaiting the moral justice of more clear-eyed generations.

The recent split-screen images of massive, Black-led, multiracial BLM demonstrations alongside armed white rioters storming the Capitol are as American as the collision between racial slavery and abolition democracy. Recognizing this makes the task ahead easier, not more difficult. Our nation's relative ineffectiveness in eradicating systemic racism and white supremacy can be explained largely as a result of the myths and lies that have been embraced—paradoxically, across racial, class, and partisan divides. The presidency of Barack Obama found its taproot in the kind of racial optimism that American exceptionalism had fostered, and his otherwise lucid analysis of American history became blinkered whenever the subject of white supremacy arose. It would take the BLM movement, the rise of Donald Trump, and the martyrdom of George Floyd, Breonna Taylor, and so many others to awaken Obama and much of the rest of the nation from a slumber that imagined the Black suffering in American history as a kind of children's bedtime story that could safely be told from the distance of adulthood.

The January 6, 2021, Capitol riot offered demonstrable proof that the clash between reconstruction and redemption is continuing in the twenty-first century. America's Third Reconstruction is simply the latest chapter in a long struggle pitting multiracial democracy against the forces of white supremacy. The mob that bullied its way through barricades, bludgeoned Capitol police officers, and defiled the Capitol itself illustrates Reconstruction's complex afterlife. The scenes recalled the organized white violence in Wilmington, North Carolina, in 1898, when the resumption of white political rule was secured through lies, threats, coercion, and murder.

Still, those who insisted after January 6 that "this is not who we are" were not entirely incorrect. The wildly unhinged redemptionist efforts to overturn a federal election is not *all* of who we are. On November 10, 2021, 123 years after the Wilmington massacre and coup d'état, the city finally buried Joshua Halsey, a Black man who in 1898 had been shot fourteen times and buried in an unmarked grave. The forty-seven-year-old father of four never lived to see an America not threatened by his dreams. But perhaps his descendants might. Wilmington's shame is the nation's shame, and our efforts to bring truth, justice, and reconciliation to these dark parts of our past underscore how a nightmare can still be a dream.[2]

THE THIRD RECONSTRUCTION

I tried to process America's racial and political reckoning of 2020 through the lens of history. I've tried to do the same in these pages. As a scholar of the twentieth-century Black freedom struggle, I found myself inexorably drawn back to the nineteenth century, too, while endeavoring to make sense of the twenty-first. Reconstruction's afterlife continues to shape American democracy and our national freedom dreams. This afterlife is most usefully recognized in the narratives we tell ourselves about the past. Those narratives are integral to who we believe we in fact are. Freedom is America's most precious aspirational legacy. But legacies are more than simple choices made by individuals. They are the by-products of collective decisions made—or not made—in specific historical circumstances. Reconstruction attempted to redefine the meaning of freedom for all Americans. Blacks, as formerly enslaved people whose labor proved instrumental to the production of wealth and the provision of liberties they could scarcely enjoy themselves, defined freedom as personal dignity. During Reconstruction they labored mightily to have their intrinsic human dignity recognized by local, state, and national institutions. Black dignity serves, then, as a precursor to effective claims of citizenship. It took a cataclysmic civil war to make the prospect of Black citizenship viable. Dignity provided the resilience, tenacity, and courage to make freedom dreams that included citizenship possible.

George Floyd died from a knee pressed against his neck. He could easily have been just another unknown victim. After all, racial violence—sometimes deployed by law enforcement, at other times by faceless institutions—causes Black people to die prematurely every day. But for a viral cellphone video, just over nine excruciating minutes long, the world might never have known Floyd's name.

CONCLUSION: FREEDOM

Struggling to the very end, unable to breathe, gasping for air, and pleading for his life, Floyd improbably inspired the biggest political mobilization on behalf of Black dignity and citizenship in American history. Americans in more than two thousand cities gathered in largely peaceful demonstrations to proclaim that Black lives matter, and their protests produced a shock of recognition from oppressed people across the nation and around the world. These rebellions became an unprecedented and collective outpouring of grief, outrage, and radical compassion. The large number of white people, in small towns and big cities, joining the protests imbued Black Lives Matter as a social justice movement with an urgency perhaps heretofore unwitnessed in American history.

America's Third Reconstruction offers a new opportunity to forge national policies that will lead to racial justice, and to build the "Beloved Community"—free of racial injustice, poverty, and violence—that Martin Luther King Jr. spent his entire life pursuing. The focus on Black dignity—the recognition of the inherent humanity of all Black people and the creation of institutions that reflect this truth—offers the nation a chance to reimagine how we think about freedom and citizenship. Since George Floyd's death, we have already witnessed political victories on behalf of racial justice that might otherwise have taken decades to achieve. From the reimagining of public safety, which has led some cities to reallocate police budgets to programs to prevent violence, provide housing, and eradicate poverty, to the dismantling of the ancient memorials to racism, which are being replaced by emancipationist symbols dedicated to reconstruction in our own time, things are afoot that show change is possible. A new political world is being created.

THE THIRD RECONSTRUCTION

In the First Reconstruction, Black Americans emerged as the improbable architects of the nation's second founding. Before Barack Obama captivated America's democratic imagination, there was Frederick Douglass, a formerly enslaved Black genius who became one of the most photographed figures of his era, a militant abolitionist and a political seer who challenged American democracy to its very core. Ida B. Wells was the precursor to contemporary criminal justice reform movements, her anti-lynching crusade marking her as perhaps the most courageous Black activist of the late nineteenth century. Douglass, a staunch feminist, mentored Wells at the start of her career. His lifelong quest for Black citizenship dovetailed with her thirst for political dignity capable of preventing Black bodies from swinging from southern trees. The Third Reconstruction, like the First, represents the possibility of literal and figurative national rebirth, renewal, and reimagining.

The nation now has an opportunity to reimagine its past, present, and future. Black citizenship and dignity are the essence of the political and moral project that forms the most important issue of our time. The citizenship Barack Obama projected to the world from above required the dignity insisted upon by BLM activists and organizers from below. The backlash to both mainstream and radical efforts by Black Reconstructionists reflects a tragic history that finds redemptionists, time and again, emerging victorious in the narrative war that defines our political reality, our economic priorities, and our moral and ethical compass. And so in the face of backlash—a new Lost Cause advocating simultaneously for voter suppression, the criminalization of Black communities, and

censorship efforts to limit the stories we tell to a new generation—
the work of reconstruction must continue.

The members of the new generation of Black grassroots organizers, led by Black women, have honored the hard truths about
past reconstruction efforts, and about how, however well inten-
tioned, they left parts of the Black community behind. They call
forth ancestral genius and failure, pride and disappointment, victories and defeats, to summon the strength necessary to take full
stock of our present challenges. In their spiritual and political resilience, they resemble the student activists of the 1960s and the
sharecroppers of the 1860s. The phrase "Black Lives Matter" captured over a century and a half of struggle to build a new American project that recognizes the instrinsic dignity and humanity of
all Black people.

I believe that the struggle for Black dignity and citizenship can
be achieved in our lifetime. But it must continue even if it takes
several lifetimes. Americans of all backgrounds can choose love
over fear, community building over anxiety, equity over racial
privilege, and dignity over shame and punishment. Martin Luther
King Jr.'s "Beloved Community" encapsulates the hopes, across
time and space, of generations of Black folk, in captivity and after the coming of freedom, who dreamed of living in a nation that
loved them back. Our two earlier periods of Reconstruction ended
prematurely, wrecked by anti-Black violence, white backlash,
and the creation of more sophisticated forms of racial segregation, exploitation, and death. In each period, we have confronted
crises presenting us with stark choices: the racial violence of the
late nineteenth century, the political rebellions in places such as
Los Angeles and Detroit during the 1960s, the fires of discord that

burned more recently in Ferguson and Baltimore, and, in 2020, across the nation and around the world. Each time so far, we have embarked afterward on the wrong path. Today, in the midst of another period of Reconstruction, we have a grave political and moral choice to make. I choose hope.

ACKNOWLEDGMENTS

IN MANY WAYS *The Third Reconstruction* is the realest thing I have ever written. In this book I have attempted to channel not just history but also the memories and experiences of my own that endowed Black history with such majesty for me. By excavating my own childhood and familial stories, I hoped to be better able to share historical context regarding the struggle for Black dignity and citizenship in the past, present, and future. More than this, I hoped to convey why the act of reading, writing, and public speaking about this history became my vocation and a lifeline to imagining a different future for myself and the country.

My mother, Germaine Joseph, made this book possible. Mom has been a font of knowledge, intellectual curiosity, and discipline for me from birth. Since becoming a parent myself I have found the bits of wisdom I gleaned from her to be truly miraculous and more inspiring than ever before. She made it possible for me to find hope, dignity, and love in so many extraordinary ways that I have lost count. Thank you for being my mother and for loving me always.

I would like to thank all of the teachers, friends, and alumni at Sts. Joachim and Ann Catholic School and Holy Cross High School who helped to make this book possible. Many thanks to friends, professors, and alumni at Stony Brook University and Temple University. I had the privilege of teaching at Arizona State University, the University of Rhode Island, Brandeis University, and Tufts

ACKNOWLEDGMENTS

University before my time at the University of Texas. I appreciate the opportunities that each of these terrific institutions of higher education provided for me and my family and remain grateful.

My time in Austin has been invigorating and inspiring thanks to a group of terrific colleagues. I would like to extend my thanks to Jeremi Suri for over twenty years of friendship. Thanks as well to David Springer, Ed Dorn, Victoria DeFrancesca Soto, Kate Weaver, Paul Steckler, Gordon Abner, Mary Evans, Tori Yu, Becky Petitte, Monica Muñoz Martinez, Daina Ramey Berry, Ashley Farmer, Evan Smith, Bill Brands, Erika Bsumek, Alison Frazier, Ryan Sutton, Leighton Wilson, Len Moore, Lina del Castillo, Toyin Falola, Tanya Clement, Yoav Di-Capua, Talitha LeFlouria, Mark Lawrence, Jackie Jones, Mark Updegrove, and Abena Dove Osseo-Asare.

In addition, I would like to thank JR DeShazo, dean of the LBJ School of Public Affairs, for being such a wonderfully collaborative and visionary leader and colleague. Ann H. Stevens, dean of the College of Liberal Arts, has been a steadfast supporter.

Rich Reddick is truly a gem—a great friend, deft collaborator, and brilliant scholar whose work inspires me and whose friendship has been sustaining. A shout-out to Rich and to our students—Sai, Eddie, Will, Jay, Zia, Hailey, Tolu, Pritika, Breigh, Josh, and Sruthi—who are part of the "Imagining Anti-Racist Academic Worlds in the UK and USA." Thanks to all of our collaborators across the Atlantic and to the President's Award for Global Learning, which funded our research and pedagogy. A special thanks goes to Laura Caloudas, who as senior program coordinator for Texas Global helped us facilitate this sprawling venture.

Emily Dunklee and Chante Thompson deserve thanks for all of their excellent and hard work in helping to build and sustain

ACKNOWLEDGMENTS

the Center for the Study of Race and Democracy (CSRD). Kudos to Madi Donham, my graduate assistant, for her help on this project, and to Sarah Porter for her assistance. My student Brandon Render, now an assistant professor at the University of Utah, has been inspiring to learn with and from.

Thanks to Lisa B. Thompson for her friendship and grace. She is a fantastic colleague, a brilliant artist, and a stellar friend.

Thanks to Estevan Delgado for his inspiring work as a colleague in the Justice, Equity, Diversity, and Inclusion (JEDI) office at the LBJ School, and to Michael Paniagua for their work helping the JEDI and CSRD amplify their respective and joint missions.

My agent, Gloria Loomis, believed in this project from the start and that I was the writer to tell this story. My editor Brian Distelberg pored over every word of this book, and his care made the final product better than I could have imagined. Lara Heimert, publisher of Basic Books, welcomed the project with her customary grace, enthusiasm, and brilliance.

Thank you to the following thought leaders for being such enormous friends and advocates: Gina Prince-Bythewood, Reggie Bythewood, Jamal Joseph, Nina Shaw, Van Lathan, Charlamagne Tha God, Khalil Gibran Muhammad, Ibram X. Kendi, Jonathan Eig, Vincent Brown, Rhonda Y. Williams, Cheo Hodari Coker, Keisha N. Blain, Brett Hurt, John Berkowitz, Lawton Cummings, Jim Ritts, Craig Cummings, Marjorie Clifton, Leslie Wingo, Alison Alter, Jim Basker, Angela Vallot, Robert Schenkkan, Howard Axel, Amber Payne, Deborah Douglas, Liz Coufal, Nathan Ryan, Sherrilyn Ifill, Daron Roberts, Kendra Field, Don Carleton, Ted Gordon, Shaun Harper, C. K. Chin, Marc Lamont Hill, Rabbi Neil Blumofe, Ken Mack, Evelyn Brooks Higginbotham, Sharon Harley, Michael

ACKNOWLEDGMENTS

Hole, Bob Campbell, Tom Meredith, Lynn Meredith, Joseph Kopser, Jane Carr, Julian Zelizer, Azeem Edwin, Aisha Mahama-Rodriguez, Kelly Carter Jackson, Kelli Newman Mason, Lisa Graham, Dan Graham, and Charlayne Hunter-Gault.

Special thanks to Jeanne and Mickey Klein for their support of my work and life's mission.

Michael Eric Dyson continues to be an inspiration and source of friendship. Robin D. G. Kelley has been an intellectual North Star for decades. Thank you. Thanks to my brother Lewis Gordon, whose work continues to shine a bright light for future generations.

A special thank you to Sonia Sanchez, the iconic poet and Black Arts luminary. I had the extraordinary privilege of learning from her while a graduate student at Temple University, and my engagement with Black feminist thought in these pages is rooted in a field I began to rigorously study under Sonia's tutelage. Since that time a new generation has come to appreciate her intellectual brilliance and passionate commitment to human rights and justice.

Henry Louis Gates Jr. has been a fierce advocate, supporter, and friend to my entire family. Thank you, Skip, for your generosity of spirit, prodigious mind, and brilliant intellectual curiosity.

Thanks to Darryl Toler for being such a great friend and brother over the years. Yohuru Williams continues to inspire me as a scholar, administrator, and thought leader. Femi Vaughan continues to be a great mentor, friend, and intellectual guide. Many thanks to Larry Hughes, Derrick "Priest" Myers, Curtis Byrd, Michael Williams, Mark Barnes, Sal Mena, and Chris and Ina Pisani for their supportive friendship.

My daughter Aya's piercing intelligence, wide-eyed curiosity, and robust sense of humor grew alongside of this project. My

ACKNOWLEDGMENTS

brother, niece, and sister-in-law, Kerith, Caitlin, and Dawn, remain steadfast and loving supporters of me and my work.

My wife Laura's intelligence, compassion, empathy, and love are wonders to behold. Laura took time away from her own doctoral studies to read parts of this book, which has benefited immeasurably from our shared pursuit to make the world a better place to leave our children. Our family continues to cultivate a miraculous harvest of a blended and extended network of kin and friends. Much love to Vivi, Saylor, Julia, David, Sandy, Jeff, Quinn, June, and especially to the memories of Lucy Berkebile and Boulos Joseph.

This book capitalizes the word "Black" and leaves "white" in lowercase throughout. "Black" is capitalized because it signifies a shared historical and contemporary sense of history, identity, and culture. The term "white," in contrast, carries no such historical significance, because many ethnic identifiers (Irish, Scottish, English, and so on) have become broadly constituted as "white" over time.

INTRODUCTION: A NIGHTMARE IS STILL A DREAM

1   For an analysis of this case and the organizing around it, see LaShawn Harris, "Beyond the Shooting: Eleanor Gray Bumpurs, Identity Erasure, and Family Activism Against Police Violence," *Souls* 20, no. 1 (2018): 86–109; Keisha N. Blain, "'We Will Overcome Whatever [It] Is the System Has Become Today': Black Women's Organizing Against Police Violence in New York City in the 1980s," *Souls* 20, no. 1 (2018): 110–121.

2   C. L. R. James, *The Black Jacobins: Toussaint L'Ouverture and the San Domingo Revolution* (New York: Vintage, 1963). See also Michel-Rolph Trouillot, *Silencing the Past: Power and the Production of History* (Boston: Beacon Press, 2015 [1995]); Laurent Dubois, *Haiti: The Aftershocks of History* (New York: Metropolitan Books, 2012); Sudhir Hazareesingh, *Black Spartacus: The Epic Life of Toussaint Louverture* (New York: Farrar, Straus and Giroux, 2020); Vincent Brown, *Tacky's Revolt: The Story of an Atlantic Slave War* (Cambridge, MA: Belknap Press of Harvard University Press, 2020).

3   The term "lower frequencies" is an allusion to the last sentence in Ralph Ellison's *Invisible Man*, first published by Random House in 1952: "Who knows but that, on the lower frequencies, I speak for you?"

4   I am indebted to my mentor, the late historian Manning Marable, for this crucial understanding. See Manning Marable, *Race, Reform, and Rebellion: The Second Reconstruction and Beyond in Black America, 1945–2006* (Jackson: University of Mississippi Press, 2007).

NOTES TO THE INTRODUCTION

5 W. E. B. Du Bois, *Black Reconstruction in America* (New York: Free Press, 1998 [1935]), 166.

6 W. E. B. Du Bois, *The Souls of Black Folk* (Chicago: A. C. McClurg, 1909).

7 Du Bois, *Black Reconstruction*; Saidiya V. Hartman, *Scenes of Subjection: Terror, Slavery, and Self-Making in Nineteenth-Century America* (New York: Oxford University Press, 1997); David W. Blight, *Race and Reunion: The Civil War in American Memory* (Cambridge, MA: Belknap Press of Harvard University Press, 2001). See also Greg Grandin, *The End of the Myth: From the Frontier to the Border Wall in the Mind of America* (New York: Metropolitan Books, 2019). For an incisive history of the reception of *Black Reconstruction* among mainstream academics who supported a racist interpretation of America's post–Civil War landscape, see David Levering Lewis, *W. E. B. Du Bois: The Fight for Equality and the American Century, 1919–1963* (New York: Henry Holt, 2000), 350–378.

8 Bruce Levine, *Thaddeus Stevens: Civil War Revolutionary, Fighter for Racial Justice* (New York: Simon and Schuster, 2021), 210, 171–236.

9 Blight, *Race and Reunion*.

10 For more on Ida B. Wells, see Mia Bay, *To Tell the Truth Freely: The Life of Ida B. Wells* (New York: Farrar, Straus and Giroux, 2010); Paula J. Giddings, *Ida, a Sword Among Lions: Ida B. Wells and the Campaign Against Lynching* (New York: HarperCollins, 2008); Naomi Murakawa, "Ida B. Wells on Racial Criminalization," in *African American Political Thought: A Collected History*, ed. Melvin L. Rogers and Jack Turner (Chicago: University of Chicago Press, 2021), 212–234; Ida B. Wells, *Crusade for Justice: The Autobiography of Ida B. Wells* (Chicago: University of Chicago Press, 2020).

11 Jacqueline Jones, *Labor of Love, Labor of Sorrow: Black Women, Work, and the Family from Slavery to the Present* (New York: Basic Books, 2009); Tera W. Hunter, *Bound in Wedlock: Slave and Free Black Marriage in the Nineteenth Century* (Cambridge, MA: Belknap Press of Harvard University Press, 2017).

12 Steven Hahn, *A Nation Under Our Feet: Black Political Struggles in the Rural South from Slavery to the Great Migration* (Cambridge, MA: Harvard University Press, 2003).

NOTES TO THE INTRODUCTION

13 Douglas A. Blackmon, *Slavery by Another Name: The Re-enslavement of Black Americans from the Civil War to World War Two* (New York: Anchor Books, 2009); Talitha L. LeFlouria, *Chained in Silence: Black Women and Convict Labor in the New South* (Chapel Hill: University of North Carolina Press, 2015); Sarah Haley, *No Mercy Here: Gender, Punishment, and the Making of Jim Crow Modernity* (Chapel Hill: University of North Carolina Press, 2016).

14 Eric Foner, *Reconstruction: America's Unfinished Revolution, 1863–1877* (New York: Perennial Library, 1989); Hahn, *A Nation Under Our Feet*; David A. Bateman, Ira Katznelson, and John S. Lapinski, *Southern Nation: Congress and White Supremacy After Reconstruction* (New York: Russell Sage Foundation; Princeton, NJ: Princeton University Press, 2018); William A. Darity Jr. and A. Kirsten Mullen, *From Here to Equality: Reparations for Black Americans in the Twenty-First Century* (Chapel Hill: University of North Carolina Press, 2020).

15 Blight, *Race and Reunion*, 64–97.

16 Blight, *Race and Reunion*; Hahn, *A Nation Under Our Feet*.

17 Edward E. Baptist, *The Half Has Never Been Told: Slavery and the Making of American Capitalism* (New York: Basic Books, 2014).

18 James Baldwin, *The Fire Next Time* (New York: Dial Press, 1963); Eddie S. Glaude, *Begin Again: James Baldwin's America and Its Urgent Lessons for Our Own* (New York: Crown, 2020); Peniel E. Joseph, *The Sword and the Shield: The Revolutionary Lives of Malcolm X and Martin Luther King Jr.* (New York: Basic Books, 2020).

19 Kathleen Belew, *Bring the War Home: The White Power Movement and Paramilitary America* (Cambridge, MA: Harvard University Press, 2018).

20 Thomas A. Guglielmo, *Divisions: A New History of Racism and Resistance in America's World War II Military* (New York: Oxford University Press, 2021); Farah Jasmine Griffin, *Harlem Nocturne: Women Artists and Progressive Politics During World War II* (New York: Basic Civitas, 2013); Jane Dailey, *White Fright: The Sexual Panic at the Heart of America's Racist History* (New York: Basic Books, 2020).

21 John F. Kennedy, "Televised Address to the Nation on Civil Rights," June 11, 1963, John F. Kennedy Presidential Library and Museum, www

.jfklibrary.org/learn/about-jfk/historic-speeches/televised-address
-to-the-nation-on-civil-rights.

22 Peniel E. Joseph, *Waiting 'til the Midnight Hour: A Narrative History of Black Power in America* (New York: Macmillan, 2007).

23 Keeanga-Yamahtta Taylor, *Race for Profit: How Banks and the Real Estate Industry Undermined Black Homeownership* (Chapel Hill: University of North Carolina Press, 2019).

24 Angela Y. Davis, *Abolition Democracy: Beyond Prison, Torture and Empire* (New York: Seven Stories Press, 2005).

25 Michael B. Katz, ed., *The Underclass Debate: Views from History* (Princeton, NJ: Princeton University Press, 1993). For an important essay on the significance of Davis's work to notions of abolition, democracy, and justice, see Neil Roberts, "Angela Y. Davis: Abolitionism, Democracy, Freedom," in Rogers and Turner, *African American Political Thought*, 660–684.

26 Angela Y. Davis, "Reflections on the Black Woman's Role in the Community of Slaves," in *Words of Fire: An Anthology of African-American Feminist Thought*, ed. Beverly Guy-Sheftall (New York: New Press, 1995), 200–216; Angela Y. Davis, "Abolition Democracy," in *The Meaning of Freedom and Other Difficult Dialogues* (San Francisco: City Lights Books, 2012), 105–106.

27 Michelle Alexander, *The New Jim Crow: Mass Incarceration in the Age of Colorblindness* (New York: New Press, 2011).

28 Michael Eric Dyson, *The Black Presidency: Barack Obama and the Politics of Race in America* (New York: Houghton Mifflin Harcourt, 2016); Claude A. Clegg III, *The Black President: Hope and Fury in the Age of Obama* (Baltimore: Johns Hopkins University Press, 2021).

29 I am inspired in this endeavor by works rooted in a Black radical tradition that has sought alternatives to racial capitalism, white supremacy, racism, sexism, patriarchy, and other systems of structural and identity-based modes of colonialism, imperialism, and oppression. See Cedric J. Robinson, *Black Marxism: The Making of the Black Radical Tradition* (Chapel Hill: University of North Carolina Press, 2000 [1983]); Robin D. G. Kelley, *Hammer and Hoe: Alabama Communists During the Great Depression* (Chapel Hill: University of North Carolina Press, 1990); Manning Marable, *How Capitalism*

Underdeveloped Black America (Boston: South End Press, 1983); Dayo F. Gore, *Radicalism at the Crossroads: African American Women Activists in the Cold War* (New York: New York University Press, 2011); bell hooks, *Killing Rage: Ending Racism* (New York: Henry Holt, 1995); Michael O. West, William G. Martin, and Fanon Che Wilkins, eds., *From Toussaint to Tupac: The Black International Since the Age of Revolution* (Chapel Hill: University of North Carolina Press, 2009); Michael C. Dawson, *Black Visions: The Roots of Contemporary African American Political Ideologies* (Chicago: University of Chicago Press, 2001); Stephen M. Ward, *In Love and Struggle: The Revolutionary Lives of James and Grace Lee Boggs* (Chapel Hill: University of North Carolina Press, 2016); Farah Jasmine Griffin, *Read Until You Understand: The Profound Wisdom of Black Life and Literature* (New York: W. W. Norton, 2021); Laurence Ralph, *Renegade Dreams: Living Through Injury in Gangland Chicago* (Chicago: University of Chicago Press, 2014); Joy James, ed., *The Angela Y. Davis Reader* (Malden, MA: Blackwell, 1998).

30 For other books that grapple with national history and memory, see Glaude, *Begin Again*; Annette Gordon-Reed, *On Juneteenth* (New York: Liveright, 2021); Trouillot, *Silencing the Past*; Monica Muñoz Martinez, *The Injustice Never Leaves You: Anti-Mexican Violence in Texas* (Cambridge, MA: Harvard University Press, 2018).

CHAPTER 1: CITIZENSHIP

1 Peniel E. Joseph, *Dark Days, Bright Nights: From Black Power to Barack Obama* (New York: Basic Books, 2010); Ricky Jones, *What's Wrong with Obamamania? Black America, Black Leadership, and the Death of Political Imagination* (New York: SUNY Press, 2008); William Jelani Cobb, *The Substance of Hope: Barack Obama and the Paradox of Progress* (New York: Walker and Company, 2010).

2 Keisha N. Blain, *Until I Am Free: Fannie Lou Hamer's Enduring Message to America* (Boston: Beacon Press, 2021), 52–58; John Dittmer, *Local People: The Struggle for Civil Rights in Mississippi* (Urbana: University of Illinois Press, 1994), 272–302.

3 Michael Eric Dyson, *The Black Presidency: Barack Obama and the Politics of Race in America* (New York: Houghton Mifflin Harcourt, 2016), 85–86.

4 Heather Cox Richardson, *How the South Won the Civil War: Oligarchy, Democracy, and the Continuing Fight for the Soul of America* (New York: Oxford University Press, 2020).

5 Barack Obama, *Dreams from My Father: A Story of Race and Inheritance* (New York: Crown, 2004).

6 Ben Calhoun, "Nearly a Quarter of a Million Fill Grant Park for Obama Victory Rally," WBEZ Chicago, November 5, 2008, www.wbez.org/stories/nearly-a-quarter-of-a-million-fill-grant-park-for-obama-victory-rally/3aff1ad4-1bcc-4566-b852-4d803cf8a8a4.

7 William A. Darity Jr. and A. Kirsten Mullen, *From Here to Equality: Reparations for Black Americans in the Twenty-First Century* (Chapel Hill: University of North Carolina Press, 2020); Dyson, *Black Presidency*.

8 Barack Obama, *A Promised Land* (New York: Crown, 2020).

9 Claude A. Clegg III, *The Black President: Hope and Fury in the Age of Obama* (Baltimore: Johns Hopkins University Press, 2021), 98.

10 Obama, *Promised Land*, 77; Clegg, *Black President*; David W. Blight, *Frederick Douglass: Prophet of Freedom* (New York: Simon and Schuster, 2018).

11 Sidney Blumenthal, *All the Powers of Earth: The Political Life of Abraham Lincoln, 1856–1860* (New York: Simon and Schuster, 2019), 355–359.

12 James M. Washington, *A Testament of Hope: The Essential Writings and Speeches of Martin Luther King, Jr.* (New York: HarperCollins, 1991), 217.

13 Washington, *Testament of Hope*, 217, 243.

14 For critiques of the Vietnam War by civil rights and Black Power leaders, see Ashley Farmer, "'Heed the Call!' Black Women, Anti-Imperialism, and Black Anti-War Activism," *Black Perspectives* (blog), August 3, 2016, www.aaihs.org/heed-the-call-black-women-anti-imperialism-and-black-anti-war-activism; Simon Hall, *Peace and Freedom: The Civil Rights and Antiwar Movements of the 1960s* (Philadelphia: University of Pennsylvania Press, 2005); Peniel Joseph, *Stokely: A Life* (New York: Basic Books, 2014), 173–196.

15 Peniel E. Joseph, *The Sword and the Shield: The Revolutionary Lives of Malcolm X and Martin Luther King Jr.* (New York: Basic Books, 2020); Tommie Shelby and Brandon M. Terry, eds., *To Shape a New World: Essays on the Political Philosophy of Martin Luther King, Jr.*

(Cambridge, MA: Belknap Press of Harvard University Press, 2018); Gary Dorrien, *Breaking White Supremacy: Martin Luther King Jr. and the Black Social Gospel* (New Haven, CT: Yale University Press, 2018).

16 Dyson, *Black Presidency*, 85.

17 David Remnick, *The Bridge: The Life and Rise of Barack Obama* (New York: Alfred A. Knopf, 2010), 23; Clegg, *Black President.*

18 See Steven Hahn, *A Nation Under Our Feet: Black Political Struggles in the Rural South from Slavery to the Great Migration* (Cambridge, MA: Harvard University Press, 2003). See also William J. Barber II and Jonathan Wilson-Hartgrove, *The Third Reconstruction: How A Moral Movement Is Overcoming the Politics of Division and Fear* (Boston: Beacon Press, 2016).

19 For a deeper history of postwar America, see Peniel E. Joseph, *Waiting 'til the Midnight Hour: A Narrative History of Black Power in America* (New York: Macmillan, 2007); Peniel E. Joseph, ed., *The Black Power Movement: Rethinking the Civil Rights–Black Power Era* (New York: Routledge, 2006); Peniel E. Joseph, ed., *Neighborhood Rebels: Black Power at the Local Level* (New York: Palgrave Macmillan, 2010). See also Peniel E. Joseph, ed., "Black Power Studies I," *Black Scholar* 31 (Fall–Winter 2001): 1–66; Peniel E. Joseph, ed., "Black Power Studies II," *Black Scholar* 32 (Spring 2002): 1–66; Jeanne Theoharis, *The Rebellious Life of Mrs. Rosa Parks* (Boston: Beacon Press, 2013); Jeanne Theoharis, *A More Beautiful and Terrible History: The Uses and Misuses of Civil Rights History* (Boston: Beacon Press, 2018); Risa L. Goluboff, *The Lost Promise of Civil Rights* (Cambridge, MA: Harvard University Press, 2007); Kenneth W. Mack, *Representing the Race: Creating the Civil Rights Lawyer* (Cambridge, MA: Harvard University Press, 2012); Matthew J. Countryman, *Up South: Civil Rights and Black Power in Philadelphia* (Philadelphia: University of Pennsylvania Press, 2006); Claude Andrew Clegg III, *The Life and Times of Elijah Muhammad* (Chapel Hill: University of North Carolina Press, 2014); Brian Purnell, *Fighting Jim Crow in the County of Kings: The Congress of Racial Equality in Brooklyn* (Lexington: University Press of Kentucky, 2015); Christopher S. Parker, *Fighting for Democracy: Black Veterans and the Struggle Against White Supremacy in the Postwar South* (Princeton, NJ: Princeton University Press, 2009); Beryl

Satter, *Family Properties: How the Struggle over Race and Real Estate Transformed Chicago and Urban America* (New York: Metropolitan Books, 2009); Greta de Jong, *You Can't Eat Freedom: Southerners and Social Justice After the Civil Rights Movement* (Chapel Hill: University of North Carolina Press, 2016); Thomas J. Sugrue, *Sweet Land of Liberty: The Forgotten Struggle for Civil Rights in the North* (New York: Random House, 2008); Julian E. Zelizer, *The Fierce Urgency of Now: Lyndon Johnson, Congress, and the Battle for the Great Society* (New York: Penguin Press, 2015); Nikhil Pal Singh, *Black Is a Country: Race and the Unfinished Struggle for Democracy* (Cambridge, MA: Harvard University Press, 2004); Barbara Ransby, *Ella Baker and the Black Freedom Movement: A Radical Democratic Vision* (Chapel Hill: University of North Carolina Press, 2003); Robin D. G. Kelley, *Race Rebels: Culture, Politics, and the Black Working Class* (New York: Free Press, 1994); Robin D. G. Kelley, *Freedom Dreams: The Black Radical Imagination* (Boston: Beacon Press, 2002); Nancy MacLean, *Freedom Is Not Enough: The Opening of the American Workplace* (New York: Russell Sage Foundation; Cambridge, MA: Harvard University Press, 2006); Yohuru Williams, *Black Politics / White Power: Civil Rights, Black Power, and the Black Panthers in New Haven* (New York: Brandywine Press, 2000); David L. Chappell, *Waking from the Dream: The Struggle for Civil Rights in the Shadow of Martin Luther King, Jr.* (New York: Random House, 2014); Ari Berman, *Give Us the Ballot: The Modern Struggle for Voting Rights in America* (New York: Picador, 2015); Brenna Wynn Greer, *Represented: The Black Imagemakers Who Reimagined African American Citizenship* (Philadelphia: University of Pennsylvania Press, 2019); Marcia Chatelain, *Franchise: The Golden Arches in Black America* (New York: Liveright, 2021); Louis Menand, *The Free World: Art and Thought in the Cold War* (New York: Farrar, Straus, and Giroux, 2021).

20 "Barack Obama's Remarks to the Democratic National Convention," *New York Times*, July 27, 2004, www.nytimes.com/2004/07/27 /politics/campaign/barack-obamas-remarks-to-the-democratic -national.html; Matthew F. Delmont, *Why Busing Failed: Race, Media, and the National Resistance to School Desegregation* (Berkeley: University of California Press, 2016), 187.

21 David Walker's "Appeal to the Coloured Citizens of the World," written in 1829, makes this crucial point about Black folks being defined apart from humanity. See Melvin L. Rogers, "David Walker: Citizenship, Judgment, Freedom, and Solidarity," in *African American Political Thought: A Collected History*, ed. Melvin L. Rogers and Jack Turner (Chicago: University of Chicago Press, 2021), 67. See also Eddie S. Glaude, *Begin Again: James Baldwin's America and Its Urgent Lesson for Our Own* (New York: Crown, 2020), 7–9; Isabel Wilkerson, *Caste: The Origins of Our Discontents* (New York: Random House, 2020); Frank B. Wilderson III, *Afropessimism* (New York: Liveright, 2020); Lewis R. Gordon, *Bad Faith and Antiblack Racism* (Amherst, NY: Humanity Books, 1995); Lewis R. Gordon, *Fanon and the Crisis of European Man: An Essay on Philosophy and the Human Sciences* (New York: Routledge, 1995); Lewis R. Gordon, *Fear of Black Consciousness* (New York: Farrar, Straus and Giroux, 2021).

22 Michelle Alexander, *The New Jim Crow: Mass Incarceration in the Age of Colorblindness* (New York: New Press, 2011); Khalil Gibran Muhammad, *The Condemnation of Blackness: Race, Crime, and the Making of Modern Urban America* (Cambridge, MA: Harvard University Press, 2010); Keeanga-Yamahtta Taylor, *Race for Profit: How Banks and the Real Estate Industry Undermined Black Homeownership* (Chapel Hill: University of North Carolina Press, 2019); Elizabeth Hinton, *America on Fire: The Untold History of Police Violence and Black Rebellion Since the 1960s* (New York: Liveright, 2021); Elizabeth Hinton, *From the War on Poverty to the War on Crime: The Making of Mass Incarceration in America* (Cambridge, MA: Harvard University Press, 2016); Saidiya V. Hartman, *Scenes of Subjection: Terror, Slavery, and Self-Making in Nineteenth-Century America* (New York: Oxford University Press, 1997); Mehrsa Baradaran, *The Color of Money: Black Banks and the Racial Wealth Gap* (Cambridge, MA: Belknap Press of Harvard University Press, 2017); Andre M. Perry, *Know Your Price: Valuing Black Lives and Property in America's Black Cities* (Washington, DC: Brookings Institution Press, 2020).

23 Eric Foner, *Reconstruction: America's Unfinished Revolution, 1863–1877* (New York: Perennial Library, 1989); Hahn, *A Nation Under Our Feet*; David A. Bateman, Ira Katznelson, and John S. Lapinski,

Southern Nation: Congress and White Supremacy After Reconstruction (New York: Russell Sage Foundation; Princeton, NJ: Princeton University Press, 2018).

24 Dan Petty, "On Elections Eve, 85,000 in Va. at Obama's Final Campaign Rally," CBS News, November 5, 2008, www.cbsnews.com /news/on-elections-eve-85000-in-va-at-obamas-final-campaign -rally; Ewen MacAskill, "Tired Obama Addresses Huge Virginia Crowd at Final Campaign Rally," *Guardian*, November 4, 2008, www.theguardian.com/world/2008/nov/04/uselections2008-barackobama; Mike Davis, "Obama at Manassas," *New Left Review* 56 (March/April 2009), https://newleftreview.org/issues/ii56 /articles/mike-davis-obama-at-manassas.

25 See Douglas A. Blackmon, *Slavery by Another Name: The Reenslavement of Black Americans from the Civil War to World War Two* (New York: Anchor Books, 2009); Talitha L. LeFlouria, *Chained in Silence: Black Women and Convict Labor in the New South* (Chapel Hill: University of North Carolina Press, 2015); Sarah Haley, *No Mercy Here: Gender, Punishment, and the Making of Jim Crow Modernity* (Chapel Hill: University of North Carolina Press, 2016). See also Ava DuVernay's important documentary, *13th* (2016).

26 Barack Obama, "Transcript: This Is Your Victory," CNN, November 4, 2008, https://edition.cnn.com/2008/POLITICS/11/04/obama .transcript.

27 Joseph, *Dark Days, Bright Nights*, 210.

28 See Alexander, *The New Jim Crow*; DuVernay, *13th*.

29 Adam Serwer, *The Cruelty Is the Point: The Past, Present, and Future of Trump's America* (New York: Random House, 2021).

30 Obama, *Promised Land*.

31 Clegg, *Black President*, 174–176.

32 For more on racial criminalization, see Muhammad, *Condemnation of Blackness*.

33 Keeanga-Yamahtta Taylor, *From #BlackLivesMatter to Black Liberation* (Chicago: Haymarket Books, 2016), 137.

34 Nick Kotz, *Judgment Days: Lyndon Baines Johnson, Martin Luther King, Jr., and the Laws That Changed America* (New York: Houghton Mifflin, 2006).

35 John F. Kennedy, "Televised Address to the Nation on Civil Rights," June 11, 1963, John F. Kennedy Presidential Library and Museum, www.jfklibrary.org/learn/about-jfk/historic-speeches/televised -address-to-the-nation-on-civil-rights; Peniel E. Joseph, "Kennedy's Finest Moment," *New York Times*, June 10, 2013, www.nytimes .com/2013/06/11/opinion/kennedys-civil-rights-triumph.html.

36 On John Lewis's personal biography, see John Lewis, with Michael D'Orso, *Walking with the Wind: A Memoir of the Movement* (New York: Simon and Schuster, 1998); Jon Meacham, *His Truth Is Marching On: John Lewis and the Power of Hope* (New York: Random House, 2021).

37 "Rep. Lewis Switches to Obama," *Los Angeles Times*, February 28, 2008, www.latimes.com/archives/la-xpm-2008-feb-28-na-endorse28 -story.html.

38 Jeff Zeleny, "Black Leader Changes Endorsement to Obama," *New York Times*, February 28, 2008, www.nytimes.com/2008/02/28/us /politics/28lewis.html; Joseph, *Dark Days, Bright Nights*, 183–187.

39 Dyson, *Black Presidency*.

40 David Levering Lewis, *W. E. B. Du Bois: The Fight for Equality and the American Century, 1919–1963* (New York: Henry Holt, 2000), 1–36.

41 Clegg, *Black President*, 244–260.

42 Barbara Ransby, *Making All Black Lives Matter: Reimagining Freedom in the 21st Century* (Berkeley: University of California Press, 2018); Patrisse Khan-Cullors and asha bandele, *When They Call You a Terrorist: A Black Lives Matter Memoir* (New York: St. Martin's Press, 2017).

CHAPTER 2: DIGNITY

1 C. L. R. James, *The Black Jacobins* (New York: Vintage, 1989).

2 Malcolm X, with Alex Haley, *The Autobiography of Malcolm X* (New York: Random House, 2015); Manning Marable, *Malcolm X: A Life of Reinvention* (New York: Penguin, 2011).

3 Komozi Woodard, *A Nation Within a Nation: Amiri Baraka (LeRoi Jones) and Black Power Politics* (Chapel Hill: University of North Carolina Press, 1999).

4 Assata Shakur, *Assata: An Autobiography* (London: Zed Books, 2014).

5   Mumia Abu-Jamal, *Live from Death Row* (New York: HarperCollins, 1996).

6   In 2021 the nation found out that the bones of the young Black children killed that day were being used, without the permission or knowledge of their relatives, by the departments of anthropology at Princeton and the University of Pennsylvania.

7   Ari Berman, *Give Us the Ballot: The Modern Struggle for Voting Rights in America* (New York: Farrar, Straus and Giroux, 2015), 286–313.

8   Patrisse Khan-Cullors and asha bandele, *When They Call You a Terrorist: A Black Lives Matter Memoir* (New York: St. Martin's, 2018); Alicia Garza, *The Purpose of Power: How We Come Together When We Fall Apart* (New York: Random House, 2020); Barbara Ransby, *Making All Black Lives Matter: Reimagining Freedom in the Twenty-First Century* (Berkeley: University of California Press, 2018); Keeanga-Yamahtta Taylor, *From #BlackLivesMatter to Black Liberation* (Chicago: Haymarket Books, 2016).

9   Michelle Alexander, *The New Jim Crow: Mass Incarceration in the Age of Colorblindness* (New York: New Press, 2011).

10   For M4BL's current policy platform, see Movement for Black Lives, "Vision for Black Lives," https://m4bl.org/policy-platforms.

11   Martin Luther King Jr., "Beyond Vietnam—A Time to Break Silence," April 4, 1967, American Rhetoric Online Speech Bank, www.americanrhetoric.com/speeches/mlkatimetobreaksilence.htm.

12   Barack Obama, "Statement by the President," July 14, 2013, White House of Barack Obama, Office of the Press Secretary, https://obamawhitehouse.archives.gov/the-press-office/2013/07/14/statement-president.

13   "Transcript: President Obama Addresses Race, Profiling and Florida Law," CNN, July 19, 2013, www.cnn.com/2013/07/19/politics/obama-zimmerman-verdict/index.html.

14   Garza, *The Purpose of Power*; Ransby, *Making All Black Lives Matter*; Khan-Cullors and bandele, *When They Call You a Terrorist*, 204. See also Angela Y. Davis, *The Meaning of Freedom and Other Difficult Dialogues* (San Francisco: City Lights Books, 2012); Taylor, *From #BlackLivesMatter to Black Liberation*; Christopher J. Lebron, *The Making of Black Lives Matter: A Brief History of an Idea* (New York:

Oxford University Press, 2017); Jesmyn Ward, ed., *The Fire This Time: A New Generation Speaks About Race* (New York: Scribner, 2016); Marc Lamont Hill, *Nobody: Casualties of America's War on the Vulnerable, from Ferguson to Flint and Beyond* (New York: Atria Books, 2016); Marc Lamont Hill, *We Still Here: Pandemic, Policing, Protest, and Possibility* (Chicago: Haymarket Books, 2020); Akiba Solomon and Kenrya Rankin, *How We Fight White Supremacy: A Field Guide to Black Resistance* (New York: Bold Type Books, 2019); Wesley C. Hogan, *On the Freedom Side: How Five Decades of Youth Activists Have Remixed American History* (Chapel Hill: University of North Carolina Press, 2019); Colin Kaepernick, ed., *Abolition for the People: The Movement for a Future Without Policing and Prisons* (New York: Kaepernick Publishing, 2021); Heather McGhee, *The Sum of Us: What Racism Costs Everyone and How We Can Prosper Together* (New York: One World, 2021); Danté Stewart, *Shoutin' in the Fire: An American Epistle* (New York: Convergent Books, 2021).

15 Elizabeth Hinton, *America on Fire: The Untold History of Police Violence and Black Rebellion Since the 1960s* (New York: Liveright, 2021); Peniel E. Joseph, *Waiting 'til the Midnight Hour: A Narrative History of Black Power in America* (New York: Macmillan, 2007).

16 See, for example, Jelani Cobb, with Matthew Guariglia, eds., *The Essential Kerner Commission Report: The Landmark Study on Race, Inequality, and Police Violence* (New York: Liveright, 2021).

17 Alexis De Veaux, *Warrior Poet: A Biography of Audre Lorde* (New York: W. W. Norton, 2004), 255, 306.

18 Martha S. Jones, *Vanguard: How Black Women Broke Barriers, Won the Vote, and Insisted on Equality for All* (New York: Basic Books, 2020), 111–116.

19 Julilly Kohler-Hausmann, *Getting Tough: Welfare and Imprisonment in 1970s America* (Princeton, NJ: Princeton University Press, 2017).

20 Elizabeth Hinton, *From the War on Poverty to the War on Crime: The Making of Mass Incarceration in America* (Cambridge, MA: Harvard University Press, 2016).

21 David W. Blight, *Frederick Douglass: Prophet of Freedom* (New York: Simon and Schuster, 2018), 474.

22 Phillip Agnew, "What President Obama Told Me About Ferguson's Movement: Think Big, but Go Gradual," *The Guardian*, December

5, 2014, www.theguardian.com/commentisfree/2014/dec/05/obama
-ferguson-movement-oval-office-meeting.

23 Scott Horsley, "Obama Visits Federal Prison, a First for a Sitting
President," NPR, July 16, 2015, www.npr.org/sections/itsallpolitics
/2015/07/16/423612441/obama-visits-federal-prison-a-first-for-a
-sitting-president; "Remarks by the President at the NAACP Conference," White House of President Barack Obama, July 14, 2015,
https://obamawhitehouse.archives.gov/the-press-office/2015/07/14
/remarks-president-naacp-conference.

24 Frank B. Wilderson III, *Afropessimism* (New York: Liveright, 2020).

25 Wilderson, *Afropessimism*; Derrick Bell, *Faces at the Bottom of the
Well: The Permanence of Racism* (New York: Basic Books, 1992).

26 W. E. B. Du Bois, *Black Reconstruction in America* (New York: Free
Press, 1998 [1935]); David W. Blight, *Race and Reunion: The Civil War
in American Memory* (Cambridge, MA: Belknap Press of Harvard
University Press, 2001).

27 Jeanne Theoharis, *The Rebellious Life of Mrs. Rosa Parks* (Boston:
Beacon Press, 2015); Danielle L. McGuire, *At the Dark End of the
Street: Black Women, Rape, and Resistance—A New History of the
Civil Rights Movement from Rosa Parks to the Rise of Black Power*
(New York: Vintage, 2011).

28 Clayborne Carson, *In Struggle: SNCC and the Black Awakening of the
1960s* (Cambridge, MA: Harvard University Press, 1995).

29 Carson, *In Struggle*; Wesley Hogan, *Many Minds, One Heart: SNCC's
Dream for a New America* (Chapel Hill: University of North Carolina
Press, 2008); John Dittmer, *Local People: The Struggle for Civil Rights
in Mississippi* (Urbana: University of Illinois Press, 1995); Charles
Payne, *I've Got the Light of Freedom: The Organizing Tradition and
the Mississippi Freedom Struggle* (Berkeley: University of California
Press, 1995); Faith Holsaert, Martha Prescod Norman Noonan, Judy
Richardson, Betty Garman Robinson, Jean Smith Young, and Doro-
thy M. Zellner, eds., *Hands on the Freedom Plow: Personal Accounts
by Women in SNCC* (Urbana: University of Illinois, 2010); Cleveland
Sellers, *The River of No Return: The Autobiography of a Black Militant
and the Life and Death of SNCC* (New York: William Morrow, 2018);
Adam Parker, *Outside Agitator: The Civil Rights Struggle of Cleveland*

Sellers Jr. (Spartanburg, SC: Hub City Press, 2018); James Foreman, *The Making of Black Revolutionaries* (Seattle: University of Washington Press, 1997).

30 Michael Eric Dyson, *Is Bill Cosby Right? Or Has the Black Middle Class Lost Its Mind?* (New York: Basic Books, 2006).

31 Barbara Ransby, *Ella Baker and the Black Freedom Movement: A Radical Democratic Vision* (Chapel Hill: University of North Carolina Press, 2003).

32 James Baldwin, "A Negro Assays the Negro Mood," *New York Times Sunday Magazine*, March 12, 1961, 25.

33 Holsaert et al., *Hands on the Freedom Plow*.

34 David M. Oshinsky, *"Worse than Slavery": Parchman Farm and the Ordeal of Jim Crow Justice* (New York: Free Press, 1997).

35 Carson, *In Struggle*; Kate Clifford Larson, *Walk with Me: A Biography of Fannie Lou Hamer* (New York: Oxford University Press, 2021); Keisha N. Blain, *Until I Am Free: Fannie Lou Hamer's Enduring Message to America* (Boston: Beacon Press, 2021); Joseph, *Waiting 'til the Midnight Hour*.

36 Joseph, *Waiting 'til the Midnight Hour*, 241–244, 298–302.

37 Malcolm X, with Haley, *Autobiography of Malcolm X*; Marable, *Malcolm X*; Les Payne and Tamara Payne, *The Dead Are Arising: The Life of Malcolm X* (New York: Liveright, 2020); Peniel E. Joseph, *The Sword and the Shield: The Revolutionary Lives of Malcolm X and Martin Luther King Jr.* (New York: Basic Books, 2020); Garrett Felber, *Those Who Know Don't Say: The Nation of Islam, the Black Freedom Struggle, and the Carceral State* (Chapel Hill: University of North Carolina Press, 2020).

38 Peniel E. Joseph, *Stokely: A Life* (New York: Basic Books, 2014); Stokely Carmichael (Kwame Ture), *Stokely Speaks: From Black Power to Pan-Africanism* (Chicago: Chicago Review Press, 2007).

39 Charles V. Hamilton and Kwame Ture, *Black Power: The Politics of Liberation in America* (New York: Penguin, 1969).

40 Joseph, *Stokely*; Stokely Carmichael, with Ekwueme Michael Thelwell, *Ready for Revolution: The Life and Struggles of Stokely Carmichael (Kwame Ture)* (New York: Scribner, 2003); Brandon Terry, "Stokely Carmichael and the Longing for Black Liberation: Black

Power and Beyond," in *African American Political Thought: A Collected History*, ed. Melvin L. Rogers and Jack Turner (Chicago: University of Chicago Press, 2021), 593–630.

41 Joseph, *Waiting 'til the Midnight Hour*, 175–178, 205–240; Rhonda Y. Williams, *Concrete Demands: The Search for Black Power in the 20th Century* (New York: Routledge, 2015); Joshua Bloom and Waldo E. Martin Jr., *Black Against Empire: The History and Politics of the Black Panther Party* (Berkeley: University of California Press, 2013); Donna Jean Murch, *Living for the City: Migration, Education, and the Rise of the Black Panther Party in Oakland, California* (Chapel Hill: University of North Carolina Press, 2010); Robyn C. Spencer, *The Revolution Has Come: Black Power, Gender, and the Black Panther Party in Oakland* (Durham, NC: Duke University Press, 2016).

42 Steven Hahn, *A Nation Under Our Feet: Black Political Struggles in the Rural South from Slavery to the Great Migration* (Cambridge, MA: Harvard University Press, 2003), 177–189; Eric Foner, *Reconstruction: America's Unfinished Revolution, 1863–1877* (New York: Perennial Library, 1989); David Zucchino, *Wilmington's Lie: The Murderous Coup of 1898 and the Rise of White Supremacy* (New York: Grove Press, 2020).

43 Heather Ann Thompson, *Blood in the Water: The Attica Prison Uprising of 1971 and Its Legacy* (New York: Pantheon, 2016).

44 Peniel E. Joseph, ed., *The Black Power Movement: Rethinking the Civil Rights–Black Power Era* (New York: Routledge, 2006); Peniel E. Joseph, ed., *Neighborhood Rebels: Black Power at the Local Level* (New York: Palgrave Macmillan, 2010); Joseph, *Waiting 'til the Midnight Hour*; Joseph, *Stokely*; Peniel E. Joseph, *Dark Days, Bright Nights: From Black Power to Barack Obama* (New York: Basic Books, 2010); James Edward Smethurst, *The Black Arts Movement: Literary Nationalism in the 1960s and 1970s* (Chapel Hill: University of North Carolina Press, 2005); Jeffrey O. G. Ogbar, *Black Power: Radical Politics and African American Identity* (Baltimore: Johns Hopkins University Press, 2004); Ibram H. Rogers, *The Black Campus Movement: Black Students and the Racial Reconstitution of Higher Education, 1965–1972* (New York: Palgrave Macmillan, 2012); Alondra Nelson, *Body and Soul: The Black Panther Party and the Fight Against Medical*

Discrimination (Minneapolis: University of Minnesota Press, 2012); Shirletta J. Kinchen, *Black Power in the Bluff City: African American Youth and Student Activism in Memphis, 1965–1975* (Knoxville: University of Tennessee Press, 2016).

45 Carson, *In Struggle*; Ransby, *Ella Baker*; Doug McAdam, *Freedom Summer* (New York: Oxford University Press, 1988); Holsaert et al., *Hands on the Freedom Plow*; Wesley C. Hogan, *Many Minds, One Heart: SNCC's Dream for a New America* (Chapel Hill: University of North Carolina Press, 2007); McGuire, *At the Dark End of the Street*; Carmichael, with Thelwell, *Ready for Revolution*; David Halberstam, *The Children* (New York: Fawcett Books, 1998); Susan Youngblood Ashmore, *Carry It On: The War on Poverty and the Civil Rights Movement in Alabama, 1964–1972* (Athens: University of Georgia Press, 2008); Emilye Crosby, ed., *Civil Rights History from the Ground Up: Local Struggles, a National Movement* (Athens: University of Georgia Press, 2011).

CHAPTER 3: BACKLASH

1 Adam Serwer, *The Cruelty Is the Point: The Past, Present, and Future of Trump's America* (New York: Random House, 2021), 38–75.

2 Ta-Nehisi Coates, *We Were Eight Years in Power: An American Tragedy* (New York: Random House Publishing Group, 2017), xiii.

3 In her book *The Sum of Us: What Racism Costs Everyone and How We Can Prosper Together* (New York: One World, 2021), Heather McGhee discusses the contemporary version of this historical phenomenon.

4 Coates, *We Were Eight Years in Power*.

5 See, for example, Edward E. Baptist, *The Half Has Never Been Told: Slavery and the Making of American Capitalism* (New York: Basic Books, 2014); Sven Beckert, *Empire of Cotton: A Global History* (New York: Alfred A. Knopf, 2014); Daina Ramey Berry, *The Price for Their Pound of Flesh: The Value of the Enslaved, from Womb to Grave, in the Building of a Nation* (Boston: Beacon Press, 2017); Leon F. Litwack, *Trouble in Mind: Black Southerners in the Age of Jim Crow* (New York: Vintage, 1999); Douglas A. Blackmon, *Slavery by Another Name: The Re-Enslavement of Black Americans from the Civil War to World War II* (New York: Anchor Books, 2009); Deborah Gray White, *Too Heavy*

a Load: Black Women in Defense of Themselves, 1894–1994 (New York: W. W. Norton, 1999); Ibram X. Kendi, *Stamped from the Beginning: The Definitive History of Racist Ideas in America* (New York: Nation Books, 2016).

6   David A. Bateman, Ira Katznelson, and John S. Lapinski, *Southern Nation: Congress and White Supremacy After Reconstruction* (New York: Russell Sage Foundation; Princeton, NJ: Princeton University Press, 2018), 9; Manisha Sinha, *The Slave's Cause: A History of Abolition* (New Haven, CT: Yale University Press, 2016), 567–571; David Blight, *Frederick Douglass: Prophet of Freedom* (New York: Simon and Schuster, 2018). See also Craig Steven Wilder, *Ebony and Ivy: Race, Slavery, and the Troubled History of America's Universities* (New York: Bloomsbury Press, 2013); Ethan J. Kytle and Blain Roberts, *Denmark Vesey's Garden: Slavery and Memory in the Cradle of the Confederacy* (New York: New Press, 2018); Kristin Waters, *Maria W. Stewart and the Roots of Black Political Thought* (Jackson: University of Mississippi Press, 2022); Jim Downs, *Maladies of Empire: How Colonialism, Slavery, and War Transformed Medicine* (Cambridge, MA: Belknap Press of Harvard University Press, 2021); Laurent Dubois and Richard Lee Turits, *Freedom Roots: Histories From the Caribbean* (Chapel Hill: University of North Carolina Press, 2019); Jessica Marie Johnson, *Black Women, Intimacy, and Freedom in the Atlantic World* (Philadelphia: University of Pennsylvania Press, 2020); and Alice L. Baumgartner, *South to Freedom: Runaway Slaves to Mexico and the Road to the Civil War* (New York: Basic Books, 2020) for histories that expand the geography, intellectual and political terrain, periodization, and domestic and global political actors that shaped the world during and after racial slavery in the Americas and beyond.

7   Douglas A. Blackmon, *Slavery by Another Name: The Re-enslavement of Black Americans from the Civil War to World War II* (New York: Anchor Books, 2009); Talitha L. LeFlouria, *Chained in Silence: Black Women and Convict Labor in the New South* (Chapel Hill: University of North Carolina Press, 2015); Sarah Haley, *No Mercy Here: Gender, Punishment, and the Making of Jim Crow Modernity* (Chapel Hill: University of North Carolina Press, 2016).

8 David Zucchino, *Wilmington's Lie: The Murderous Coup of 1898 and the Rise of White Supremacy* (New York: Grove Press, 2020); Steven Hahn, *A Nation Under Our Feet: Black Political Struggles in the Rural South from Slavery to the Great Migration* (Cambridge, MA: Harvard University Press, 2003).

9 Hahn, *A Nation Under Our Feet*, 288–313; Stephen Kantrowitz, *More than Freedom: Fighting for Black Citizenship in a White Republic, 1829–1889* (New York: Penguin, 2012), 411.

10 Hahn, *A Nation Under Our Feet*; Eric Foner, *Reconstruction: America's Unfinished Revolution, 1863–1877* (New York: Perennial Library, 1989); Kimberlé Williams Crenshaw, Luke Charles Harris, Daniel Martinez HoSang, and George Lipsitz, eds., *Seeing Race Again: Countering Colorblindness Across the Disciplines* (Berkeley: University of California Press, 2019); Philip Dray, *Capitol Men: The Epic Story of Reconstruction Through the Lives of the First Black Congressmen* (New York: Houghton Mifflin, 2008), 351.

11 Peniel E. Joseph, *Waiting 'til the Midnight Hour: A Narrative History of Black Power in America* (New York: Macmillan, 2007); Melvin L. Rogers and Jack Turner, *African American Political Thought: A Collected History* (Chicago: University of Chicago Press, 2021); Richard Rothstein, *The Color of Law: A Forgotten History of How Our Government Segregated America* (New York: Liveright, 2017); Ira Katznelson, *When Affirmative Action Was White: An Untold History of Racial Inequality in Twentieth-Century America* (New York: W. W. Norton, 2005).

12 Elizabeth Hinton, *From the War on Poverty to the War on Crime: The Making of Mass Incarceration in America* (Cambridge, MA: Harvard University Press, 2016); Michelle Alexander, *The New Jim Crow: Mass Incarceration in the Age of Colorblindness* (New York: New Press, 2011); Bryan Stevenson; *Just Mercy: A Story of Justice and Redemption* (New York: One World, 2014); Julilly Kohler-Hausmann, *Getting Tough: Welfare and Imprisonment in 1970s America* (Princeton, NJ: Princeton University Press, 2017); Heather Ann Thompson, *Blood in the Water: The Attica Prison Uprising of 1971 and Its Legacy* (New York: Pantheon, 2016).

NOTES TO CHAPTER 3

13 Greg Grandin, *The End of the Myth: From the Frontier to the Border Wall in the Mind of America* (New York: Metropolitan Books, 2019); Manning Marable, *Race, Reform, and Rebellion: The Second Reconstruction and Beyond in Black America, 1945–2006* (Jackson: University of Mississippi Press, 2007); Danielle Allen, *Cuz: The Life and Times of Michael A.* (New York: Liveright, 2017); Elizabeth Hinton, *America on Fire: The Untold History of Police Violence and Black Rebellion Since the 1960s* (New York: Liveright, 2021).

14 Michael Eric Dyson, *Come Hell or High Water: Hurricane Katrina and the Color of Disaster* (New York: Basic Civitas, 2006); Douglas Brinkley, *The Great Deluge: Hurricane Katrina, New Orleans, and the Mississippi Gulf Coast* (New York: William Morrow, 2006).

15 Michael W. Flamm, *Law and Order: Street Crime, Civil Unrest, and the Crisis of Liberalism in the 1960s* (New York: Columbia University Press, 2005).

16 For more on liberal law-and-order politics, see Naomi Murakawa, *The First Civil Right: How Liberals Built Prison America* (Oxford: Oxford University Press, 2014).

17 Peniel E. Joseph, *Dark Days, Bright Nights: From Black Power to Barack Obama* (New York: Basic Books, 2010), 184–185. For the politics of racial backlash in the 1990s, see Marable, *Race, Reform, and Rebellion*, 216–237; Andrew Hacker, *Two Nations: Black and White, Separate, Hostile, Unequal* (New York: Ballantine Books, 1995); Stephen Steinberg, *Turning Back: The Retreat from Racial Justice in American Thought and Policy* (Boston: Beacon Press, 1995).

18 Tressie McMillan Cottom, *Thick: And Other Essays* (New York: New Press, 2019); Barbara Ransby, *Making All Black Lives Matter: Reimagining Freedom in the 21st Century* (Berkeley: University of California Press, 2018); Marc Lamont Hill, *We Still Here: Pandemic, Policing, Protest, and Possibility* (Chicago: Haymarket Books, 2020); Don Lemon, *This Is the Fire: What I Say to My Friends About Racism* (New York: Little, Brown, 2021).

19 Serwer, *The Cruelty Is the Point*, 46.

20 John Cassidy, "Donald Trump's Dark, Dark Convention Speech," *New Yorker*, July 22, 2016, www.newyorker.com/news/john-cassidy /donald-trumps-dark-dark-convention-speech; Alex Altman, "Midnight

in America: Donald Trump's Convention Speech Paints Grim Picture," *Time*, July 22, 2016, https://time.com/4418398/donald-trump-convention-speech; Peniel Joseph, "What's Fueling the Republican Fury," CNN, July 23, 2016, www.cnn.com/2016/07/23/opinions/race-and-the-rnc-opinion-peniel-joseph/index.html.

21 Joseph, "What's Fueling the Republican Fury."

22 McGhee, *The Sum of Us*; Hinton, *America on Fire*.

23 Barack Obama, *A Promised Land* (New York: Crown, 2020).

24 Obama, *A Promised Land*; Barack Obama, *The Audacity of Hope* (New York: Crown, 2006).

25 Michael Eric Dyson, *The Black Presidency: Barack Obama and the Politics of Race in America* (New York: Houghton Mifflin Harcourt, 2016), 177–179; "Read President Obama's Commencement Address at Morehouse College," *Time*, June 2, 2016, https://time.com/4341712/obama-commencement-speech-transcript-morehouse-college.

26 Dyson, *Black Presidency*, 154–187; Claude A. Clegg III, *The Black President: Hope and Fury in the Age of Obama* (Baltimore: Johns Hopkins University Press, 2021), 71–75, 180–195.

CHAPTER 4: LEADERSHIP

1 See for example, Thomas Fisher, *The Emergency: A Year of Healing and Heartbreak in a Chicago ER* (New York: One World, 2022).

2 Nate Cohn and Kevin Quealy, "How Public Opinion Has Moved on Black Lives Matter," *New York Times*, June 10, 2020, www.nytimes.com/interactive/2020/06/10/upshot/black-lives-matter-attitudes.html; Ibram X. Kendi, "Is This the Beginning of the End of American Racism?," *The Atlantic*, September 2020, www.theatlantic.com/magazine/archive/2020/09/the-end-of-denial/614194.

3 Peniel E. Joseph, *The Sword and the Shield: The Revolutionary Lives of Malcolm X and Martin Luther King Jr.* (New York: Basic Books, 2020).

4 Ashley D. Farmer, *Remaking Black Power: How Black Women Transformed an Era* (Chapel Hill: University of North Carolina Press, 2017); Barbara Ransby, *Ella Baker and the Black Freedom Movement: A Radical Democratic Vision* (Chapel Hill: University of North Carolina Press, 2003); Keisha N. Blain, *Set the World on Fire: Black*

Nationalist Women and the Global Struggle for Freedom (Philadelphia: University of Pennsylvania Press, 2018).

5 Monique W. Morris, *Pushout: The Criminalization of Black Girls in Schools* (New York: New Press, 2016); Beth Richie, *Arrested Justice: Black Women, Violence, and America's Prison Nation* (New York: New York University Press, 2012).

6 Mariame Kaba, *We Do This 'Til We Free Us: Abolitionist Organizing and Transforming Justice* (Chicago: Haymarket Books, 2021); Andrea J. Ritchie, *Invisible No More: Police Violence Against Black Women and Women of Color* (Boston: Beacon Press, 2017); Patrisse Khan-Cullors and asha bandele, *When They Call You a Terrorist: A Black Lives Matter Memoir* (New York: St. Martin's, 2018); Keisha N. Blain, *Until I Am Free: Fannie Lou Hamer's Enduring Message to America* (Boston: Beacon Press, 2021); Barbara Ransby, *Making All Black Lives Matter: Reimagining Freedom in the 21st Century* (Berkeley: University of California Press, 2018); Farah Jasmine Griffin, *Read Until You Understand: The Profound Wisdom of Black Life and Literature* (New York: W. W. Norton, 2021).

7 Eddie S. Glaude Jr., *Exodus! Religion, Race, and Nation in Early Nineteenth-Century Black America* (Chicago: University of Chicago Press, 2000); Isabel Wilkerson, *The Warmth of Other Suns: The Epic Story of America's Great Migration* (New York: Vintage, 2011); James H. Meriwether, *Proudly We Can Be African: Black Americans and Africa, 1935–1961* (Chapel Hill: University of North Carolina Press, 2009); Ibram X. Kendi and Keisha N. Blain, eds., *Four Hundred Souls: A Community History of African America, 1619–2019* (New York: One World, 2021); Russell Rickford, *We Are an African People: Independent Education, Black Power, and the Radical Imagination* (New York: Oxford University Press, 2016).

8 The Kaiser Family Foundation estimated twenty-six million in a survey conducted from June 8 to 14, 2020. Other polls estimated the number of Black Lives Matter protesters in American cities by the end of June 2020 at fifteen million, eighteen million, and twenty-three million. See Larry Buchanan, Quoctrung Bui, and Jugal K. Patel, "Black Lives Matter May Be the Largest Movement in U.S. History," *New York Times*, July 23, 2020, www.nytimes.com/interactive/2020/07/03/us/george-floyd-protests-crowd-size.html.

9   "USA: Law Enforcement Violated Black Lives Matter Protesters' Human Rights, Documents Acts of Police Violence and Excessive Force," Amnesty International, August 4, 2020, www.amnesty.org /en/latest/press-release/2020/08/usa-law-enforcement-violated -black-lives-matter-protesters-human-rights.

10 Jelani Cobb, with Matthew Guariglia, eds., *The Essential Kerner Commission Report: The Landmark Study on Race, Inequality, and Police Violence* (New York: Liveright, 2021). For a history of the creation of the Kerner Report, see Steven M. Gillon, *Separate and Unequal: The Kerner Commission and the Unraveling of American Liberalism* (New York: Basic Books, 2018). For a comprehensive historical and policy updating of the report's finding, see Fred Harris and Alan Curtis, eds., *Healing Our Divided Society: Investing in America Fifty Years After the Kerner Report*, An Eisenhower Foundation Book (Philadelphia: Temple University Press, 2018).

11 See Elizabeth Hinton, *America on Fire: The Untold History of Police Violence and Black Rebellion Since the 1960s* (New York: Liveright, 2021); Peniel E. Joseph, *Stokely: A Life* (New York: Basic Books, 2014).

12 Larry Buchanan, Quoctrung Bui, and Jugal K. Patel, "Black Lives Matter May Be the Largest Movement in U.S. History," *New York Times*, July 3, 2020, www.nytimes.com/interactive/2020/07/03/us/george -floyd-protests-crowd-size.html; Peniel E. Joseph, "How Black Lives Matter Transformed the Fourth of July," CNN, July 2, 2020, www .cnn.com/2020/07/02/opinions/black-lives-matter-fourth-of-july -joseph/index.html; Peniel E. Joseph, "What Black Children Will Learn from George Floyd's Death," CNN, June 2, 2020, www.cnn .com/2020/06/02/opinions/what-black-children-will-learn-from -george-floyds-death-joseph/index.html.

13 Nikole Hannah-Jones, Caitlin Roper, Ilena Silverman, and Jake Silverstein, eds., *The 1619 Project: A New Origin Story* (New York: One World, 2021).

14 Kaba, *We Do This 'Til We Free Us*.

15 Paula J. Giddings, *Ida, a Sword Among Lions: Ida B. Wells and the Campaign Against Lynching* (New York: HarperCollins, 2008), 15–39; Mia Bay, *To Tell the Truth Freely: The Life of Ida B. Wells* (New York: Hill and Wang, 2009).

16 Naomi Murakawa, "Ida B. Wells on Racial Criminalization," in *African American Political Thought*, ed. Melvin L. Rogers and Jack Turner (Chicago: University of Chicago Press, 2021), 212–234.

17 Giddings, *Ida*, 188–210; Bay, *To Tell the Truth Freely*, 82–108.

18 Giddings, *Ida*, 238–239; Bay, *To Tell the Truth Freely*, 122–129; Khalil Gibran Muhammad, *The Condemnation of Blackness: Race, Crime, and the Making of Modern Urban America* (Cambridge, MA: Harvard University Press, 2010); Sarah Haley, *No Mercy Here: Gender, Punishment, and the Making of Jim Crow Modernity* (Chapel Hill: University of North Carolina Press, 2016).

19 Giddings, *Ida*, 476–479; Bay, *To Tell the Truth Freely*, 268–273; David Blight, *Frederick Douglass: Prophet of Freedom* (New York: Simon and Schuster, 2018), 721–722

20 Barbara Ransby, *Ella Baker*; Blain, *Until I Am Free*, ix.

21 Angela Y. Davis, *An Autobiography* (New York: International Publishers, 1988); Angela Y. Davis, *Blues Legacies and Black Feminism: Gertrude "Ma" Rainey, Bessie Smith, and Billie Holiday* (New York: Pantheon, 1998); Angela Y. Davis et al., eds., *If They Come in the Morning: Voices of Resistance* (New York: Signet Books, 1971).

22 Dan Berger, *Captive Nation: Black Prison Organizing in the Civil Rights Era* (Chapel Hill: University of North Carolina Press, 2014).

23 Audre Lorde, "Age, Race, Class, and Sex: Women Redefining Difference," in *Words of Fire: An Anthology of African-American Feminist Thought*, ed. Beverly Guy-Sheftall (New York: New Press, 1995), 289; Martha S. Jones, *Vanguard: How Black Women Broke Barriers, Won the Vote, and Insisted on Equality for All* (New York: Basic Books, 2020); Paula Giddings, *When and Where I Enter: The Impact of Black Women on Race and Sex in America* (New York: Bantam, 1984); Deborah Gray White, *Too Heavy a Load: Black Women in Defense of Themselves, 1894–1994* (New York: W. W. Norton, 1999); Kimberly Springer, *Living for the Revolution: Black Feminist Organizations, 1968–1980* (Durham, NC: Duke University Press, 2005); Bettye Collier-Thomas and V. P. Franklin, eds., *Sisters in the Struggle: African American Women in the Civil Rights–Black Power Movement* (New York: New York University Press, 2001); Farmer, *Remaking Black Power*; Blain, *Set the World on Fire: Black Nationalist Women and the*

Global Struggle for Freedom (Philadelphia: University of Pennsylvania Press, 2018); Mia Bay, Farah J. Griffin, Martha S. Jones, and Barbara D. Savage, eds., *Toward an Intellectual History of Black Women* (Chapel Hill: University of North Carolina Press, 2015); Daina Ramey Berry and Kali Nicole Gross, *A Black Woman's History of the United States* (Boston: Beacon Press, 2020).

24 Richie, *Arrested Justice*, 148–150.

25 Ransby, *Making All Black Lives Matter*; Richie, *Arrested Justice*; Sandra E. Weissinger, Dwayne A. Mack, and Elwood Watson, eds., *Violence Against Black Bodies: An Intersectional Analysis of How Black Lives Continue to Matter* (New York: Routledge, 2017).

26 Hannah-Jones et al., *The 1619 Project*; Heather McGhee, *The Sum of Us: What Racism Costs Everyone and How We Can Prosper Together* (New York: One World, 2021); Ruth Wilson Gilmore, *Golden Gulag: Prisons, Surplus, Crisis, and Opposition in Globalizing California* (Berkeley: University of California Press, 2007). See also Erik McDuffie, *Sojourning for Truth: Black Women, American Communism, and the Making of Black Left Feminism* (Durham, NC: Duke University Press, 2011); Dayo Gore, *Radicalism at the Crossroads: African American Women Activists in the Cold War* (New York: New York University Press, 2012).

27 Alicia Garza, *The Purpose of Power: How We Come Together When We Fall Apart* (New York: Random House, 2020); Khan-Cullors and bandele, *When They Call You a Terrorist*; Davis et al., *If They Come in the Morning*.

28 Joey L. Mogul, Andrea J. Ritchie, and Kay Whitlock, *Queer (In)Justice: The Criminalization of LGBT People in the United States* (Boston: Beacon Press, 2011); Weissinger et al., *Violence Against Black Bodies*; Darnell L. Moore, *No Ashes in the Fire: Coming of Age Black and Free in America* (New York: Bold Type Books, 2018).

29 Guy-Sheftall, *Words of Fire*; Kimberlé Williams Crenshaw, "Mapping the Margins: Intersectionality, Identity Politics, and Violence Against Women of Color," in *The Public Nature of Private Violence: The Discovery of Domestic Abuse*, ed. Martha Albertson Fineman and Roxanne Mykitiuk (New York: Routledge, 1994); Kimberlé Williams Crenshaw, Luke Charles Harris, Daniel Martinez HoSang,

and George Lipsitz, eds., *Seeing Race Again: Countering Colorblindness Across the Disciplines* (Berkeley: University of California Press, 2019); Gore, *Radicalism at the Crossroads*; Patricia Hill Collins, *Black Feminist Thought: Knowledge, Consciousness, and the Politics of Empowerment* (New York: Routledge, 1991); Imani Perry, *Looking for Lorraine: The Radiant and Radical Life of Lorraine Hansberry* (Boston: Beacon Press, 2018); Daphne A. Brooks, *Liner Notes for the Revolution: The Intellectual Life of Black Feminist Sound* (Cambridge, MA: Harvard University Press, 2021); Ransby, *Making All Black Lives Matter*; Keeanga-Yamahtta Taylor, *From #BlackLivesMatter to Black Liberation* (Chicago: Haymarket Books, 2016); Richie, *Arrested Justice*; Garza, *The Purpose of Power*; Khan-Cullors and bandele, *When They Call You a Terrorist*; Kaba, *We Do This 'Til We Free Us*; Morris, *Pushout*.

30 Kate McGee, "Texas 'Critical Race Theory' Bill Limiting Teaching of Current Events Signed into Law," *Texas Tribune*, June 15, 2021, www.texastribune.org/2021/06/15/abbott-critical-race-theory-law; "The 1619 Project Curriculum," Pulitzer Center, accessed January 19, 2022, https://pulitzercenter.org/lesson-plan-grouping/1619-project-curriculum.

31 Peniel E. Joseph, "America Is on a Brink Like None Since the Civil War," CNN, July 31, 2020, www.cnn.com/2020/07/31/opinions/1619-project-tom-cotton-slavery-joseph-opinion/index.html.

32 Annette Gordon-Reed, *On Juneteenth* (New York: Liveright, 2021); Clint Smith, *How the Word Is Passed: A Reckoning with the History of Slavery Across America* (New York: Little, Brown, 2021).

33 W. E. B. Du Bois, *Black Reconstruction in America* (New York: Free Press, 1998), 182; David W. Blight, *Race and Reunion: The Civil War in American Memory* (Cambridge, MA: Belknap Press of Harvard University Press, 2001).

34 Sanya Mansoor, "93% of Black Lives Matter Protests Have Been Peaceful, New Report Finds," *Time*, September 5, 2020, https://time.com/5886348/report-peaceful-protests, www.nytimes.com/article/george-floyd-protests-timeline.html.

35 Kaba, *We Do This 'Til We Free Us*.

36 Hinton, *America on Fire*, 257–308; Mariame Kaba, "Yes, We Mean Literally Abolish Police," *New York Times*, June 12, 2020, www

.nytimes.com/2020/06/12/opinion/sunday/floyd-abolish-defund
-police.html.

37 Jones, *Vanguard*; Guy-Sheftall, *Words of Fire*; Giddings, *When and Where I Enter* and *Ida*; Bay, *To Tell the Truth Freely.*

38 Stacey Abrams, *Our Time Is Now: Power, Purpose, and the Fight for a Fair America* (New York: Henry Holt, 2020).

39 Naomi Murakawa, *The First Civil Right: How Liberals Built Prison America* (Oxford: Oxford University Press, 2014), 140–141; Michael Javen Fortner, *Black Silent Majority: The Rockefeller Drug Laws and the Politics of Punishment* (Cambridge, MA: Harvard University Press, 2015); James Forman Jr., *Locking Up Our Own: Crime and Punishment in Black America* (New York: Farrar, Straus, and Giroux, 2017).

40 Melissa Harris-Perry, "Stacey Abrams on Voting Rights, COVID-19, and Being Vice President," *Elle*, April 15, 2020, www.elle.com/culture/career-politics/a32132819/stacey-abrams-on-voting-rights-covid-19-and-being-vice-president.

41 Ta-Nehisi Coates, "The Life Breonna Taylor Lived, in the Words of Her Mother," *Vanity Fair*, August 24, 2020, www.vanityfair.com/culture/2020/08/breonna-taylor; Jones, *Vanguard*; Guy-Sheftall, *Words of Fire*; Giddings, *When and Where I Enter* and *Ida*; Bay, *To Tell the Truth Freely.*

42 Ransby, *Making All Black Lives Matter*, 5–10.

43 Ransby, *Making All Black Lives Matter*; Taylor, *From #BlackLivesMatter to Black Liberation*; Peniel E. Joseph, "Black Lives Matter's Big Step," CNN, August 3, 2016, www.cnn.com/2016/08/03/opinions/black-lives-matter-movement-report-joseph/index.html; "Vision for Black Lives," M4BL, https://m4bl.org/policy-platforms, accessed December 19, 2021.

44 Jones, *Vanguard*; Deborah Gray White, *Too Heavy a Load: Black Women in Defense of Themselves, 1894–1994* (New York: W. W. Norton, 1999); Evelyn Brooks Higginbotham, *Righteous Discontent: The Women's Movement in the Black Baptist Church, 1880–1920* (Cambridge, MA: Harvard University Press, 1994); Bettye Collier-Thomas, *Jesus, Jobs, and Justice: African American Women and Religion* (New York: Alfred A. Knopf, 2010); Giddings, *When and Where I Enter.*

45 "Read President Obama's Speech at the 2020 Democratic National Convention," *Los Angeles Times*, August 20, 2020, www.latimes.com /politics/story/2020-08-20/president-obama-speech-dnc-2020; Chandelis Duster, "Obama Cautions Activists Against Using the 'Defund the Police' Slogan," CNN, December 2, 2020, www.cnn .com/2020/12/02/politics/barack-obama-defund-the-police/index .html.

46 James Baldwin, *The Fire Next Time* (New York: Vintage, 1991), 105.

CONCLUSION: FREEDOM

1 "Read: Youth Poet Laureate Amanda Gorman's Inaugural Poem," CNN, January 20, 2021, www.cnn.com/2021/01/20/politics/amanda -gorman-inaugural-poem-transcript/index.html.

2 Maria Cramer, "A Black Man Killed by a White Mob in 1898 Finally Receives a Funeral," *New York Times*, November 10, 2021, www.nytimes .com/2021/11/10/us/joshua-halsey-funeral-wilmington-massacre .html; David Zucchino, *Wilmington's Lie: The Murderous Coup of 1898 and the Rise of White Supremacy* (New York: Grove Press, 2020).

INDEX

INDEX

INDEX

INDEX

dehumanization of Blacks
American national character, 55–56
exceptionalism normalizing, 22
redemptionist policy of the South,
144–152
democracy
the afterlife of Reconstruction shaping,
226
assault on the Capitol as attack on,
217–219
Du Bois on the relationship between
race and, 10–11
Haitians' struggles for, 76–79
Lost Cause narrative, 107
Obama's racial optimism for America,
42–45, 48–49, 58–65
Panthers' call for radical
transformation, 122–123
pro-democracy movements in Haiti,
76–77
reconstructionist framework for
establishing, 15–22
South Carolina's disenfranchisement of
Black voters, 134–135
Trump's redemptionist assault, 154–158
views on Black citizenship and identity,
46–47
Democratic National Convention (1968),
42
Democratic National Convention (2004),
37–38, 50, 53
Democratic National Convention (2008),
39–40
Democratic Party
Black voters' frustration with
Republicans and, 160
Black women's support, 177, 208–209
Clinton's vacillation on Black equality,
151–152
Georgia's runoff election, 217
post-Obama identity, 132–133
redemptionism, 21
vice-presidential nomination, 205–211
white supremacists' alliance with, 124,
144
See also Obama, Barack

dignity, Black
Black community in New York, 79–80
Black Lives Matter movement, 87–89
BLM's inclusive approach to Black
identity politics, 128–130
BLM's radical call for, 119–120
civil rights era activism, 108–115
exceptionalism limiting the prospects
for, 224
influences and examples, 75–79
Malcolm X's history and mission,
116–118
police violence against Blacks, 95–96
radical Black activists, 84–86
reconstructionist framework for
establishing, 15–22
redemption politics weaponizing white
grievances, 145
Do the Right Thing (1989), 7–8
domestic violence against Black women,
191
double consciousness, 9–10, 79, 178
Double V campaign, 23–24
Douglass, Frederick
abolition democracy, 30, 186
Black voting rights, 15
Johnson's condescension to Blacks,
104
public view of, 228
the role of the ballot in Black
citizenship, 47
Douglass, Stephen, 47
Dreams from My Father (Obama), 41–42
Dred Scott, 138
Du Bois, W.E.B., 1(quote)
abolition democracy, 15
American exceptionalism
contradicting, 54
double consciousness, 9–11
history of the 1619 Project, 196–197
incompleteness of Reconstruction, 106
the politics of Black solidarity, 70
Wells's friction with, 186–187
Duke, David, 158
Dunham, Madelyn, 63
Dunning, William Archibald, 11

INDEX

INDEX

INDEX

INDEX

INDEX

Parks, Rosa, 108
Philadelphia, Pennsylvania: radical Black
  activists, 83–86
Plessy v. Ferguson, 143–144
police surveillance by the Black Panthers,
  122–124
police violence, 2–3, 41
  arrest of Henry Louis Gates Jr., 62
  assault on the Capitol, 217–219
  BLM protests and policy reform
    demands, 13–14, 200–203
  during the civil rights era, 95–96
  Freedom Summer murders, 113–114
  Lee's cinematic portrayal, 7–8
  the murder of Breonna Taylor, 204–205
  the murder of George Floyd, 226–227
  the murder of Trayvon Martin, 86–87,
    89–90
  the murders of Alton Sterling and
    Philando Castile, 131–132
  the murders of Michael Brown, Eric
    Garner, and Freddie Gray, 94–95
  1968 Democratic National Convention,
    42
  Obama's meeting with community
    activists, 102
  origins of Black Lives Matter, 93–94
  Trump celebrating, 131–133
  See also Floyd, George; violence, racial
political representation
  Abrams and Harris, 205–210
  Obama's presidential campaign and
    victory, 38–40
  See also Obama, Barack
postracial America, 44–45, 60–61, 64, 216
Powell, Colin, 149
power relations, redemptionists' view of,
  17–18
Presidential Reconstruction, 52–53,
  140–141
prison system. *See* criminal justice system
protests and demonstrations
  assault on the Capitol, 217–219
  the deaths of Michael Brown, Eric
    Garner, and Freddie Gray, 94–95
  globalization of BLM protests, 203–204

King's assassination, 179–180
  removing Confederate monuments and
    flags, 213–214
  2020 protests over George Floyd's
    murder, 175–181
  See also Black Lives Matter
Public Enemy, 2, 7–8
public service, politics as, 49–50

Queer politics, 97–98
  Black Trans Lives Matter march,
    194–195
  BLM's inclusive method and agenda,
    128–130
  post-civil-rights era leadership and
    mobilization, 192–194
  See also Black Lives Matter

race relations: optimism over Obama's
  election, 46
racial injustice
  the murder of Trayvon Martin, 88–92
  Obama's racial optimism and
    incrementalism, 162–164
  "postracial" America, 44–45
  Wells's anti-lynching campaign,
    184–186
racial optimism
  BLM activists' message, 103, 105
  Obama presidency, 45, 59, 61, 64, 72, 106,
    161–163, 224
  redemption-reconstruction duality,
    135–136
racial profiling: Gates's arrest, 62
radical abolition democracy, 30–33, 89
Radical Reconstruction, 12, 28, 130,
  142–143
Radical Republican Congress, 140–141
Reagan, Ronald, 76
  Black feminist leadership countering
    racial cruelty, 191–192
  championing redemptionist policies,
    148–149
  Davis's fugitive status, 30–31
  War on Drugs, 103
Reconstruction Amendments, 44, 52–53, 143

273

INDEX

INDEX

early reconstructionists fighting, 17, 23–24

effects of white supremacy on racial equality, 167, 199, 202–203

Lee's cinematic portrayal, 7

Obama's racial optimism, 59

overt racism under Trump, 27–28

persistence of, 7, 26–28, 32, 56, 83

post-civil-rights America, 147–148

shaping Gen Xers, 2–4

1619 Project demands, 197

SNCC activism, 112

Trump's redemptionist narrative, 165

Sellers, Cleveland, 111–112

Selma, Alabama, 51

separate but equal doctrine, 143–144

Service Employees International Union (SEIU), 77

Shakur, Assata, 84

sharecropper activism, 110

Shelby v. Holder, 26–27, 86

Sister Souljah, 152

1619 Project, 171, 195–198

slavery

Dred Scott's life, 136–137

Haitian Revolution, 4–5, 79

Obama's reconstructionist political vision, 53–54

post-Reconstruction perpetuation of, 139–140

ratification of the Thirteenth Amendment, 33

reconstructionist political vision, 54–55

1619 Project, 195–196

systemic racism replacing slavery in the South, 223–224

See also Thirteenth Amendment

Smith, Barbara, 190

Soledad Brother (Jackson), 126

Sotomayor, Sonia, 220

Stand Your Ground Law (Florida), 90–91

Sterling, Alton, 131

Stevens, Thaddeus, 11–12, 141

Stony Brook University, New York, 82–83

structural racism

Biden's campaign addressing, 206–209

BLM calling for an end to, 97, 181

Second Reconstruction attack on, 34

the Trump presidency embodying, 199–200

See also redemptionists; systemic racism

Student Nonviolent Coordinating Committee (SNCC), 109–116, 120–122, 127–130

Supreme Court, US

Brown decision, 13, 25, 33, 44

dismantling the Voting Rights Act, 132–133

Jackson's confirmation, 221–222

Plessy v. Ferguson, 143–144

Reconstruction-era denial of Black human dignity, 107–108

Scott v. Sandford, 137

Shelby v. Holder, 26–27, 86

Sotomayor's swearing in of Harris, 220

systemic racism

Abu-Jamal's incarceration, 84–85

American exceptionalism, 22, 224–225

Black feminism, 193

Black Lives Matter weaponizing civil disobedience, 97–98, 174

Black respectability politics, 109–110

built environment, 213–214

the murder of George Floyd, 180

the murder of Michael Brown, 94

redemptionist perspectives of Black equality, 152

SNCC relations with white activists, 120–121

See also white privilege

Talented Tenth of America's Black population, 109–110

Taney, Roger, 137

Taylor, Breonna, 204–205

Tea Party: racist attacks on Obama, 61

Temple University, 83

terrorist groups

Lost Cause narrative, 107

racial violence in the South, 141–142

Trump's campaign attacking people of color, 157–158

INDEX

PENIEL E. JOSEPH is the Barbara Jordan Chair in Ethics and Political Values; founding director of the Center for the Study of Race and Democracy; associate dean for justice, equity, diversity, and inclusion at the LBJ School of Public Affairs; and professor of history at the University of Texas at Austin. He is the author and editor of award-winning books on African American history, including *The Sword and the Shield* and *Stokely: A Life*. He lives in Austin, Texas.